PUTTING BACK
THE STYLE

PUTTING BACK THE STYLE

Edited by Alexandra Artley

EVANS BROTHERS LIMITED

Endpapers: (front) Georgian terrace in Bedford Square, London; (back) 1930s detached house with characteristic pantiles and shutters. Title page: Room setting of the Arts and Crafts period. Half-title page: Entrance to weather-boarded cottage built *c.* 1800 in Sandgate.

Published by Evans Brothers Limited
Montague House, Russell Square
London, WC1B 5BX

Copyright © Swallow Publishing Limited 1982
First published 1982

Conceived and produced
by Swallow Publishing Limited
32 Hermes Street, London N1

Consultant Editor
Alexandra Artley

Editor
Sarah Snape

Researchers
Scott Reyburn, Charles Wagner

Illustrator
David Tetley

Designer
David Young

ISBN 0 237 45603 6

All statements in this book giving information or advice are believed to be true and accurate at the time of going to press, but neither the authors nor the publishers can accept any legal liability for errors or omissions.

Set in Monophoto Baskerville
by BAS Printers, Hampshire
Printed in Italy
by New Interlitho

Contents

Introduction

Nowadays, most people would rather live in an old house. Most estate agents know that too. Ten or fifteen years ago, 'modernisation' was a major selling point in estate agents' literature, and the rather spurious stream-lining of old houses was considered to be a great asset. Today, the words 'many period features retained' work their magic in the hearts of prospective buyers.

Despite the disgraceful and wholesale demolition of vast tracts of traditional houses in British towns and cities during the 1960s and '70s, a large quantity of eighteenth, nineteenth, and early twentieth-century housing stock has survived. The purpose of this book is to help owners or prospective owners understand these houses, however modest such buildings may appear to be.

Before we go any further, one sad fact should be underlined. It has been estimated that approximately one-half of the population of this country is now living in flats or houses built since 1945. Most of these new housing developments are part of the terrible post-war social and architectural experiment carried out on the working-class people of Britain who did not have the political awareness to avoid the destruction of their traditional communities and lifestyle. When you sit in your 'period' home, glass in hand reading this book, *always remember that to live in almost any house built before the Second World War is now a great privilege in Britain.*

With privilege comes duty: to your house, to your neighbours and to the environmental health of the country at large. The pinstripe vandalism and professional visual illiteracy of the 1960s and '70s must never happen again. Already there are too few decent buildings left and the new Modernist slums are as bad as the old. One of the best things you could do, to help yourself and old buildings, is to join one or more of the hard-working architectural conservation societies listed on page 188 of this book.

The first duty of the aware householder is to restore and care for his house in such a way as to avoid any *irreversible* mutilation or disfigurement which would reduce still further the dignity and usefulness of the traditional housing stock which remains. Always remember that one day your house will pass into new hands. Try to leave something for those who come after you to live in and enjoy.

That is where this book comes in. In the past decade, many hundreds of books and still more scholarly articles have been written on various aspects of architectural history and interior design. With a few very localised exceptions, these books have dealt with rather grand buildings: the magnificent houses of the mighty and those of the great connoisseurs of history. These books are fascinating, but knowing how to re-assemble a one-ton chandelier, or noting how Mr. Capability Brown literally moved mountains to improve the view, is not much use to the average householder trying to restore his badly mutilated 1840s villa in Hackney.

Successful restoration cannot ever be achieved unless you first understand the plan and original purpose of your house and you have an emotional grasp of it as an organic whole. In the past, before rooms were knocked together to make 'multi-use spaces', old houses consisted of a large number of rooms clearly separated from each other and used for very specific purposes. The British like privacy outside and inside their houses. Being able to shut the door on other members of your family is still a great asset in a house. If your house has been 'opened out' in any way, the first job is to replace those dividing walls and to restore the original plan as far as possible. Unless this is done, the spaces in each room will never feel right.

The one exception to this is the basement, which usually varies considerably from house to house. Some original partitions may have to come down here to provide a reasonably sized kitchen. If the kitchen was originally sited in the basement it is usually preferable to keep it there. If it is well lighted there is no reason why it should not become a 'family room', in which people breakfast, have lunch and in which children's meals are served. If space permits, however, it is always best to try to reserve one small room on the ground floor as a formal dining room. It does not matter if it is small, dark or north-facing, as it will be used exclusively after dark anyway. Guests find it rather dismal to arrive for dinner and then be asked to troop down to dine in a basement while staring gloomily at the Aga. A bit of style has returned to dining, and even a tiny dining room can be a place in which to let rip one's more exotic interior design fantasies.

Having restored the original plan of your house, the next step is to make good any missing or mutilated decorative details. This is not something which can be done in a trice. Some people seem to think that any bit of moulding or curvacious bracket will do as long as the wall is not left plain. That is quite wrong, as decorative details and the exact placing of them are matters of tremendous historical precision. The same applies to fireplaces. Any fireplaces and grates you restore should be roughly the same period as your house. When looking for fireplaces from architectural salvage companies or direct from demolition sites, try to gauge the comparative importance of the room you want the fireplace for. A drawing room is a formal room and would have quite a grand fireplace: it would not do to buy a bedroom fireplace for it. Even between bedrooms there would be degrees of importance in the original fittings.

If you are very confused about what details should have appeared in a particular area of your house, ask to see inside another house in the same street. The chances are you will find what you are looking for, as well as discovering who your neighbours are. The same applies to the exterior of the house. In most streets at least one original fanlight, balcony, or pane of stained glass will have survived. This will provide you with an authentic pattern when you start enquiring for replacements from architectural salvage firms.

Decorative features which should be always replaced are the wooden shutters behind ground-floor and first-floor windows. Although shutters are often difficult to track down, they are worth pursuing. Not only do they look marvellous but they provide excellent security.

When you are considering external details, remember too that many local history societies will be only too delighted to show you photographs and

documents relating perhaps to the very street in which you now live. One of the pleasures of refurbishing your house properly is that you can become your own architectural historian and make practical use of what you discover.

When you have restored the plan of your house, its decorative details, fireplaces, doors and door furniture and so on, you can begin on the decoration and furnishing. People are often more concerned about 'authenticity' in wallpaper design than they are about the correct architectural detailing of their houses. The truth is that 'authenticity' in interior design and, in particular, 'authenticity' of colour, is a very vexed question on which most experts violently disagree. Even in this comparatively short book, experts occasionally contradict each other on minor but controversial matters. Within the general guidelines given in this book, the best answer is to do what is most graceful to live with.

There are some minor 'don'ts', however, for people who like rules. The *scale* of your furniture should always be considered in relation to the period of your house; and you should try to avoid certain rather dated types of lighting. Spotlights on tracks and down-lighters, for example, immediately smack of late Modernist architects' homes. Fitted carpets and coffee tables are also rather dubious these days. Coffee tables were originally Moorish in origin and appeared in men's smoking rooms, or in oriental rooms, in large artistic houses of the 1880s. In stream-lined form, they next appeared in smart '20s flats, as early Modernist architects liked very low furniture which their creaky elders could not easily sit down on or rise from. They are quite out of place in eighteenth and most nineteenth-century houses.

One last point concerns the general level of decoration and furnishing you attempt to do. Many people make the mistake of swotting up very grand interiors and then trying to copy them with lesser financial means. This can sometimes work if you are a brilliant fantasist or a very gifted designer with theatrical flair, but it is full of pitfalls. Doing up your house above its station and yours is in rather bad taste, and can sometimes produce quite comical effects. 'Queen Anne at the front, Mary Ann behind', old tabbies used to say. If you come to understand your house by studying local history and you love it for its own sake, you will repair its anatomy first. The decorative flesh on the bones will then grow consistently and confidently from that.

Understanding Your House

Before you can successfully restore your house, you must first understand its original purpose, plan and decorative detailing. In this section, three experts provide the essential background information. **Dan Cruickshank** traces the development of the Georgian speculative terraced house; **Gavin Stamp** discusses the merits of the Victorian terraced house; and **Roderick Gradidge** looks at the influence of the Arts and Crafts movement on early twentieth-century houses.

The Georgian Terraced House

The origins of the Georgian terraced house lie in the mid-seventeenth century, and its progeny were still being constructed in the suburbs of our towns and cities until the early years of this century. That a particular building type should have lasted so long says a lot for the logic that lay behind its design.

More than any other factor, the design of the Georgian terraced house was based on constraints; those of money, space and building regulations. The inventive energy generated by efforts to reconcile these daunting problems is what made the terraced house the ingenious mixture of display, elegance, convenience and cosy comfort that it had become by the end of the Georgian period.

Plans

By 1700, the terraced house had evolved so that, typically, it rose three storeys above ground level, had a basement, and was topped by an attic. It had two rooms per floor with the first-floor front room being the major room of the house. This would embrace the entire width of the house (since the stairs were usually placed at the rear of the house) and, in accordance with Italian Renaissance ideas, this floor would be treated as the *piano nobile* (or main floor of the building) and have a slightly higher ceiling height than other floors in the house.

The position of the staircase was vital in deciding the plan of Georgian terraced houses. Its design was varied and experimental until the second decade of the eighteenth century, when a design which offered a little grandeur and much economy of space—the 'dog leg'—was settled upon. The 'dog leg' is a staircase that rises from floor to floor by the use of two flights of stairs running parallel and linked by a landing or winding treads. It allowed the first flight of stairs to be visible from the front door and could be designed to 'cut a dash' with a curved handrail, well profiled newel posts, carved tread ends, and by the display of panelling and chair-rail mouldings. Subsequent flights of the staircase, as it progressed up the house, could be modified to suit the pocket of the builder or occupier.

The grand manner might (and usually did) continue from the first half-landing to the first-floor landing but after that, as the staircase became more of a family affair leading mainly to bedrooms, the dog leg would revert to the older (and cheaper) newel stair made up entirely of winders (stairs spiralled around a newel post) or, more usually, flyers (straight stairs) with winders instead of landings.

Balusters also became simpler as the staircase rose and open strings (the sloping piece of wood running at each side of the stair tread), which became fashionable in the second decade of the eighteenth century, gave way to the more archaic, and easy to construct, closed string. To attain even more grandeur, the first flight could lead to an elegant half-landing with the second flight to the first floor not returning directly alongside the first flight but with a well in between. Often, when fitted into terraced houses, this type of stair ended at first-floor level with a spacious balustraded gallery running where the flight to the second floor would be expected to begin. Access to the higher floors (in this design) would be via a modest secondary staircase.

By the mid-eighteenth century the typical plan of

the medium-cost London terraced house was as follows: rooms back and front on each of the five floors, dog-leg stairs and flues on party walls.

There was, however, an important variation of this plan, and that was the closet. The closet was a cunning device evolved in the second decade of the eighteenth century to give narrow-fronted houses an extra room per floor without blocking the windows of the back rooms.

How the Georgian House was Used

But, closet or no closet, the uses to which the major rooms of the typical eighteenth-century house were put were fairly standard. Variations were generally due to the profession of the occupant. A weaver, for example, might use the attics for his looms and a merchant the ground floor for an office. Generally, the pattern of occupation from the mid-seventeenth century to the mid-nineteenth century was to have the main kitchen in the front basement, with the back room used for bread ovens or storage with, perhaps, vaults for brewing, logs or, after about 1750, pavement vaults for coal storage. On the ground floors would be the back and front parlours—the normal focus of family life—or one parlour and a dining room, which would usually be the front room. The first floor would contain the main drawing room and possibly the dining room if the ground floor was all given over to parlours. There might also be a parlour or even a bedroom on the first floor if the dining room were on the ground floor. Later in the eighteenth century it became fashionable to link these two rooms (and occasionally the ground-floor rooms) by double doors. Almost invariably the main rooms on all these floors would front on to the street. The front room was largest, since the back room would have been robbed of space to accommodate the staircase. The second floor and attics would be given over to bedrooms, with the attics used mainly for the accommodation of children or servants.

Top: Although the details of this early eighteenth-century staircase hark back to the late seventeenth century, it was not unusual to find upper flights of stairs like this as late as 1725 in London. The more elaborate staircase (left) comes from a good quality house of the 1720s.

Interior Decoration

In 1714, when George I came to the throne, the seventeenth-century fashion to cover main rooms of even modest houses with timber panelling was still dominant. However, the late seventeenth century preference for oak had given way to cheaper pine, and the choice of moulding to embellish panelling changed. Oak, when used (as it still was after 1700 for especially prestigious works), was usually left naked and waxed—all else was painted.

Panelling and Wooden Detailing

The pre-1700 method of fixing panels into frames with bolection moulding was still occasionally used in the early Georgian period (mainly in slightly backward country districts); but generally, by 1714, the ornate bolection method had given way to a system which was followed throughout the country. Panels slatted in sequence into a frame, made of stiles (vertical members) and rails (horizontal members), and the whole fixed together with wooden pegs. The edges of the frame which met the panel were embellished in a formalised, hierarchical manner.

In the main rooms (ground and first) of an ambitious terraced house, raised and fielded panels were fitted into a frame embellished with ovolo mouldings at its edges. In lesser rooms in ambitious houses, or in main rooms in more modest houses, plain panels were fitted into ovolo-embellished frames. In simple rooms, plain panels went into plain frames, and in extremely modest rooms in medium houses—such as top-floor servant bedrooms—panelling might be merely planks fitted between posts, enriched with bead mouldings.

Above the panelling was a wooden cornice which, in grand rooms, could be embellished with dentils and, in more modest rooms, be of a simple Doric type.

The skirting at floor level also had an important role, for it was modelled on the mouldings used at the base of plinths. All this work would be painted, for naked, pale and knotted pine had an unfortunate appearance to the early eighteenth-century eye, weened on the rich tones of English oak. White lead was the usual medium for interior as well as exterior timbers in the eighteenth century, and the colours varied according to which pigments were available or fashionable. But as well as plain lead-based paint (which would have had a semi-gloss finish), graining (to look like oak, walnut or other exotic woods) was popular, as was the marbellising of certain features. Wallpaper was commonly used from the late seventeenth century and, one must assume, was used in combination with panelling. Around 1740 'dead' (that is matt) paint became fashionable, but this coincided with the fall from fashion of panelling, and must mostly have been used on plaster walls.

One timber that was never painted was mahogany. A very expensive and rare wood in the early eighteenth century, it was only used for small or important details, like stair handrails—and then only

The many different types of moulding provide useful dating tools. For example, it is known that bolection moulding was fashionable between 1660–1700, and reeding between 1795–1825.

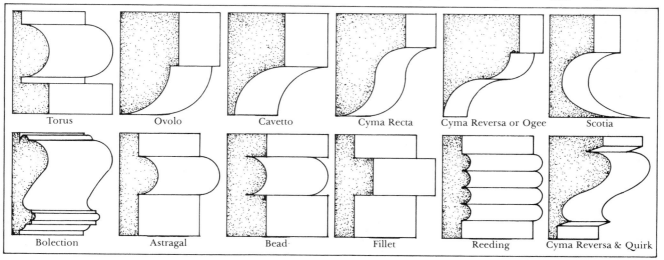

| Torus | Ovolo | Cavetto | Cyma Recta | Cyma Reversa or Ogee | Scotia |
| Bolection | Astragal | Bead | Fillet | Reeding | Cyma Reversa & Quirk |

Detail of shutters and window soffit c. 1800.

The Use of Plaster

After the late 1740s, the London terraced house was never panelled, unless it was the cheapest possible building, and simple panels were used as the most economic and utilitarian means of providing partitions between rooms.

From 1750 until the end of the Georgian period, plaster was the preferred material for both wall-covering and decoration. The typical first-floor room of a terraced house of 1760 would be Palladian in its proportioning and its decoration, with a touch of Rococo or even Gothick or Chinoiserie thrown in. Walls would be plastered, and either painted or hung with floral patterned or Chinese wallpaper above painted dados. In grander houses, silk might take the place of paper. The cornice would be of plaster, and the ceilings could display a free assymetrical Rococo design as could the fireplace surround. The fireplace itself, like any internal door case, would still be largely Palladian—columns, scrolls, and correctly decorated cornices.

By 1770, the Adam-inspired neo-Classical revolution had taken place. New sources of inspiration for designs, such as Robert Wood's *Ruins of Balbec* (1757) and Stuart's and Revett's *Antiquities of Athens* (1762) had a greater influence on the design of interiors than on façades, and made the established Palladian and Renaissance-derived decoration look extremely old hat. The Palladian bones survived, but on to the skeleton of cornice, chair rail and skirting the neo-Classical designer grafted the new, light, playful and highly coloured motifs and compositions of the Adam brothers.

The typical drawing room of 1775 would have a shallow moulded ceiling displaying favourite Adam motifs of anthemion leaves, or have painted panels linked by slender floral swags arranged in concentric bands, bats'-wings or spider-web patterns. All would be highly coloured with light blues, light greens, yellows or deep reds dominating. The cornices, also highly coloured, could be rearranged so that the emphasis was put on the soffit of the corona, which would be highly decorated and extend some distance into the ceiling. The walls of the room would be of similar colour to the range used in the ceiling, while chair rails, skirtings, doors, and window shutters would display various Adam motifs rendered in gesso and carved wood. The fireplace, usually of marble but of wood and gesso in modest houses, would display

in fairly grand houses. However, by the end of the century, dark Cuban mahogony was supplanted by lighter, redder, and more available mahogony, so that handrails, in even modest houses, were often wrought of this timber.

Pine panelling was used in London into the mid-1740s, though less exclusively and with modified details. Changes were small at first. The ovolo which held the panels in the frame sprouted an extra fillet around 1735, and by 1740 the typical panelled room had a dado beneath a chair rail of flush planks; the chair rail itself would have a simple cornice profile, and the cornice to the room would, as likely as not, be of plaster and enriched with Ionic modillions beneath the corona. The panels themselves tended to be wider in proportion, as did the stiles and rails, and composed in an irregular manner. For example, the long wall of a room would not be clad with a row of panels of equal width, as was normal in the early eighteenth century, but perhaps by two wide panels, one narrow panel, two wide and so on. At this time the simple cornice fire surround became popular. Earlier in the century, simple ovolo moulds, with no mantelshelf, were common, as were wood or marble surrounds, embellished only with a concave moulding on the outer edge and a bead moulding on the inner edge.

Adam lightness and originality with standard Palladian cornice profiles, reduced in bulk by substituting delicate moulding.

Within the fireplace would be fixed a cast-iron grate—of Carron or Coalbrookdale manufacture—which would also display fashionable neo-Classical motifs. In grand rooms this might be a free-standing grate, or in lesser rooms a hob grate fitted with metal plates or hobs to warm food and kettles.

Before the Industrial Revolution made the mass-production of cast iron possible, coal was burnt in hob grates made of a mixture of stone (for the side plates or hob) and iron for the bars. Before this still, when coal was expensive and when wood was commonly burned (which it was in London until the mid-eighteenth century), fireplaces were open, usually with curved backs to create better draughts, and furnished with iron fire dogs on which the logs were laid. Curiously, later hob grates, those of around 1825, were similar in form to those earlier mixtures of stone and iron—the sides were flat and the coal held in place by flat, or slightly curved bars.

But if the grate reverted in form, the rest of the room most decidedly did not. By 1810, a typical modest terraced drawing room would be papered and have, perhaps, a rudimentary chair rail. The cornice would be slight—perhaps a soffit containing a

honeysuckle or rose or a band of reeding. The door surrounds, if there were any, might be provided with scanty moulding. The fireplace would almost certainly be of a reeded pattern, with roundels or masks at the corners. In the best houses, the surround would be of naked marble, while in lesser houses or rooms, it would be of stone (usually painted or marbellised), or of wood and gesso.

By the end of the Georgian period, in the 1830s, the interior, like the exterior, began to take on a mongrel appearance. Greek revival was mixed with Gothic revival, and all bore the signs of that confusion of taste and style which was to characterise the architecture of the forthcoming age.

Exteriors

The aspect of the terraced house that changed the most during the Georgian period was its major public face, the elevation to the street. The typical London house of 1725 would have a flat front elevation, while slightly grander examples might have a rubbed-brick profiled string course at first-floor level, or still display a few Baroque touches such as brick or stone keystones in window arches (a feature popularised in the late seventeenth century London building boom), or a cut-brick cornice and pilasters. By 1725 flat brick window arches, which were general until about 1720, had given way to segmental arches (which remained the fashion until about 1730) and the façade was given polychromatic appeal by the mix of purple and brown or occasionally yellow bricks for the main work, with window jambs, corner quoins and arches being wrought in red stocks. The brick bond used in the construction of these houses, in both London and the provinces, was generally Flemish, as indeed it was to be right into the 1830s. However, for reasons of economy—a consideration near to the heart of the speculative builder—the Flemish bond used in London terraced houses was not really Flemish bond at all. Only occasionally did the header bricks actually bond into the brick piers behind. In this way a cheaply built 9-inch wall could be made to resemble a substantial Flemish-bond wall.

Late eighteenth-century cast-iron hob grate, typical of those manufactured by Carron. The painted-stone fire surround dates from the time the house was built in the 1720s.

Foundations

Foundations generally consisted of beaten-down earth made up with a little rubble or domestic waste (though oak piers were occasionally used for better class work). On this base walls were raised on shallow brick footings corbelled out to give a little extra spread, and sunk perhaps two feet below basement level. Later on in the eighteenth century, when more ambitious speculations were common and whole streets rather than groups of houses were undertaken by the same builder, the system of foundation-digging was rationalised. Basements were half dug, say to the level of three feet, and the earth thrown on to the site of the future street. This created a terrace roughly 6 feet above the newly created basement level, which would be strengthened and on which the walls would be raised. For this reason many domestic gardens in areas developed in London in the late eighteenth century are some feet below the street and represent the natural level of the site.

Window Treatments

Window sashes, flush or recessed, in the façade of the mid-1720s were still set in fully visible box-sashes and generally held twelve panes of Crown or Newcastle glass arranged in frames three panes wide. Only nine panes might be used in top, square windows, or fifteen in deep first-floor windows, which by the late eighteenth century could contain up to eighteen panes of glass. The first-floor window became more elongated, in accordance with a proportioning system which reflected both the social importance of the various levels and the Classical ideals of the Renaissance. Typically the first-floor windows would the largest, with the ground-floor windows similiar and the second and third progressively shallower. As the century progressed, the geometry which underlay this proportioning system became increasingly formalised so that even the most ignorant builder could produce an elegantly and well-proportioned façade.

But it was not only the general disposition of major elements that leaned heavily on Classical precedents.

A house in Kings Cross, London. Built c 1825, it displays interesting features typical of its period. For example the first-floor windows are set within an arch, and the balconies are of mass-produced anthemion pattern.

Details also were based on Italian Renaissance ideas. Glazing bars to windows, broad (1 inch to $1\frac{3}{4}$ inches) in the early years of the century, were composed of an astragal moulding capped with a fillet, and door cases, hand-wrought and carved, and individual at first, after 1715 gradually became more Classically correct and standardised under the influence of architectural pattern books spreading the Palladian word.

The Roof

Somewhat ironically, above all this Classical finery, and only slightly hidden by the Portland stone-capped parapet, lurked the traditional and somewhat rustic pitched roof. Until Welsh slates became generally available after the construction of the canal system in the 1770s, the usual roof covering for

terraced houses in London was either plain peg tiles or pantiles, both of which required, unlike close-fitting slates, to be laid on a steep pitch to be watertight. In the very early years of the eighteenth century, a steep single pitch was common. This entailed relatively massive but straightforward construction, and provided enough room for an attic lit with dormers. By the 1720s a double-pitched roof (known as an M roof) was favoured—that is two small versions of the single-pitched roof, with ridges running parallel to the façade. This form ensured that less roof would be visible from the street and that smaller (and thus cheaper) timbers could be used than in a single-pitched roof. If accommodation was required in a double-pitched roof then a mansard roof was needed, which meant that each slope of each pitch was divided into two angles with the lower slope being steeper. This created head room within the pitches.

Another popular roof in the second quarter of the eighteenth century was the double roof. Similar in principle to the double-pitched roof, this form had its ridges running at right-angles to the façade. The roof was prevented from presenting an ungainly gable end to the street by the use of a hip.

Most of these forms were common throughout the eighteenth century, with only pitches changing. But by the early nineteenth century, as speculative builders became even more cost conscious, an extremely cheap form of terraced roof was developed that contained no structural truss at all. Two single pitches ran from a central beam set at right angles to the façade up into extended party walls. This form, with no structural strength of its own, was vulnerable to even slight structural movement in the house, which could crack the gutter running along the central beam.

Colour

By 1740, the London terraced house had toned down considerably in colour. Grey/brown bricks were used in preference to purple/red; gone were red-brick dressings to windows (although red-brick arches were still usual and indeed lingered on in occasional use

right to the end of the Georgian period in London), and hand-carved and turned-timber door surrounds were replaced by simpler, more austere designs, often in stone.

By the mid 1750s this tendency towards a cool colouring (grey bricks, light cream paint and white Portland stone), coupled with nobly proportioned and austere façades, reached its peak both in London and fashion-conscious provincial towns such as Bath.

The external eaves cornice reappeared, but in stone, and usually in a Doric variation called a block cornice. It was used as a part of an elevational treatment that recalled the fact that the Georgian terraced façade was proportioned and detailed as if it were a Classical temple-front embellished with a properly proportioned colonnade.

Fanlights

The mid-eighteenth century saw the large-scale introduction of an item that has become synonymous with the design of domestic Georgian architecture—the fanlight. The entrance halls of houses in the first half of the eighteenth century were occasionally lit by glass panels above the front door but generally the door reached to the soffit of the door case. Certainly there was no formal or usual way of glazing or

Top: Detail of a house of the 1820s in London. The fanlight is an off-the-peg design which the builder could have ordered from a catalogue.

Right: A fanlight c 1770 in an early eighteenth-century house.

A door in Bedford Square, Bloomsbury. Constructed to a highly uniform design of c 1770, the entrances to the houses in the square are all embellished with doors of Coade artificial stone. This design was advertised through Coade's catalogue and can be found in houses throughout London and parts of the South-East.

guarding these apertures, just a couple of iron bars fitted with spikes to keep thieves out. By 1750, the characteristic fan glazing patterns had appeared, first with stout lead or timber bars but gradually with more delicate and varied designs so that, by the end of the Georgian period, the fan pattern was just one of many designs available for decorating this useful aperture.

Coade Stone

Elevational changes were rapid after 1760, due largely to the Adam brothers' reinterpretation of Classical decoration. The stone-block cornice and plain string courses were replaced with decorated bands or shallow pilasters wrought in that revolutionary material, Coade stone. Coade, an artificial stone, was manufactured in large quantities in Lambeth from 1769. The Adam brothers were amongst the first architects to use Coade in large quantities when they employed it to decorate their Adelphi development in the very early 1770s.

The standard terraced front of about 1772 would display the elegant Palladian proportions of the 1750s, but be embellished by a mass-produced Coade stone-string course at first-floor level, displaying perhaps a Vitruvian scroll and sporting a Coade-stone door surround of rusticated blocks and a river-god keystone ordered from the Coade's pattern book. Surrounded by this Coade door decoration would be another specimen of early mass-production, the lead and cast-iron fanlight which was, by the late eighteenth century, becoming the most decorative element of the façade. The house could also be embellished at first-floor level with balconies which, in the following decade, would have been purchased via a catalogue from the foundry masters at Carron, Falkirk or at Coalbrookdale.

The Mass-Produced Georgian House

By the late eigthteenth century, it was not just decorations that were being run off in endless repetition, but whole streets. The typical small speculative builder, content to run up pairs or small groups of houses, gave way to big operators such as the Adam brothers, and a little later, John Nash and James Burton, who undertook to build not only entire streets but even districts of London.

Mass-produced ornaments were essential to embellish the increasingly austere designs of these mass builders. But there was a stronger force than taste or even economy behind this external growing austerity. This was the massive Building Act of 1774.

This act, which repealed all previous acts, enshrined the refined taste of the 1770s in legal statutes. Any latent desire on the part of builders for more decoration was quashed. To prevent the spread of

fires, sash boxes had to be, after 1774, not only set 4 inches back, but also recessed behind the bricks of the window jambs. Bow windows could not protrude more than 10 inches in streets 30 feet wide or more. Most importantly, to regularise house building, minimum standards of construction were laid down. These took the form of four classes—or rates—of houses (based on volume and cost), with each rate carrying a code of construction to which each newly built house had to conform.

A second-rate London house of 1790 was of yellow brick (though reddy-browns were occasionally still used for elevational work and generally used for concealed work). It would consist of three storeys over the basement, and the door would be a round-headed brick arch decorated with a Coade-stone keystone. The door would contain a cast fanlight with, possibly, a slender string course between ground and first floors. The windows themselves—headed by cut-brick arches which would usually, by now, be wrought of rubbed first-rate stock bricks the same colour as the façade rather than in specially fine rubbing bricks—would be furnished with exceedingly slender glazing bars.

By 1810, the second-rate house had changed—mostly in the direction of uniformity. Yellow bricks were obligatory; first-floor windows would drop down to floor level to allow easy access to a cast-iron balcony running the length of the first floor. The entrance

Built around 1810 by the builder James Burton, this terrace in Bloomsbury shows many of the characteristics of the late Georgian speculative terrace, including almost overpowering uniformity and regularity of elevation set off by slight variations in details such as balconies, fanlights and area railings.

would be round-headed with the only embellishment being the fanlight and, possibly, slender pilasters which, like the front door itself, might display Regency motifs such as reedings, rosettes and lion masks. The rest of the ground floor was likely to be stuccoed and perhaps lined out with fake ashlar joints, frescoed to look like weathered Bath stone or even rusticated below a stone-string course.

The second-rate terraced house of 1825 was, perhaps, a slightly more decorated version of that of 1810. A few overblown and ill-wrought decorations in the Greek revival or other exotic manner may appear, such as a Greek Doric porch in plaster and brick, and cast-iron verandas of bold design. The terraced form itself was being questioned by speculative builders.

Larger developments would include free-standing villas (often with shallow pitched roofs with deep overhanging eaves), semi-detached houses, houses linked by single-storey entrance blocks and numerous other permutations, as well as the traditional terrace.

After 1830 the battle of the styles—Greek revival versus early Gothic—put a stop to the unselfconscious development of the Classically detailed and proportioned terraced house. Gradually architects became persuaded that architecture had a moral value and that it was their job to sift out a style appropriate to the aspirations of their age and the greatness of the British Empire. The Victorian era had begun.

Elevations of a second-rate house of 1820. Taken from the 1823 edition of Peter Nicholson's The Practical Builder.

The Victorian House

The ordinary Victorian house has had a bad press. Victorian houses were often ridiculed by architects and critics at the time they were built; they were dismissed as stuffy and over-ornamented by the early twentieth-century children of Victorian parents, who were reacting against the whole Victorian age; and they have been regarded as representative of the awfulness of nineteenth-century industrialism by social and architectural reformers. As a result, although the vile slums of nineteenth-century industrial cities were almost always run-down Georgian houses, acres and acres of monotonous but solid Victorian terraces have been ruthlessly swept away by town planners in the prejudiced belief that they are insanitary.

Because they are sometimes large and have had to be divided up into flats, Victorian houses were mercilessly modernised in the 1960s. Purely to conform with contemporary taste, chimney pieces and picture rails were swept away; panelled doors were rendered flush; colour and texture were overwhelmed by white paint. But most Victorian houses remain serviceable, adaptable and, above all, very well built; they can still be, as they were designed to be, family homes. Less blinkered generations can today appreciate them both for their solidity and for their design and detail; we would no more think of destroying the original features of Victorian houses today than we would those of Georgian houses, and the chimney pieces which once ended up in junk shops having been ripped out by builders and trendy architects are now being sought after for restoration purposes. 'Victorian' is no longer a pejorative term.

Victorian architecture is usually associated with monuments—churches and town halls, museums and railway stations—but a vast number of houses were also built in the period 1837–1901. These were ordinary houses, constructed in response to the massive increase in population in Britain in the nineteenth century. Owing to the advent of the railways and other forms of cheap public transport, London and all the other large cities grew and grew, and round the inner core of Georgian and earlier building there arose large developments of Victorian housing— terraced housing nearer the centre and leafy suburbs further out. Indeed, the suburb and the suburban house as we now understand them are essentially Victorian creations.

A significant proportion of the population still live in Victorian houses—whether by necessity or by choice—but not in the sort described in the architectural history books. The Victorian houses which have been written up and analysed, documented and listed, are country houses or the grand town house or villa for the aristocracy or the wealthy. These are usually the work of a known, named architect, and would have been published in the *Builder* or the *Building News*, the two most important Victorian architectural periodicals. However, as in the eighteenth century, most houses built for the middle, lower-middle and working classes were not designed by an architect—or at least, not by an architect of any distinction—and, as with Georgian houses, they were speculative developments. Many writers have seen something essentially reprehensible in building as commercial speculation, and imply that ordinary people were compelled to live in dreary, repetitive, mediocre housing. But speculation is always uncertain and developers, who put their money at risk, inevitably have to respond to public demand and aspirations if they are to succeed. There can be no doubt that the ordinary Victorian house was popular, desirable and efficient in its day. Only a small proportion of these houses were planned for a large domestic staff; most families who could afford servants would, perhaps, have had one maid, and the average Victorian house is of a size which makes them perfectly convenient and manageable today. Apart from the plumbing and sanitary arrangements and the absence of electricity, there is nothing out of date about an ordinary—unspoiled—Victorian house.

Most Victorian houses were extremely conservative in style and in plan and it took many decades for the work of the *avant-garde* architect to affect the speculative builder. A high proportion of Victorian houses were built in terraces, and the Georgian and Regency tradition continued well into Victoria's reign: Mr. Pooter's house—'The Laurels', Brickfield Terrace, Holloway—could have been either late Georgian or early Victorian. Until towards the end of the century, terraced houses were being built with regularly spaced rectangular windows which derive from the standard Georgian terrace, whether they were of brick or faced all over in painted stucco—the enduring legacy of John Nash. Such houses have the standard plan of a staircase on one side and two rooms on each floor, at front and back; possibly a rear extension on one or more floors, incorporating bathrooms

A house of the early 1840s in De Beauvoir Town in north-east London. At some stage the windows of the first floor have lost their plaster surround, or architrave. Until 1981 the interior of this house was virtually unaltered. It was then 'modernised' by builders who threw out original doors and windows, and the present occupant has also had to replace chimney pieces and internal plaster cornices. Unfortunately, the new front door was already installed and is of poor neo-Georgian design, wrong in proportion and thin in detail. It lacks a decorative fanlight above.

Opposite: No 18, Stafford Terrace, Kensington, London, run by the Victorian Society as a museum and open to the public. This house has four floors and a basement, in a terrace built for the prosperous middle classes in 1868–74. The plate glass in the sash windows is original, as are the front railings, and door. The only alteration to the exterior is the addition of the late Victorian glass Wardian Cases, or miniature conservatories, with decorative tiles. With the exception of the bay windows rising through three floors, the plan of the house is almost identical to that of a standard Georgian terraced house.

(perhaps) and sculleries. In comparison with Georgian terraces, however, such houses are sometimes bigger in scale and often more elaborately ornamented with Classical detail; nor are they laid out so formally, with large squares between the straight streets; for the influence of the 'picturesque' resulted in many terraces being curved.

There were some innovations, however. The columned projecting porch in front of the entrance door appeared in Belgravia in the early nineteenth century and continued to be used in the stuccoed terraces of Bayswater and Kensington right up until the 1870s. If there was no porch the front door would be recessed. Improved technology also allowed larger sheets of plate glass to replace the smaller Georgian panes by the 1840s, a development greatly encouraged by the abolition of Window Tax in 1851.

A conspicuous feature of the Victorian house is the bay window. These, breaking forward from the wall plane and allowing more light and a wider field of vision than the conventional window, were used by the Elizabethans and occasionally appeared in the eighteenth century; they were commonplace by the mid-nineteenth century. Usually opening out from a drawing room, they appear in the terraced house on either one storey or combined in two to make a tall projecting bay. These had the advantage of breaking up the street line and making houses more complex in shape; to the Victorian, the regular, reticent 'hole-in-the-wall' Georgian terrace—typified by Gower Street—was intolerably boring and gloomy. The typical Victorian bay window has sides canted at 45 degrees and is lit with sliding sash windows of single or double sheets of plate glass.

The nineteenth century was obsessed with style, as there was no one modern style which was generally accepted and conventional. The early Victorians had a choice of Greek, Italian, Gothic or even Egyptian. However, there was one style which, in the middle of the century, was carried to dominance on a tide of religious fervour and Romanticism: Gothic. The Gothic revival captured all the brightest architects in the 1840s, '50s and '60s, and they used the style for churches, country houses, schools, town halls, law courts and even railway hotels. Eventually, the Gothic revival affected the ordinary speculative builder, but the results were not such that could be approved by the fervent partisans of the style. By 1872 John Ruskin, author of the *Seven Lamps of Architecture* (1849), complained from his house in Denmark Hill in South London that 'I have had indirect influence on nearly every cheap villa-builder between this and Bromley; and there is scarcely a public-house near the Crystal Palace but sells its gin and bitters under pseudo-Venetian capitals copied from the Church of the Madonna of Health or of Miracles. And one of my principal notions for leaving my present home is that it is surrounded everywhere by the accursed Franken-stein monsters of, *in*directly, my own making.'

Very few houses were literally Gothic, with pointed windows, buttresses and an elaborate skyline: only a few expensive country houses and many vicarages. Some detached suburban houses were built in the Gothic style, such as the celebrated examples in north Oxford, but, on the whole, the style was thought to be too 'churchy' for an ordinary house and such houses are exceptional. But the Gothic revival did influence the ordinary terraced house, in a more subtle manner. The porch might have carved naturalistic capitals, the windows might be flanked by thin columns, or incised geometrical decoration might appear in the elab-orately chamfered lintels above windows and doors. A

striking effect was achieved by the use of 'polychromy'—different coloured bricks in stripes or patterns—which was a result of the interest in Italian Gothic stimulated by Ruskin's *Stones of Venice*. Further interest to the wall surface was often given by a course of special moulded bricks, or terracotta, or by a course of bricks laid at an acute angle, all of which, combined with carved decoration, made a façade much more ornamental and deliberately drew attention to the wall surface.

The most distinctive feature of this so-called 'Gothic' type of house was not truly Gothic at all. This was the use of the segment-headed window, rather than openings with a rounded, pointed or straight top. The gently curved window lintel—usually raised on 'haunches'—might either be in a single piece of stone or formed by a brick arch, possibly with bricks of variegated colour, as 'structural honesty' and the enhancement of constructional elements was an important element in Victorian architectural philosophy.

Rows of houses with some of the above elements were being built until well into the twentieth century and, in a simplified and standard form, they constitute the typical late Victorian ordinary house, whether built by speculative builders for the middle and lower middle classes, or by one of the housing trusts for the working classes. Sometimes such houses are known as 'Bye-law terraces', as they conformed to the provisions of the Public Health Act of 1875, which insisted on good drainage and sanitation and discouraged basements for occupation. In London, where building was regulated by successive London building acts, a typical terrace would be faced in red brick with the yellow London stock bricks used for the rear portions and the general construction. The low pitched roof, above eaves and not now hidden by a parapet, would be of grey slate—the standard urban roofing material of the eighteenth and nineteenth centuries. The houses are of two bays: one for the front door (opening

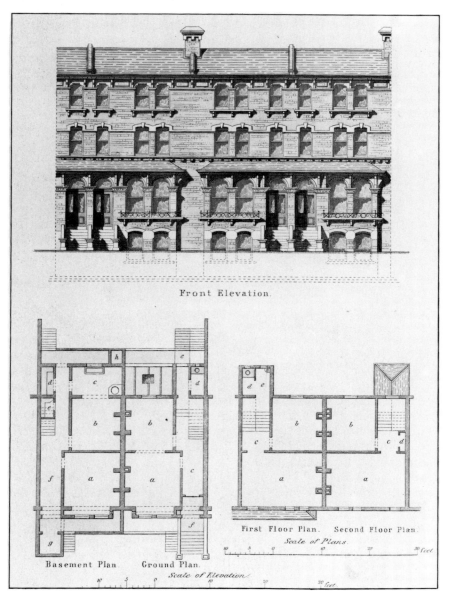

Front Elevation.

Basement Plan.   Ground Plan.
Scale of Elevation.

First Floor Plan.   Second Floor Plan.
Scale of Plans.

A design for a three-storey terraced house with a basement, designed by the firm of Shaw & Lockington, Architects and Surveyors, and published in E. L. Blackburne's Suburban and Rural Architecture *of 1869. In style and plan, these are very typical of standard mid-Victorian speculative builders' houses. Apparently of red brick, they may have been built in London. The plan shows little departure from that of a standard Georgian London terraced house. In the Basement,* a *is the breakfast-room,* b *the kitchen and* c *the scullery; on the Ground Floor,* a *is the dining-room,* b *(separated by folding doors) a study and* d *a water closet; on the First Floor,* a *is the drawing room,* b *a bedroom and* d *a WC; and on the Second Floor are bedrooms. The estimated cost of such a house was £350.*

off a small front yard or garden now that there is no basement or area), the other consisting of bay windows on one or two floors.

In plan, such houses show virtually no departure from the standard Georgian house, which has a staircase rising on one side and a 'dog-leg' corridor going past to the narrower rear extension. The extension shares the party wall on one side only, and thus allows additional space for the back yard and for light to reach the inner rooms in each pair of houses. The two reception rooms on the ground floor consist of drawing and dining room, with a kitchen and scullery to the rear; on the first floor are bedrooms, with a bathroom in the rear extension.

The front door might have ornamental stained glass in its glazed open panels. All internal surfaces were plastered, with a simple cornice where wall meets ceiling and, possibly, an ornamental 'rose' in the centre of the reception room ceilings. Doors are panelled; rooms have a wooden skirting board and picture rail, carefully detailed with mouldings, like the staircase with its elaborate newel post. The principal rooms have chimney pieces of wood, stone, slate or marble according to status and class of house. In style these tend to be a more florid and decorative development of the Classical forms of the eighteenth century. Within would probably be one of the mass-produced cast-iron grates. About internal decorations it is difficult to generalise as fashions changed, but wall surfaces would be painted or wallpapered in a variety

Above and right: The end house in a terrace in Macclesfield, built in 1885 by local architect Jabez Wright, who made his house wider than the rest as it was for his own use. The roof is of slate and the red brickwork is relieved by raised and decorative bands of white and dark grey bricks. Stone quoins are used to finish off the corner. The fireplace in the dining room had been removed, and had to be replaced with this simple Classical chimney piece and mantel and a cast-iron arched surround with a built-in grate.

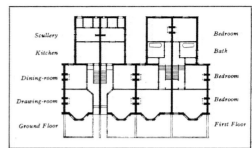

A terraced house in Chiswick, West London, c 1876. The design is very conservative compared with the houses in Bedford Park nearby, although built at exactly the same time. The influence of the Gothic revival is minimally evident in the chamfering of the window and door lintels. The large panes of glass in the sash windows and the decorative tiles on the roof ridge are original. Fire regulations required that the party walls rise above the roof line. The roof is of slate; the walls of London stock brick.

Opposite left: A terraced house of c 1880 in Barons Court, West London. This house tries to look slightly more countrified than the one in Chiswick (left) by means of the Queen Anne gable and the decorative terracotta tiles between the upper and lower bay windows. The stained glass above the front door is original, but the painting of the house is not. The owner is intending to repaint the external joinery in maroon and cream, which will be more in keeping with the period.

of dark colours and patterns.

By no means were all Victorian houses of the standard, conservative, terraced type, however. With the intense individualism of Victorian life, the respect for family life and the desire for privacy and quiet, the detached house was the ideal, but economics demanded that many of these were semi-detached. These descended from the villas of Regent's Park and those built by the Georgians along the Thames and just outside towns and cities. Like the Georgian villa, the Victorian villa aspired to rural picturesqueness

and the country life, but was essentially urban in character. The semi-detached villa was cheaper and usually smaller than the proper villa, but was decidedly a cut above the terraced house. However, although in theory the semi-detached villa allowed a free and more flexible plan, in practice most such houses employed the standard Georgian terrace plan and were built in regular rows, the only difference from the terrace being that there were gaps between each pair of houses, where the entrances were placed. This arrangement did, nevertheless, allow each pair to have a different architectural treatment, securing that variety which the Victorians so welcomed. In cities such as Bristol, semi-detached houses were the standard form of Victorian suburban development while in different parts of London large estates of such houses were built: lower-middle-class ones in Hackney and larger and more expensive examples in Blackheath.

Right: Half of a semi-detached house in Bedford Park, London, built in 1880. Except for the front fence, the house is in its original state, with the small panes of glass in the window in the fashionable Queen Anne style. The gable rises above the coved cornices and its centre is faced in rough-cast plaster. This house is much more advanced in style, and individual in plan, than the typical speculator's house of the period.

The detached, private house in a garden was the middle-class Victorian ideal. The picturesque eccentricities of such houses have been taken by many writers as typical of the Victorian age but, in fact, such houses were in a minority and less typical than the type of terraced house already described. However, because such houses were more expensive and were often individually commissioned from an architect,

25

A group of three houses on a steeply sloping site in Bristol, a city where many of the Victorian middle-class houses were single villas or semi-detached properties. Built c 1860, the style is an odd mixture of round-arched and segment-headed windows, and the collision between the rusticated relieving arch and the low-pitched bargeboards on the right-hand gable is not a success. The house on the left has had a new window of the wrong shape inserted, and has been insensitively refaced in Bath stone ashlar, while the massive garden retaining walls are of rubble stone. Oddly, the building is not exactly symmetrical and the plans of the three houses not identical.

they were always more up to date in fashion, and exhibit the domestic application of the various styles employed by *avant-garde* architects. Italianate villas can be found in St. John's Wood, Gothic houses in north Oxford and, in London suburbs such as Sydenham and Hampstead, eclectic mixtures of styles can be enjoyed. The streets in such suburbs were more picturesquely laid out and in some planned residential developments, such as sylvan Birkenhead Park, the semi-rural tradition of Regent's Park was maintained.

Architectural developments in the 1860s and 1870s encouraged the development of the detached house. In those decades a large number of young architects, most notably Philip Webb and Norman Shaw, reacted against the rigidity and ponderousness of the Gothic revival and sought to develop a more homely and free domestic architecture. For inspiration they looked to country cottages, barns and farmhouses and, for town buildings, to houses of the seventeenth and even the eighteenth centuries. The result in the country was the 'Old English' style: tall brick chimneys, tile-hung gables, half-timbering and rough cast. In the town, the Queen Anne style was used: an eclectic mixture of Classical features, Georgian sash-windows, Dutch gables, with red brickwork and tiled roofs—a reaction against London stock brick and slate roofs. Older Gothicists such as Sir Gilbert Scott could not bear this new style, and could not understand why old-fashioned features such as

casement windows with leaded-light panes, or windows with small panes with wooden glazing bars, were adopted instead of modern plate glass—failing to understand that both the architects and their middle-class clients were rejecting the modern Victorian age. They wished to escape from the city and flee into the country, to houses which looked countrified, Romantic, homely and old.

Inspired by this essentially reactionary vision, a school of domestic architecture flourished in England which was the envy of the rest of the world. Its first historian was a German, Hermann Muthesius, who in his book *Das Englische Haus* (1904–5; translated as *The English House*, 1979) described and illustrated the work of such architects as Shaw, Webb, Ernest George, Voysey and Lutyens. Although these architects were working usually for the upper middle classes in the country and outer suburbs, their work did eventually influence the ordinary house. This was first evident in Bedford Park, a suburb in West London designed for middle-class families of moderate means and built in 1875–86. Most of the houses were designed by Norman Shaw or his followers; they are detached, semi-detached or in terraces, but all are detailed in the new Queen Anne and 'Old English' styles, with Dutch, or tile-hung gables, Classical details, small-paned sash windows and plans which were more free than those of the typical Victorian house.

A design for a pair of villas in the 'Anglo-Italian' style, built at Milton in Kent by E. L. Blackburne. This plate was published in Blackburne's Suburban and Royal Architecture *of 1869. The houses were to be built in polychromatic brickwork. On the plans, in the Basement,* a *is the kitchen,* b *the scullery,* c *the pantry,* d *the coal cellar and* e *the servant's WC; on the Ground Floor,* b *is the drawing room or 'Front Parlour',* c *the dining room and* d *the WC; on the First Floor,* b *and* c *are bedrooms and* d *the servant's room. The tower was proposed for a study, or for an additional servant's room. The basic arrangement of the plan is typical of many semi-detached Victorian houses.*

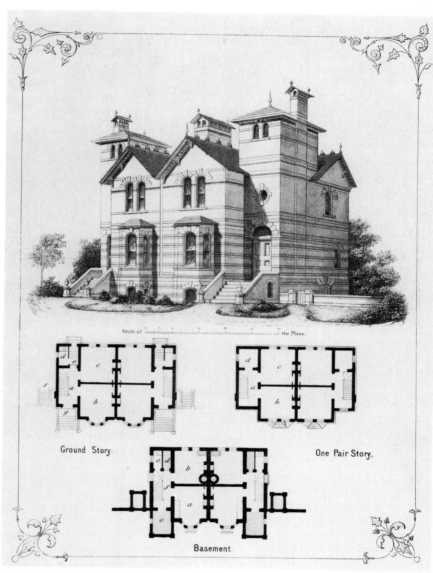

Muthesius considered that Bedford Park 'signifies neither more nor less than the starting point of the smaller modern house, which immediately spread from there over the whole country'. One legacy was the planned 'Garden Suburb' or the 'Garden City', in which the suburban ideal was allied to the English Utopian and anti-urban tradition; examples are Hampstead Garden Suburb in London; Letchworth; and the estates of the London County Council described by Roderick Gradidge in the next section. A more important legacy was the ordinary suburban house of the twentieth century: detached or semi-detached, with bow or bay windows, gables, tall chimneys and other details deriving from the work of Shaw or Voysey. However, Bedford Park and the work of Shaw also affected the type of ordinary speculative housing already described. By the end of the century, suburban terraces could have gables above their bay windows—some even tile-hung—and timber porches in a 'vernacular', half-timbered style. Sometimes the upper part of a window is filled with small panes and glazing bars—in deliberate and attractive contrast to the large pane below. In such houses, the decorative tiles around the fireplace or the stained glass in the front door may reflect the influence of *Art Nouveau*—that turn-of-the-century Continental

A group of houses of c 1880 in Bedford Park, London by the architect E. J. May, showing the application of Norman Shaw's Queen Anne style to a terrace. Each house has individual features with Dutch gables of varied design; in the hands of the speculative builder the same window forms and brick details were often used, but repetitively. The terrace is of red brick with a red-tiled roof, in conscious reaction to the drab grey-brown of the typical Victorian London house built of stock brick or stucco, with a slate roof. The wooden railing design of the centre two houses is original.

style which only affected decorative details in England.

The other type of housing which the Queen Anne movement influenced was the flat. For most of the nineteenth century the English disliked this Continental type of urban housing; even Muthesius believed that 'flat-dwelling can only be regarded as an emergency substitute for living in a private house' and 'that to live in a private house is in every way a higher form of life'. Most Englishmen would have agreed with him, but in 1880 Norman Shaw designed Albert Hall Mansions, a block of flats which was the forerunner of the many blocks built in late Victorian and Edwardian London. These have tall gables above their tiers of bay windows and balconies, and are built of red-brick or terracotta. Internally, such mansion flats had spacious plans, designed for domestic staff, but even today, when individual flats have usually been subdivided, they have well-proportioned rooms with decorative chimney pieces and tall windows which open onto balconies. They are probably the best flats which have ever been widely built in London.

Before such buildings became respectable in late Victorian England, it was only the working classes who lived in tall, tenement buildings in densely-populated inner-urban areas. These were built by the several charitable housing trusts, such as the Peabody Trust. Today, many of these artisan blocks have been sold to private occupiers and they make perfectly satisfactory urban dwellings. Naturally, these buildings were not finished as well as were private houses, but even the Peabody Buildings of the 1860s were a great improvement on the poor housing of the time. They were solidly built and compare favourably today with the public housing built since 1945. Although architectural embellishment was kept to a minimum and the open iron staircases clearly indicated the building's status, the rooms were finished with chimney pieces and picture rails. By the end of the century, such buildings were more decorative, being built in different coloured brick and stone and with Classical details deriving from Shaw and the Queen Anne style. Restored and sympathetically decorated, flats in these buildings can be as comfortable and pleasant today as the ordinary Victorian house.

The literature on the ordinary Victorian house is not extensive. To establish original details and finishes, as well as to find out where you can inspect unspoiled surviving examples, it is possible to refer to the various handbooks used by the Victorian speculative builder. These, with titles like *The Mason's, Bricklayer's Plasterer's and Decorator's Practical Guide* or *The Practical House Carpenter*, were essentially revised and updated versions of eighteenth-century manuals. Books of suggested house designs, with details, were sometimes published by architects, and designs for ordinary houses occasionally appear in the pages of the *Builder* or *Building News*. Modern historians have been almost exclusively concerned with the special, architect-designed house—usually for the wealthy and usually in the country or an exclusive suburb—and few have looked at the ordinary (typical) Victorian house. S. E. Rasmussen's *London: The Unique City* (1937) examines the ordinary London house of the eighteenth and nineteenth centuries, and Donald Olsen's *The Growth of Victorian London* (1976) surveys several middle- and working-class suburbs. The same author contributed to *The Victorian City* (1973), edited by H. J. Dyos and M. Wolff. J. M. Richards' *Castles on the Ground* (1946) was a sympathetic review of the suburb; John Gloag's *Victorian Taste* (1972) looked at ordinary suburbs. Detailed analyses of particular housing developments can be found in the more recent volumes of the *Survey of London* which cover the whole nineteenth century.

Of particular value is *The Victorian Villas of Hackney* (1981) by Michael Hunter, which examines the dating and details—inside and out—of typical houses in one London borough, applying the observations on style and building methods to the whole country. There were, of course, regional variations in Victorian housing, although they were less than in earlier centuries as the railways allowed the easy and cheap movement of building materials. Nevertheless, the typical Victorian house in London was of brick, while in many cities in the west and north of England it was of stone. But wherever they are, they display features which are characteristic and which deserve respect and careful restoration.

Arts and Crafts and Afterwards

Whilst few of us are lucky enough to live in a Tudor cottage, with its ancient glow and welcoming sense of enclosure—or in a Georgian house, whose elegant proportions give a cool sense of rightness—nonetheless the houses built between about 1890 and 1930 often have many of these characteristics—sometimes indeed combining a Tudor welcome with the solid proportions of the Georgians. At that time architects and house builders cared more for these things than at any other period of history. British architects then were acknowledged as the best in the world, and to most of them the successful design of houses, both big and small, was the highest peak of their ambition.

Where architects lead, builders usually follow. The result was a period of building where 'the English House' was admired and imitated throughout the world. Since it was a period of great wealth in this country, literally thousands of carefully handcrafted houses—each designed to fit comfortably into its environment, be it a Georgian town street or a Cotswold hillside—were built and they still survive, still lived-in in the way that they were designed to be lived in. The people who own them appreciate them for their comfort and conformity, but probably few appreciate the subtlety and skill that has gone into their making.

This does not just apply to 'one-off' houses, because for the first time during this period, local authorities started to build housing estates. More often than not, these estates were designed by architects who went into the design of local authority housing because of their high ideals. Indeed, often these architects were quite as talented as their better-known contemporaries in the private sector. The result is that the housing estates put up by the London County Council and other local authorities just before and just after the

First World War are as good as any housing estate ever erected at any time anywhere in the world. Even the ordinary builder's semi-detached houses put up between the wars were deeply influenced by the architecture of the Arts and Crafts architects, although they may not have understood some of the ideals of the masters. This is possibly why the inter-war 'semi' has such an enduring hold on the public. The fact that a vast majority of all privately owned houses in Britain today fall into one of the above categories

does not mean that we should not care for this part of our building heritage just as carefully as we do for buildings of an earlier period.

Recently some terrible things have been happening to the houses of this period—largely because people do not appreciate what it is that they possess. Because there are so many buildings of this period, people feel that it does not matter if one or two buildings are altered. But so often the estates—and not just the architect-designed estates—were designed to make a

These semi-detached houses in West London, built in a vernacular Georgian style in light red brick, are typical of the humane and well detailed houses built by the London County Council just before and after the First World War. The well proportioned sash and casement windows harmonise with the carefully chosen and well-laid bricks, under a red pantile roof. Simple and charming.

An identical, balancing pair of houses has been individually 'improved' by their proud new owners since houses on the former council estate have been sold off. On both sides the fine wooden-framed windows with glazing bars have been ripped out and replaced by blank sheets of glass, which look out over a motorway fly-over and so have to be shielded with elaborately draped curtains. The excellent brickwork has been covered on one side with a dull grey render, achieving precisely the brutal character which the public is said to reject in modern architecture. The right-hand house is covered in plastic-stone panelling creating an effect which, because it is so ludicrous, must lower the value of the house—not what the proud owner intended. Anybody who treated a house in a Georgian terrace in this way would be regarded as a vandal; good uniform houses of the nineteenth and twentieth centuries deserve equal respect.

cohesive whole, and one insensitive alteration can destroy the whole carefully organised pattern of the street. Most at risk perhaps are the beautiful small estates put up by the local authorities just after the First World War. These 'homes for heroes' have only recently been sold to tenants who have in many cases lived in the house all their lives, who not unnaturally want to 'improve' their home now that it is their own. Grasping salesmen have recognised an untilled field and have forced onto these people a number of largely useless and certainly very unsightly additions.

The most horrifying 'improvement' of all is the facing of the whole of the front of the house—which was often originally built of carefully laid bricks—with an absurd crazy-paving pattern. What purpose this is supposed to have, or indeed what it is supposed to represent, it is difficult to imagine. The only person who can get any benefit from this eyesore is the salesman, no doubt chuckling in his neo-Georgian gem paid for by his gullible householder.

Almost as bad and perhaps more insidious, because it is backed by pseudo-science and publicity by commercial firms, is the hard selling of commercial double-glazing. Anyone who lives in an ordinary street will know the way the door mat is littered almost daily with insistent claims and offers from double-glazing firms. The result of this standardised double glazing is almost always destructive to the look of the house.

It is doubtful that anyone reading this book would be responsible for such horrors, or indeed would buy a house which had been treated in this manner. If you are landed with this sort of thing it is essential to reinstate the glazing bars or the leaded lights, both of which are almost always removed by double-glazing firms. It is possible to find out what sort of glazing was originally in the house by looking at the other houses in the road. If double glazing is essential then it is often cheaper merely to repeat the existing wood windows on the inside face of the room. If both inner and outer windows are correctly sealed then a higher degree of insulation will have been achieved, whilst retaining the character of the house. It is not so easy to cope with crazy-paving on the front wall. Possibly the best solution would be to render the whole façade and then paint it in a suitable manner. If the house should be in a predominantly brick estate it might be possible to face the house with paviours (thin bricks normally used for pavements). This however would be very expensive, and potential buyers of such mistreated houses should be warned of this.

Although such drastic treatment may be rare, all houses that come on the market have over the years been subjected to small unsightly alterations. In the last forty years the rage for modernisation has particularly affected the inter-war house. Flush doors replace the original high-waisted panel doors, picture rails are removed, leading is taken out of the windows, brass knobs are replaced with plastic or aluminium lever handles, and of course in every case the bathroom and the kitchen have been modernised. So perhaps, with all this alteration, it would be as well to consider two types of house built in 1910 and which exist still in their pristine state. I have chosen 1910 as this was the high point of the small individual house, and it was to these houses that the builders of the estates of the 1920s and '30s looked back.

The Neo-Georgian House

First let us look at a house influenced by Edwin Lutyens and the Georgian revival which he helped, with his friend J. M. Barrie, to create. Lutyens had designed the sets for Barrie's play *Quality Street* in 1902. The house is rectangular, in the centre there is a front door with a pediment, possibly supported on finely carved volutes. To either side the sash windows balance, though the elevations are not entirely symmetrical; there may be a bay window to one side, or perhaps at the position of the staircase there will be a tall window rising between the two floors. There is almost certainly a service wing, which may even contain a garage running off to one side. Nonetheless the overall effect is of architectural balance, and all the details have the elegant refinement that we find in true eighteenth-century buildings.

Inside it is much the same. The rooms are well proportioned, though possibly slightly lower than a true Georgian room, and there will be good Classical cornices and well-proportioned doors with wide, moulded architraves. The dining room will possibly be panelled, and most of the fireplaces downstairs will be framed in a simple bolection mould. The bedroom fireplaces are in pale green or purple tiles, with a cast-iron surround—not to a mass-produced pattern, as so often happened in Victorian times, but in an elegant design which is in character with the house and may well have been designed by the original designer of the house. It is important that these fireplaces, which are especially vulnerable since they are no longer needed

A pair of neo-Georgian houses of c 1930 on Western Avenue in London, one of the new arterial roads which encouraged massive suburban speculative housing developments between the wars. Influenced by the work of architects like Lutyens and Clough Williams-Ellis, these houses are perhaps a little prim but surprisingly distinguished. The little touches like the urns on the parapet and the carefully designed chimneys help to differentiate these houses from their less imaginative neighbours.

in a centrally heated house, should be saved on every possible occasion, since they are an important part of the character of the house, and often show the architect at his best.

On the ground floor in the main rooms the floors are usually designed to be of polished wood, either hard-wood floorboards or parquet. It is best to leave these as they are; close carpeting is as unsuitable for the neo-Georgian house as it is for the genuine seventeenth-century house. The first floor may have simple deal boards, which of course were intended for carpeting; or, if the house is of a superior quality, then it is possible that the wide floorboards will be of oak, which was intended to be polished. This is particularly true of upstairs corridors, where carpet runners were much more common than close carpeting.

One usually finds these neo-Georgian houses relatively unaltered, unless they have been lived in by the singularly foolish or the very rich. This is because the room shapes are simple, and ordinary people still find them easy to live in. If the downstairs fireplaces have been removed, or architraves taken off, these can always be replaced relatively cheaply, and it is usually possible to find something in the house to copy. Similarly the sash windows can be replaced relatively easily should the double-dealing double-glazing merchants have been at them. It is surprising how

often staircase balustrades are boarded up but it is also surprising how often this is all that is done, and the removal of a hardboard panel will display the turned balustrades in all their original glory.

These neo-Georgian houses are usually well built of brick, often with a damp-proof course and cavity brickwork under a simple hipped roof. They should give little worry as far as ordinary maintenance is concerned, though of course all tiled roofs need attention after about sixty years. Particular care should be taken to see that the nailing of the tiles has not rusted.

Houses like these, which have the cool elegance of a Georgian house, should be painted in much the same way that a Georgian house would be treated, though perhaps white should be used more lavishly than might be now thought proper in a true Georgian house. Pale creams are also very suitable as indeed are any pastel colours. It was in neo-Georgian houses that these colours were first used, and they respond to such treatment. Pale lilac walls set against white architraves and windows are particularly effective. Regency stripe or Georgian-influenced wallpapers would also be entirely appropriate decoration. Indeed, if it is still available in your area, the 'porridge' wallpaper which was so reviled by the fashionable in the early 1960s would also be suitable, though perhaps the use of

Another pair of semi-detached houses on Western Avenue, London. By removing all the glazing bars on the ground floor windows and replacing them with sheets of glass, the whole elevation has been ruined. Like its neighbours, these houses have a tiled roof and are built of light-red brick, with courses of thin tiles used to accentuate the corners.

A pair of semi-detached houses of c 1930. Little remains in the house on the left of the original, rather pleasant, design which can be seen in the house on the right. The fake-stone panels will inevitably crack off after a few winter frosts. The enormous sheets of glass replacing the leaded arched windows let in the cold and look out on to a particularly noisy stretch of an arterial road. The new roof is partly flat and does not follow the pitched roofs of the main part of the house, which will lead to leaks between the junction of the two roofs. In a few years' time a small fortune will have to be spent in correcting these so-called 'improvements'.

decorative friezes might be avoided except in inter-war houses where they would be entirely suitable. Lutyens himself experimented with much more daring colour schemes in his neo-Georgian houses. He painted his wall gloss black and contrasted this by picking out architectural features in scarlet gloss, at the same time staining his floors green. But perhaps only a house with the sort of character that Lutyens, or one of his followers like Harold Falkner, was able to design would be able to stand up to this sort of treatment. But nonetheless, the period just before 1914 was also the period of the Russian Ballet, with its use of clashing scarlets and oranges set against black and deep purple, and also the period when the Post-Impressionists first came to England. All this had a loosening effect on the use of colour in the period around the First World War, but it was not long before interiors reverted to paler and more refined

A pair of houses in a terrace in West London. A typical 'up-market' pair of London houses; both have been altered. On the left, a garage door has been rather surprisingly converted into a bay window in a sensitive manner, the new windows matching the old dormers. On the right-hand house, the leading has been removed from the first floor windows which means that they have lost the lightness of those on the left. The rough-plaster external finish is original, but it would probably not have been coloured.

colours which remained in favour until the appearance of *House and Garden* colours, with their much brighter effects, in the early 1960s.

The Arts and Crafts House

Our second house has none of the refinement of the neo-Georgian house that we have just been looking at, though perhaps it has more character and gusto. The Arts and Crafts movement started as an attempt to return to honest English vernacular building. It was only by chance, almost by accident, that the neo-Georgian style developed from the true local vernacular. To William Morris, and his friend Philip Webb, both of whom had been trained in the office of the great Gothic revival architect G. E. Street, Classicism symbolised all that was commercial and vile in Victorian England. It was only at the end of their careers that they came to see that the simple Georgian house, albeit with its Classical details, was as much a part of the vernacular tradition as was the ordinary old country cottage. However their first love was these simple vernacular cottages—built somewhere between the end of the Middle Ages and the arrival of Queen Anne on the throne. They were built in a style that we would probably today call Tudor. In stone country, like the Cotswolds and Derbyshire, the house would be built in that material. If it were an expensive house it would be roofed in stone slates and there would be stone lintels with Tudory drips over the stone-mullioned windows; if it were cheaper,

then it would have been thatched, with ordinary timber lintels over leaded windows. In forest country the house would have been built with great baulks of timber and the walls filled in with wattle and daub (plaster reinforced with strips of wood). Here the roof would almost certainly be thatched, while for more expensive houses there would be elaborate displays of timberwork and much carving. Bricks were rarely used for ordinary houses until the eighteenth century, but flint with brick dressings and reed-thatch roofing was common enough in Norfolk.

The rooms of these cottages would be low and very simple. Often large timber beams, sometimes carved, would support the ceiling joists plastered over (nowadays too often stripped). There would be a great deep fireplace or ingle where, in a wealthy house, huge joints of meat would be turned on a spit. Up a twisting narrow staircase one or two ill-lit bedrooms with small dormers would be tucked into the roof. All the equipment of the house would be locally made by craftsmen, who could turn their hand to a multitude of crafts. Everything had a cohesion of style, which was much admired in the late Victorian period, when it sometimes seemed that any style would do.

If this may today seem a rather sentimental approach to early house building, this was the view put about by William Morris and his followers, and their influence was colossal. As late as 1904 that great artist, garden designer, photographer and crafts woman, Gertrude Jekyll, in her delightful book *Old West Surrey*, illustrates every conceivable country

...tefact, from a wooden mousetrap to old villagers' ...hite smock-frocks', which she had found still in ...ily use around her home at Munstead outside ...odalming.

With such masters pressing the style it was of course ...ot long before architects tried to create the type of ...uilding that they all so admired. Often they ...cceeded—like that great furniture-maker Ernest ...imson in his cottages in Charnwood Forest—in ...creating at great expense all the characteristics of a ...nd-built country cottage. Other architects were ...rhaps not quite so dedicated as Gimson to the ...rsuit of absolute authenticity. They took up the ...yle and, after giving perhaps more consideration for ...acticalities (in one of the Gimson cottages it is ...ecessary to go through the main bedroom to get to ...e other bedrooms), modern neo-Tudor was born. ...his Arts and Crafts style survived right up to 1939.

Harold Falkner, who could handle the vernacular ...yle as easily as he could the Georgian, produced ...me extraordinarily cranky 'hand-built' Tudor ...ouses just outside Farnham in the late 1930s. Oliver ...ill, who, as well as designing in Lutyens's Georgian ...yle, designed in a Modern style entirely acceptable ... doctrinaire Modernists, also designed and lived in ...ild Tudor fantasies. P. A. Barron's book *House ...esirable* (1929) is entirely given to neo-Tudor design, ...d includes Lutyens's work with other lesser-known ...chitects.

Although neo-Tudor is a style that is rather out of ...shion at the moment, it nonetheless has a number of

qualities which still appeal to the ordinary house buyer today. Often these are not architectural qualities (which is why in this period of intellectual snobbery the style is so out of fashion) but it offers the ordinary house buyer in this insecure age the same sense of security that it did during the insecure 1930s. Primarily it offers warmth and enclosure, and although there is little of the elegance that we have seen in the neo-Georgian house, this is compensated for by the sense that this type of house is more suitable to the damp and cold of a typical English day. The windows are small and leaded, perhaps with a picture of a sunset or a great galleon in the golds and reds made so popular at this time by the paintings of Frank Brangwyn. The ceilings are low, often with heavy dark oak beams, and there will be an ingle-nook with a fireplace which has a beaten copper hood set against dark red or green tiles. Possibly the ingle itself will have a little leaded window that looks out onto the garden.

It was quite common in this style, particularly in the work of Baillie Scott or Raymond Unwin, for all the rooms on the ground floor to flow into each other. The ingle in the living hall is divided by a high settle from the staircase. The dining room, seen through an arch, has its own deep bay window, and tucked round the corner, perhaps even with another bay window, is the study, where there may be a small fitted desk reminiscent, as is so much else in the house, of a Durer engraving. Perhaps all the rooms will be tied together with a painted or stencilled wide frieze, below which will be a plate rack held up on paired brackets on which pewter and copper plates glitter in the firelight. There is not a great deal of furniture; possibly just one gate-legged table on a carpet on the polished wood floor. On the table is a large copper bowl crammed with roses, and the garden door, which opens directly from the hall, looks out onto a pergola dripping with roses beyond a herbaceous border.

The staircase winds up to a gallery, which looks down onto part of the living hall which in places runs up two storeys. Because of this the bedrooms can be rather small, and there is probably not room for a four-poster bed under the eaves. But each room has an oak door with its ledging and bracing showing into the room. On the passage side, the door is made of four large planks possibly with their edges moulded, which run straight up and down without any lippings. The latches are also made of oak, with a string to lift the latch from outside and an oak plug which slides to lock the door. All the oak is stained and polished, and the walls are in a rough stippled plaster which probably looks best painted white or a pale cream. Wallpaper was rarely used in these houses, but since William Morris's influence was paramount in creating the style, his marvellous patterned fabrics, particularly the printed linen and not the cheaper screen prints, go perfectly in these surroundings. Whilst fitted carpets are suitable in bedrooms, the best architects used polished floor boards often 14 inches wide, and these should of course be displayed, as should the good floor boards or floor tiling downstairs. It is possible that the original decorative friezes have been destroyed over the years, but it is a simple matter to find suitable friezes in a book of contemporary patterns, and have them replaced with stencils.

There were a large number of books published between 1890 and 1930 concerned with the de-

coration of this type of house, and since they were ve popular they can still often be picked up cheaply second-hand book shops. By looking at these books will soon be clear what the ideals of the builders of t neo-Tudor homes were, and how their buildin should be treated. Their titles usually made a gre play on the word 'Home', such as: *Modern Hom* (1909) by Raffles Davidson; *Art and Craft of Hor Making* (1913) by Edward Gregory; *Modern Domes. Architecture and Decoration*, Studio Year Book 19 (Colour Plates); *Our Homes and How to Beautify The* (1902) by H. J. Jennings; *The British Home of Tod.* (1904), *Flats, Urban Houses and Cottage Homes* (1907 *The Modern Home* (1906), all three by W. Sha Sparrow with coloured illustrations. *Houses and Garde* (in two editions, 1906 and 1920) by M. H. Baill Scott has colour plates and a lot of good advice o colours, etc. *The Apartments of the House: The Arrangement, Furnishing and Decoration* (1900) Crouc and Butler; *Home and Garden* (1900) Gertrude Jekyl *The Art of Building a Home* (1901) Parker and Unwir and *Modern Suburban Houses* (1906) C. H. B. Quennel are all books in which architects discuss their ow work.

Because Arts and Crafts houses were designed for fantasy dream world (which perhaps still holds som of its potency today), they require love and sympath in a way that perhaps few other houses, except for ver old houses, do. But then a very old house would rarel be treated in an insensitive manner. There is littl reason why a relatively new building which is out c fashion at the moment should not be judged on its ow merits and recognised for what it is. This is, of course the rule that should always be obeyed whenever w attempt to 'put back the style': the difficulty in th case of relatively new buildings is recognising wha that style is.

Architectural Metalware

This section deals with domestic fitted metalware that is largely decorative as well as functional. The variation is wide and follows the progression of styles from the late eighteenth century to the 1930s. There are three basic headings under which most aspects should be covered: railings, balconies and balustrades; door and window furniture; and fire grates.

Restoration of original fittings should be carried out wherever possible; broad indications as to how to do this are given in the final section of this chapter. The replacement of metalwork can be expensive, so a careful consideration of design, material and scale is advisable before the fittings are to be reinstated. Much can be gained from studying other similar properties in the area, as the builder is likely to have used similar details and materials.

Railings, Balconies and Balustrades

These are the most dominant features of architectural metalwork, especially in the early nineteenth century when highly decorative balconies and canopies made of cast iron enlivened the sombre terrace. In the eighteenth century, iron had become the new wonder material whose production epitomised the Industrial Revolution. Feats of construction and technology had been performed with it, like the most famous example, the Iron Bridge at Coalbrookdale. Samuel Smiles hailed it 'This most extraordinary metal, the soul of every manufacture and the mainspring perhaps of civilised society'.

Decorative ironwork in the eighteenth century was made of scrolled and elegant wrought iron, which involved laborious smithying by hand. In 1709, Abraham Darby developed new casting techniques which were fuelled by coal instead of charcoal. Using charcoal had meant a large consumption of wood, and its increasing scarcity had prevented the expansion of the industry. The great railings around St. Paul's Cathedral were the first important examples of cast iron on any scale. They were cast in Kent by the old charcoal method in 1714 and were much disliked by Sir Christopher Wren, who had beseeched the building committee to erect a low railing of wrought iron rather than the tall bulky balusters that obscured his building. The architect Isaac Ware felt entirely differently, and in 1756 wrote: 'Cast iron is very serviceable to all builders and a vast expense is saved in many cases by using it; in rails and balusters it makes a rich and massy appearance when it has cost very little and when wrought iron, much less substantial, will cost a vast sum!' The economic factor more than anything else contributed to the sharp decline in wrought-iron production.

By the late eighteenth century, railings particularly were made of cast iron with a pattern of designs that was set until the mid-nineteenth century. At first the decorative details like the urn finials were cast. Later whole railings could be cast in sections, then assembled to the required dimension. Generally railings were made up of slender bars capped with finials in

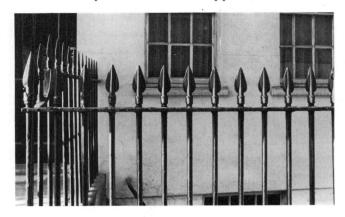

Railing of a Georgian terraced house. The pattern of spears held by one horizontal bar and set into stone is typical for the period 1770–1840.

Part of the facade of the Lancet building, Adelphi. *The lower balcony shows a curved design of vigorous repeating anthemion pattern. It was designed by the Adam brothers in the 1770s. The window guard on the upper floor also includes the anthemion motif—one of the most popular patterns up to 1840.*

the form of spears, arrows, pikes and *fleur-de-lys*, giving the impression that the house was protected by a palisade of weapons. Corners were accentuated with the ubiquitous neo-Classical urn or maybe an acorn or pine cone. Wrought iron survived longer in the case of balconies and stair balustrades, where the light framework of simple geometric design (like trellis, for example) was still executed in the material until about 1810. The small details however were applied and cast in iron, lead or brass and were occasionally gilded. An enormous demand for cast-iron balconies, window guards and balconettes (small decorative guard rails) was prompted by the large-scale speculative developments in the fashionable towns like Cheltenham and Brighton. The estates in these towns, built for the rapidly expanding middle class, were carefully planned and arranged in long terraces.

One of the earlier speculative developments in London was the Adelphi Terrace scheme, designed by

the Adam Brothers in the 1770s. They probably also designed the balconies on the main floor, which were the first to be made of cast iron. They were cast at the Carron Works in Scotland. The repeated anthemion motif is executed in rather a heavy way when compared to the window guards on the upper floors of the same house. These upper guards are of an extremely popular pattern that crops up on Georgian terraces all over England. The design is printed in L. N. Cottingham's *Smith and Founder's Director* (1823). Many nineteenth-century trade catalogues illustrated the same designs for twenty or thirty years. This means that the more conservative middle class could have safe and identifiable decoration, which implied a certain continuity.

Although Georgian terraces, with their emphasis on restraint, order and dignity, changed little in design, their decorative details became ponderously florid in the second quarter of the nineteenth century. Balcony fronts tended to be made up of small sections which were cast and assembled with a continuous piece of top rail. More curvacious and Rococo inclinations became evident. The neo-Classical repertory was breaking down into Naturalism, and the battle of the styles that raged throughout the century broke out in earnest. The ironwork of the mid Victorian villa was cast in a mongrel Gothic style. On the high-pitched roofs, open-work crestings and finials pierced the skyline; balconies and window guards shrank to low fences or single twisted horizontal bars. Railings continued in their eighteenth century form as spears though the bars were elaborated in ropework or a spiral.

It is now often difficult to assess what type of railings existed. Where houses had no basement railings were hacked down during the last war. The reason was that they went to the war effort, ostensibly to provide armaments. It was a wasted gesture—cast iron cannot be melted down and re-cast. Many Victorian streets are now a mess of crude masonry, wooden fences or tennis wire and privet hedge.

Early nineteenth-century terrace. The restraint of the facade, so typical of the terrace, 1770–1840, depends on the ironwork for decorative contrast. The balcony fronts are cast in individual sections.

Below : High Victorian elaboration—a page from the catalogue of Macfarlane, Glasgow. A varied roofline was very important and could be enhanced with ironwork crestings and finials.

The mid-nineteenth century was the high point of decorative cast-iron work. Whole buildings could be made of it, prefabricated and exported to anywhere in the world. Trade catalogues burst with all kinds of ornamental fitting. These were illustrated in a variety of styles, though the Gothic revival was dominant for domestic use. Cresting was strongly apparent at this time, in the medieval manner or in the 'Second Empire' Classicism; either style would do.

Wrought iron re-surfaced properly under the instigation of the Arts and Crafts movement. Though the principles had been laid in the 1840s by Pugin, a direct, individual and honest approach to craftsmanship took place in the late nineteenth and early twentieth century. This was probably a reaction to the opulent contortions of high-Victorian cast iron. Iron was to be an example of 'truth to material'. It was hammered, beaten and wrought—never cast. Designs were inspired by the simple and functional fittings of the seventeenth and eighteenth-century country cottage. Decorative features like balconies and railings had little place in the Arts and Crafts house except, perhaps, in an urban case where they could comprise of plain wrought upright bars. Lead rainwater heads harked back to the seventeenth century, and were often displayed inscribed with a date as well as patterning. Weather vanes were very

common, made of wrought iron and with a sharply defined silhouette.

The fashion for wrought iron survived in the traditional suburban home of the 1930s. The above-mentioned fittings that were popular from the Arts and Crafts movement remained so. The execution was of a lower standard. Finishes could be *cast* to resemble wrought work, and designs were stodgy or 'twee'. Simply scrolled gates and window guards were produced in large numbers for the 'ribbon developments'. Railings might consist of a panel set into a low wall, as in the nineteenth century. Posts of wood

between which spiked chains were slung made a convenient device for fencing the small street as they created less of a visual barrier. Outside the inter-war block of flats, or the more 'Moderne' house, the railings would appear in a jazzy, 'Odeonesque', *Art Deco* idiom. In the later 1930s, when European Modernism finally made an impact in this country, tubular metal was used for fencing. It was made up into rectangular sections and sometimes filled with wire mesh, which then could be installed interchangeably as railing, gate or balcony.

Railings can be re-cast by an iron foundry on production of a model; a single bar should do. Wrought-iron work can still be commissioned from a blacksmith, or from firms listed in the directory section. There are dealers who specialise in antique architectural metalwork, though size and proportion is a great difficulty.

Door and Window Furniture

Many mistakes seem to be made in the arrangement and selection of the metal fittings on the front door. The door itself should be of the correct scale and design. The six-panelled door was common in the eighteenth and nineteenth centuries; the two-panelled door in the Regency. Glass started to appear in the upper panels by the mid-nineteenth century.

New doors are all too often of a type that is called 'Georgian'. This is historically inaccurate, since the

Above: Edwardian commercial designs from the catalogue of Benham and Froud. These 'artistic' designs were popular for the suburban home in the early twentieth century, and survived in essence until the 1930s.

Left: Modern movement. The tubular metal railings emphasise the geometrical nature of 'contemporary' design in the 1930s. The windows are cast in metal, probably iron.

The correct arrangement of furniture for a six-panel door.

Plain door handles from a trade pattern book c 1820. Popular 1770–1840.

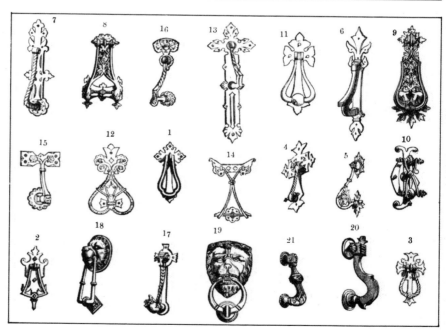

Door knockers from the trade catalogue of Hart, Son Peard and Co., about 1875. Though described as medieval, some designs are updated versions of Georgian models.

top panels are replaced by a fanlight. It looks especially ridiculous when there is a fanlight above the door already. The current prevalence for stripped and varnished doors is also incorrect in the terrace; they should be painted. The gleam of brass on the front door is very much in favour today despite the continual attention that it requires. Brass was a relatively expensive material until the mid-nineteenth century; black japanned or 'berlin' cast-iron fittings were usual and needed little maintenance. Bronze was popular in the nineteenth century and remained so through to the 1930s, when plated chromium became widespread. When replacing door furniture it should all be made of the same metal and, if possible, the same finish.

Door knockers were the most decorative feature on the front door. They first appeared, in various forms, on modest houses in the eighteenth century. The earliest types range from the simple heavy ring and a lion's mask with a ring in its mouth, to a neo-Classical urn hung with a swagged rapper. Style and treatment of door knockers changed with taste, though many designs continued to be shown in the trade catalogues throughout the nineteenth century. The most common was the slender U-shaped rapper, chastely decorated with acanthus. From about 1860 one type of door knocker incorporated a letter box, which avoided cluttering smaller doors.

A combination from the late Victorian period was the letter box and pullbar. It was more effective in that previously the large central door knob had a tendency to come adrift with the vibration from the banging of the door. The letter box itself arrived with the introduction of the penny post in 1840, as no longer did the householder have to pay for letters received. The late nineteenth-century examples were typically elaborate in design, and often cast with the word *Letters*. The plainer designs of the early twentieth century were inspired by the Arts and Crafts movement, sometimes relieved by undulating curves. Letter boxes should correctly be situated on the constructional bars of the door—not in the weaker panels. This is also true of the rest of the door furniture. The illustration on page 41 shows the most pleasing arrangement.

Numerals on the terraced house were engraved on brass plates or made up of individual brass characters. Sign-written numbers were painted in a contrasting colour to the door itself, or, where there was a porch, on the column. Enamel plaques of blue numbers on a white background made an appearance on the modest doorway in the late nineteenth century. The script chosen should match the period of the house.

Mortice locks that were concealed in the door were invented in the late nineteenth century. Before that the more conspicuous rim lock was fitted to the door, with the movement contained in a brass or iron casing. Rim locks are better on interior doors. Modern insurance usually insists on one or more mortice locks of recent make on the main outside door.

Bell pulls came into common use during the Regency, installed either in the masonry at the side of the door, or in the frame itself, or where there was a side panel. The design is usually of a knob set into a circular recessed dish. These bells were converted to electricity quite easily when the time came. Purpose-made electric bells shrank to little more than the push button. In the Craft revival, a popular design derived from the country types was a vertically placed wrought bar, with a handle fixed onto the door jamb. These enjoyed a great vogue on the beamed mock-Tudor semi-detached houses.

Door, window and cabinet furniture designed by R. L. B. Rathbone, an Arts and Crafts metalworker. The flat backplates and sinuous outlines are typical of the period 1890–1910.

Fanlights were a semi-circle of decorative wrought iron and glass above the front door. They were necessary in the terraced house of the eighteenth century to light the narrow hallway. The plainer rectangular ones with simple divisions in cast iron date from the early nineteenth century. Lanterns were sometimes let into the fanlight, leaning forward above the door to shed light onto the steps.

Plain brass door handles are most suitable for all styles of interior door, in combination with equally plain fingerplates and keyhole escutcheons. They can be made out of other materials such as ceramic, glass or wood, and frequently were in later Victorian homes. Fretted or cast fingerplates were common from the 1820s onwards. Ormolu could only be afforded by the rich and was impractical, as the gilding easily wore off.

Portières were curtains that were hung on the back of the door to help exclude the draught. They were attached by brass rods, and added the lush cosiness so important to the Victorian interior. Rustic latches and levers were highly admired by the artist-craftsmen, whose designs display a definite (and at times idiosyncratic) individual style rather than a slavish copying of earlier examples. Watered-down versions of the Arts and Crafts style were again common in the 1930s, and sometimes cast with a 'hammered finish'. Bakelite, a sort of plastic, was mass-produced at this time in a brown wood-grain effect for interior door knobs, light switches and so on. Elaborate doors (which have suffered badly with more recent 'modernisations') with intricate metalwork fascias drew attention to the entrance of a '30s flat. Interior doors sported angular chromed knobs and handles, set rather high up.

There is an enormous amount of door furniture available, and selection can be difficult. If in doubt choose the simplest designs. Beware of modern 'wrought' iron; it is better to try and get a blacksmith to execute something in the local tradition. The modern 'Louis' types of brasswork are very coarsely chased; if you must have this style of fitting, buy old ones from an antique dealer.

Window Furniture

Counterbalanced sashes were introduced at the end of the eighteenth century, and have remained in use since. The sash fastener of brass has hardly altered in design from the lever type of the early nineteenth

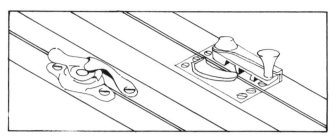

Two common types of sash-window fastener.

century; other types, such as the cheaper screw bolt, proved too fiddly. The small 'hook' sash lift, and the handles which were positioned in pairs on the underside of the upper sash, are of late nineteenth-century origin.

Tall casement windows, now known as French doors, became especially popular during the Regency, opening onto the balcony or garden. The locks were long bolts running the height of the frame and operated by a handle, made entirely in brass. Cast-iron casements were frequently put into the picturesque Victorian cottage and were either of a diamond pattern imitating leaded lights or of more complex hexagonal and octagonal shapes. Properly maintained they did not corrode. The casement window had generally replaced the sash by the 1930s. They could be made of metal and opened with lever handles. The more modernistic house also had metal windows, made famous by the firm of Crittall in Essex. The fenestration was long and low, like a tall late eighteenth-century window turned onto its side. A common feature of this type of window was the curved corner, which contributed to the nautical look of the house.

It is important to stress that the replacing of any window with modern double-glazed units can be a serious mistake—especially if they are described as 'Georgian'. The proportion and the width of the 'glazing' bars are incorrect and can ruin the period look of the house.

Fire Grates

As coal replaced wood in the fireplace in the eighteenth century, the traditional 'fire dog' with bars holding the logs disappeared. A basket, which became known as the 'dog grate', was needed to support the coal and was raised above the hearth to obtain a good draught. The better kinds were made of steel and were pierced along the apron with a pattern. The question

Dog grate of about 1780. Executed to a very high standard in engraved, chased and faceted steel, it is in the neo-Classical style of the Adam brothers. The pierced apron increased the draught.

Below : Peace and Plenty *original Victorian cast-iron mantelpiece shown with original cast insert, overmantel, fender and fire tools, all in burnished cast-iron finish. The mantelpiece features the Greek Goddesses of Harvest.*

of the draught necessary to burn the coal and to heat the room efficiently was not properly understood until the late eighteenth century, when Count Rumford invented his new fireplace. The size of its opening was much smaller, as was the neck of the flue. With his system, fireplaces had to be filled in at the sides, which were splayed to throw out heat. Rumford recommended that metal should only be used for the grate itself, as it conducts and therefore absorbs heat.

The hob grate developed from the dog grate in the late eighteenth century. It was made of cast iron and often applied with elegant neo-Classical swags, medallion heads and arabesques. The basket was still raised but the sides were filled in, creating a hob on either side to keep food and drink warm. The inside of the hearth above was lined with decorated cast plates which were a descendant of the fire-back. This grate did not accord to Rumford's principles of keeping metal down to a minimum and was probably inefficient. It did, however, remain a favourite until the late nineteenth century.

The characteristic nineteenth-century fireplace was made almost entirely of cast iron. The grate was small and inside a richly ornamented arched opening. Even the spandrels within the fire surround were made of cast iron. Tiles were common in later Victorian homes, and often constituted the only non-ferrous

Right: Vignette showing a cottage hob grate in use. From Thomas Bewick's History of British Birds *(1804).*

Right: Vignette showing a cottage hob grate in use. From Thomas Bewick's History of British Birds *(1804).*

Below right: Early nineteenth-century grate in the Gothic revival style. It was probably meant to be made entirely of metal. The slides are splayed to throw out heat.

Below left: Arts and Crafts fireplace designed by C. F. A. Voysey. The opening of the grate is very reduced, has a small hood and is set high, all to increase efficiency. From the catalogue of Thomas Elsley Limited, about 1905.

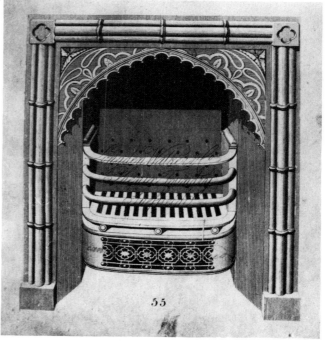

element in a fireplace which—chimney piece and all—could be made entirely of cast iron.

Stoves were not popular in England even though they were much more efficient than the wall fireplace. People complained that they gave off unpleasant fumes and dried up the air. Unlike the open fire, they created no focal point to the room.

All kinds of patented grates and fireplaces were invented in the nineteenth century. Among the more efficient were some that were hung with steel chains, which improved the draw. A closely fitting wire mesh, decorated with brass details, could do the same, and at the same time protected the carpet from spitting coals.

The 'register' was a popular system of draught control with a form of door in the flue that was invented in the nineteenth century. After 1900 improvements were made in its grate design. They were now even smaller and had no bars at the front. These grate fronts could be finished in a variety of metals and enamels.

Electricity finally provided the answer to obtaining clean and fume-free living in the form of bar fires. These could take the place of the open fire without mess or labour and be used in any part of the room, as there was no flue. The bar was held in a reflective dish of chromium-plated metal, and the whole fitting was recessed into the wall.

Gas fires first appeared in the nineteenth century, though they did not evolve until the time of the First

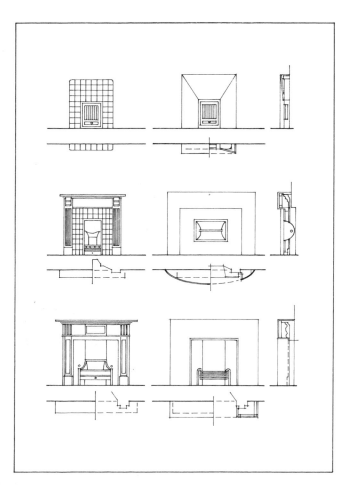

Modern fire grates of the 1930s, showing how to transform them from more traditional designs. The conversion in the middle includes an electric single-bar fire.

World War when they burned in porcelain elements and were set into surrounds of iron. Gas log fires also date back to the nineteenth century. Their current appeal lies in that they more or less successfully imitate wood or coal fires. This replaces the focal point of the room that was lost with the introduction of central heating.

There are now many dealers in antique fireplaces and grates. Shops that sell gas log fires have many period-style baskets and grates. In all cases, avoid choosing designs that are too grand for your house. Many of the fireplaces on the market are French nineteenth-century ones. Gas log fires can really only be used for effect, as much of the heat goes up the chimney.

Renovation and Maintenance

Iron

Paint can be removed from exterior ironwork by stripping with a chemical cleaner. On large-scale projects like railings, it is necessary that the whole process be carried out in sections to prevent rusting. When stripped, the iron should be wire brushed and any rust removed. The re-painting should commence with a layer of red oxide followed by the chosen colour. Most railings were painted black in the eighteenth and nineteenth centuries, though a colour described as 'garter blue' is known to have been used in the eighteenth century, and green is known in the first half of the nineteenth century. A wider variety of colours began to be used in the twentieth century. A matt finish enhances newly revealed details.

Japanning and berlin finishes were mentioned in trade catalogues in the nineteenth century. The first was a thick, resinous, glossy varnish, the second a dull matt finish which was appropriate for more complex designs. Interior cast and wrought iron should be waxed with a high-quality product that is not sticky. Steel grates have a finer surface. Strong rust removers should not be used. A fine wire wool to clean, and a mild metal polish to finish off, should ensure that the surface is not unnecessarily harmed.

Copper and Brass

Lacquer is only a good idea if the surface is not going to be touched or exposed to damp air. Door furniture should be cleaned lightly and regularly with a mild polish. This will inevitably cause wear but less so than an occasional, fierce cleaning. A good quality wax applied after cleaning will help prevent a certain amount of tarnishing. A wire brush should never be used.

Architectural Metalware

We often overlook just how much metalware there is, both in and around a 'period' house. During the 18th century, cast iron became a new wonder material and henceforth, delicate balconies and canopies sprang airily from facades, lacey fanlights and bold knobs and hinges graced entrances, and miles of elegant railings marked the perimeter of every street and square. Inside the house, centuries of decorative inventiveness, as well as mechanical ingenuity, have gone into the design of grates.

The following listings give a wide range of craftsmen who specialise in the repair, replacement and cleaning of domestic metalware, both inside and out.

Exterior Metalware

Albion Design
Albion Design have a wide range of period cast iron designs available including railings, balconies, etc., and also manufacture a comprehensive range of spiral staircases in cast iron, timber and concrete. These can be made to any height in diameters ranging from 4 feet to 7 feet.

Albion Design
12 Flitcroft Street
London WC2H 8DJ
Tel: (01) 836 0151

Almondsbury Forge
Sundays Hill
Almondsbury
Bristol
BS12 4DS
Tel: (0454) 613315

Bayswater Architectural Metalwork Co
This firm can make objects of almost any size to clients' specific designs.

Bayswater Architectural Metalwork Co Ltd
2 Pond Place
London SW3
Tel: (01) 589 4191

R Beasdale & Co
349 Caledonian Road
London N1
Tel: (01) 609 0934

H J Brooks & Co
136 Old Street
London EC1
Tel (01) 253 3887

Classic Garden Furniture
This firm has a fine selection of reproduction exterior and interior metalware, including cast iron rail heads, spiral

A selection of cast iron rail heads. Complete railings can be supplied.

staircases, lamp-posts, footscrapers, umbrella stands, door stops, etc.

Classic Garden Furniture Ltd
Audley Avenue
Newport
Shropshire
Tel: (0952) 813311

Crittall Windows
Crittalls were the leading manufacturer of steel doors and windows in the 1920s and '30s. They now manufacture some replacement parts to the original designs and offer advice on all aspects of repair and replacement of steel doors and windows.

Crittall Windows Ltd
Manor Works
Braintree
Essex CM7 6DF
Tel: (0376) 24106

Dorothea Restoration Engineers Ltd
Pearl Assurance House
Hardwick Street
Buxton
Derbyshire SK17 6DH
Tel: (0298) 3438

Kentish Ironcraft
Belhersden
Ashford
Kent
Tel: (0233) 82465

B Levy & Co
From a customer's drawing, rough sketch, sample, mock up or just an idea, B Levy & Co can manufacture practically any article in most metals, wood and certain kinds of plastics. Recent work includes the exact replicas of the cast iron Dolphin lamp-standards

These Acanthus pattern heavy cast iron railings were originally installed in the early 19th century. The restoration included remoulding the finials.

on the North Embankment of the Thames. These were produced from pattern equipment manufactured and planned by B Levy & Co and now line the South Bank.

B Levy & Co (Patterns) Ltd
8 Esterbrooke Street
Westminster
London SW1P 4NL
Tel: (01) 834 7486/1073

T Martin
The Old Nissean Forge
Newthorpe
Nottinghamshire
Tel: (07737) 3868

Richard Quinnell
Richard Quinnell are master craftsmen and specialists in the restoration of wrought and cast ironwork, and will make all kinds of replacement cast-iron decorative features, from spear-headed railings to weathervanes.

Richard Quinnell Ltd
Rowhurst Forge
Oxshott Road
Leatherhead
Surrey
Tel: (53) 75148/9

Robocraft
This forge specialises in all forms of traditional ironwork, both exterior and interior. Small candlesticks, flower pedestals, gates, railings, balustrades and lighting are available.

Robocraft
The Forge
Kington St Michael
nr Chippenham
Wiltshire
Tel: (024 975) 585

Southwell Builders (Stockwell)
This firm is engaged in the fabrication, casting and fitting of reproduction cast ironwork and the refurbishment and refixing of reclaimed ironwork. Southwell have in the past few years assembled a large range of patterns and original mouldings from which they can reproduce railings, balustrades, window guards, bootscrapers, table legs, etc. They specialise in 'one off' sets of rails, etc., mostly for private customers. They always have good stocks of railings,

A cast iron gate made to the original pattern. As well as moulding from surviving ironwork, this firm also has a large range of finial patterns.

balustrades, gates, spiral staircases, etc., in their factory in Robert Dashwood Way, but it is advisable to phone first as it is a factory, not a showroom.

Southwell Builders (Stockwell) Ltd
104a Lansdowne Way
London Sw8
Tel: (01) 622 7970/703 7740
and
The Ironworks
166 Robert Dashwood Way
Amelia Street
London SE17

Interior Metalware

J A Keenan
J A Keenan specialises in reproduction brass locks, cast from designs taken from his own, or customers', originals.

J A Keenan
3 Cranleigh Gardens
Stoke Bishop
Bristol
BS9 1HD
Tel: (0272) 682507

Lilly
This firm has a large selection of interior metal fittings in a variety of styles. The 'Antique' range of cabinet handles has

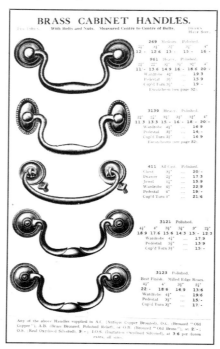

been produced from patterns used by the company for over 100 years. It is available in both polished brass and a brown relief finish.

B Lilly & Sons Ltd
Baltimore Road
Birmingham
B42 1DJ
Tel: (021) 357 1761

The following firms have large stocks of interior metalware, some with traditional designs.

J D Beardmore & Co Ltd
3/5 Percy Street
London W1P 0EJ
Tel: (01) 637 7041
and
120 Weston Road
Hove
Sussex
Tel: (0273) 71801
and
49 Park Street
Bristol
Tel: (0272) 277831

Comyn Ching & Co Ltd
110 Golden Lane
London EC1Y 0SS
Tel: (01) 253 8414

Locks & Handles
8 Exhibition Road
South Kensington
London SW7
Tel: (01) 584 6800

Stoves and Fire-Places

Many of the architectural salvage firms listed here also have large stocks of cast iron railings, balustrades and other items of architectural metalware.

Acquisitions
Acquisitions have probably one of the best stocks of old fireplaces in the country, including such gems as a special fireplace commemorating Queen Victoria's Jubilee in 1887. The process of

A page from B Lilly & Sons catalogue from early this century. The pattern shown at the top of the page is still available.

Right: An elaborate, early Victorian cast iron mantelpiece complete with insert, fender and fire tools.

restoration is slow and laborious, usually involving removal of thick layers of paint. Frequently the actual fire-back needs repair following decades of use. Often ornamental tiles will need repair or replacement, and for this purpose Acquisitions have built up one of the best collections of Victorian tiles outside the Victoria and Albert Museum. The restored fireplaces are usually sold with a burnished cast iron finish, although they can be painted if desired.

Acquistions (Fireplaces) Ltd
269 Camden High Street
London NW1 7BX
Tel: (01) 485 4955

Amazing Grates

This firm has one of the largest stocks of Georgian, Victorian and Edwardian fireplaces in London with a large showroom and adjoining workshops. All fireplaces are stripped and rebuilt with new firebricks to ensure a comfortable second lifetime, and are available in either a traditional black lead or polished pewter finish. Also available are pine mantels (both original and reproduction), old and new fire tools, fenders, hods, and a very large selection of Victorian tiles.

Amazing Grates
Phoenix House
61–63 High Road
London N2 8AB
Tel: (01) 883 9590

Edwin Arkwright

Edwin Arkwright have a range of four faithful reproductions of Victorian and Edwardian fireplaces. The castings and wood surrounds are produced using the original skills and techniques. All fireplace fenders are made in solid brass.

Edwin Arkwright Co Ltd
14–15 Charles Street
Willenhall
West Midlands
Tel: (0902) 62231/66440

Classic Garden Furniture

Classic Garden Furniture produce a fine selection of reproduction coal fired cast iron heaters, stoves, kitchen ranges and fire grates. All are produced to accurate Edwardian and Victorian designs and have a variety of accessories such as firebacks, fire tools, fire dogs and screens made to a similar standard.

The Queen *stove is one of the many designs produced in cast iron by the company.*

Classic Garden Furniture Ltd
Audley Avenue
Newport
Shropshire
Tel: (0952) 813311

Esse

Boasting a company history dating back to 1854 and such customers as Scott of the Antarctic and Florence Nightingale, Esse now produce an attractive range of four 'Victorian Heritage' cast iron stoves, which combine all the decorative features of their Victorian and Edwardian predecessors with the comfort and efficiency of modern stoves.

Esse Smith and Wellstood Ltd
Bonnybridge
Stirlingshire FK4 2AP
Tel: (032 481) 2171

Grahamston Iron Company

Many of Grahamston's products might be described as old fashioned rather than traditional in design, and consequently they would be ideal for the restoration of the 1920s and 1930s period. Products include continuous burning fires, cast iron room heaters, fire guards, and a slow combustion stove.

Grahamston Iron Company
PO Box 5
Falkirk
FK2 7HH
Tel: (0324) 22661

House of Steel Antiques

House of Steel Antiques have some 5,000 square feet of warehousing, showrooms and workshops where 300–400 original Victorian and Edwardian fireplaces are restored and on sale. They also restore and repair and polish customers' own fireplaces.

House of Steel Antiques
400 Caledonian Road
Islington
London N1 1DN
Tel: (01) 607 5889

An attractive 19th century cast iron fireplace from House of Steel Antiques. The dramatic centre piece is surrounded by flowers and ribbons.

Interoven

Interoven have an attractive range of reproduction traditional fires made from original patterns in cast iron, and also decorated fire-backs, dog grates and baskets.

The Apollo fire grate is made in solid cast iron and available in polished or matt black. It is suitable for burning all open fire solid fuels.

Interoven Ltd
70–72 Fearnley Street
Watford
Hertfordshire WD1 7DE
Tel: (92) 46761/2

King's Worthy Foundry Co

This foundry specialises in making fine quality reproduction cast iron fire grates, baskets, etc.

King's Worthy Foundry Co
Kingsworthy
Winchester
Hampshire SO23 7QG
Tel: (0962) 880841/882216

The London Architectural Salvage & Supply Co

A large selection of 18th century hob grates, 19th century combined grates/inserts, baskets, and fire dogs, is available. They also stock a large variety of stoves and cooking ranges, ranging in period from 1840–1920.

The London Architectural Salvage & Supply Co Ltd
Mark Street (off Paul Street)
London EC2A 4ER
Tel: (01) 739 0448/9

Marble Hill Fireplaces

This firm offers a large range of traditional, reproduction pine, and white and

Below: The Sandy mantelpiece is available in hand carved pine or with composition mouldings on wooden frame.

antique marble mantels. All fireplaces supplied are suitable for real, electric or gas fires. Extra depth can be given to a mantel to accommodate an electric fire when a recess into a chimney is not available.

Marble Hill Fireplaces Ltd
72 Richmond Road
Twickenham
Middlesex
Tel: (01) 892 1488

Petit Roque

This firm has a very large selection of fire grates with designs varying from

Below: The photograph shows the high relief of this fire surround. The mantel itself is made of pine and has a sheet marble inlay.

traditional to modern. 'Gothic', 'Adam' and 'Georgian' fire dogs are available together with all the necessary accessories. Items come in a variety of metals, including polished steel and wrought iron.

Petit Roque Ltd
5a New Road
Croxley Green
Rickmansworth
Hertfordshire WD3 3EJ
Tel: (87) 77968

The Stove Shop

The Stove Shop specialises in original Danish Stoves from the end of the 19th century. In addition they also have traditional English ranges as well as Swedish and French models. The stoves are restored to full working order by sand-blasting, polishing, re-bricking, casting new parts, welding, etc. Private restoration of stoves is undertaken. They also install and offer advice about the best way to run the stoves so as to obtain the maximum performance. All the stoves and ranges burn solid fuel (except pure coal and wood).

The Stove Shop
Camden Lock
Chalk Farm Road
London NW1
Tel: (01) 969 9531

Townsends

Apart from their huge stock of period

A part of Townsends showroom showing a Victorian fireplace, a wooden coal scuttle and a fireback and grate.

This interesting cast iron stove from Walcot Reclamation carries the inscription 'Electric Light' and a design symbolising a bulb.

tiles, Townsends are among London's leading suppliers of salvaged grates and fireplaces. Their stock usually dates from *c.* 1825 to the early 20th century. Townsends will sand-blast customers' own cast iron grates and will make up new surrounds from their huge stocks of Victorian and Edwardian tiles.

Townsends
1 Church Street
London NW8
Tel: (01) 724 3746
and
81 Abbey Road
London NW8
Tel: (01) 624 4756

Verine Products

Verine fireplaces are authentic marble reproductions of original 18th century classical designs such as those of Robert Adam and William Pain. Colours and designs are interchangeable between mantelpieces and there are sizes to suit large or small rooms.

Verine Products & Co
Goldhanger
Maldon
Essex CM9 8AP
Tel: (0621) 88611

Walcot Reclamation

One of the specialities of this architectural salvage firm is Georgian and Victorian fireplaces and stoves. These are renovated on the premises and are available with a large selection of fireplace surrounds and accessories.

Walcot Reclamation
108 Walcot Street
Bath
BA1 5BG
Tel: (0225) 310182

Mr Wandle's Workshop

A large selection of Victorian and Edwardian fireplaces and kitchen ranges are available. There is a comprehensive range of different finishes such as black lead, matt or eggshell black, shot-blast or painted to choice. A large range of accessories and a complete fitting service can be provided.

Mr Wandle's Workshop
200–202 Garrett Lane
London SW18 4ED
Tel: (01) 870 5873

Flooring

The floor is often the least considered aspect of an old interior. Many good rooms, where considerable trouble has been taken to get the walls and furniture right, are marred by horrible off-the-peg patterned carpet or a boring pastel-shaded wall-to-wall fitted carpet. It is well worth the effort to get the floor right, as it provides the basic unifying factor in any room and is largely responsible for the overall 'feel' of any decorative scheme.

Georgian Terraced Houses

Most floors in an old house will be made of wooden boards. In the eighteenth century such boarded floors would not have been stained and varnished or polished but left matt and either wet or dry-scrubbed. Wooden floors in their original state can still be seen in the Saloon at Uppark, Sussex, and in the Red Drawing Room at Syon House, Middlesex. The floor of the long gallery at Woburn Abbey, Bedfordshire,

has its original silvery scrubbed patina (surface texture) preserved (although it is presently covered by wall-to-wall carpeting), and so has the long gallery at Erdigg in Wales.

In the eighteenth century wooden floors were often left bare. George III, for instance, at Buckingham House, had no carpet, 'a luxury of which his Majesty deprives himself in almost every apartment, for the opinion that carpets . . . are injurious to health.' One authentic treatment for a bare boarded floor, which might not be practical where there is a lot of wear but could be pretty in a spare bedroom or even in a dining room, is a painted stencil pattern. Authentic eighteenth-century floors of this type can still be seen in England in the Chapel Drawing Room at Belton, Lincolnshire, and in the Dining Room at Crowcombe, Somerset, but traces of many others survive in the colonial houses of east-coast America, and it may be that they, with their simpler patterns, would provide the best examples to follow in a small house. Stencils

Long Gallery, Erdigg, Wales. A good example of an eighteenth-century bare-boarded floor in its original condition.

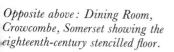

Opposite above: Dining Room, Crowcombe, Somerset showing the eighteenth-century stencilled floor.

Opposite below: Chapel Drawing Room, Belton, Lincolnshire, another rare survival of an early eighteenth-century painted and stencilled floor.

The Entrance Hall at 44 Grosvenor Square, London. The characteristic eighteenth-century stone-flagged floor with inset diamonds of slate can be copied in oil cloth or linoleum.

Below left: An eighteenth-century staircase showing patterned carpet with a plain border.

for patterned floors could be composed of stylised plants, heraldic devices, architectural features like Greek Fret or *trompe l'œil* paving. A stencilled pattern can be protected against wear by clear varnishing at regular intervals.

Patterned floor cloths are similar in spirit to decoratively painted floors and were very common in the eighteenth century. Floor cloth is a primitive and thinner form of linoleum and is canvas-backed and washable. It is ideal for entrance halls and dining rooms because it is easy to clean. In the eighteenth century it usually represented a pavement, and was marked or lined to represent stone flags. Sometimes, though, it was elaborately decorated to resemble a Roman mosaic. A modern reproduction floor cloth pavement can be seen in the Dining Room of No. 1 Royal Crescent, Bath, a house which has recently been restored as a museum by the Bath Preservation Trust. And many samples of old floor cloths can be seen at Wintherthur, in America.

The drawing room and bedrooms of a Georgian house would commonly have had carpet. Loom-weave carpet was manufactured in England from the 1740s at Wilton and Kidderminster though a great deal of carpet was also imported, largely from the Low Countries. In the eighteenth century, carpet would usually have covered the centre of the floor only leaving a space of about two feet of bare boards round the edge for the furniture to stand on. A number of lengths of carpet would be sewn together to form a square or rectangle, based on the proportions of the room and provided with a border. The provision of a plain or patterned border to a carpet was very important. Without one, a carpet tended to look like a cheap job-lot of factory remnants. As an extra refinement an additional border was painted on the woodwork of the floor round the edge of the carpet, like the inlaid borders which can be seen on the very grand floors of the galleries at Apsley House, London, and Attingham, Shropshire.

The Victorian Villa

A special feature of many Victorian houses is a paved floor of Minton tiles or Blashfield's mosaic in the entrance hall. Such floors are colourful and hard-wearing and it is silly to try to carpet over them, and vandalism to destroy them as Sir John Pope-Hennessy did with the *opus criminale* floors of the Victoria and Albert Museum in London. A tiled floor will probably be in need of repair, but most competent builders can cope with work of this type and two or three firms still make replacement tiles. (These can also be salvaged from demolition sites.)

Otherwise Victorian floors are most likely to be made of deal planks and will nearly always have been stained the dark plum-pudding colour of mahogany. They will either be varnished or polished round the edges, and have the middle of the floor carpeted. Completely fitted wall-to-wall carpets were also common in the nineteenth century, especially in draw-ing rooms where they contributed to the effect of all-

Wimpole Hall, Cambridgeshire. The hall floor was designed by Kendall in 1842 and executed in Minton's encaustic tiles. The greeting 'Salve' is a nice Victorian touch, and can still be bought on doormats.

Left: A Victorian drawing room with a floral patterned carpet and matching hearth rug contributing to the overall upholstered feel.

Opposite: An eighteenth-century panelled room with a wood-block floor covered with oriental rugs.

over upholstery. In the Victorian dining room it is almost *de rigueur* to have a Turkey pattern carpet in the middle of the floor. These are still relatively easy to get, either second-hand or in reproduction, and are in many ways the perfect carpet. A once-popular alternative floorcovering in dining rooms, entrance halls and passages and so on was linoleum. You may be lucky enough to find old linoleum still *in situ*, in which case it is worth keeping and repairing. Old linoleum can be cleaned with warm water or a commercial wax-stripper, but ammonia should not be used. Damaged areas can be repaired with shellac and holes filled with do-it-yourself sawdust composition, then painted to match the surrounding colours and varnished. Victorian-style lino can also be bought from second-hand furniture shops, old-established shops with undisturbed antediluvian stock, or straight from the manufacturers. In laying linoleum it is important to remember that it is brittle and should always be unrolled in a warm atmosphere to prevent the surface from cracking. Lino should not be glued to the floor (as it expands at a different rate to wood) but left to stretch for a fortnight or so after laying before being nailed down with carpet tacks.

Rugs are also an important feature of the Victorian interior. As well as enhancing the cosy fussiness desirable in a nineteenth-century house they serve a practical purpose, as they help to keep the house warm. Hearth rugs and little mats at the doors to all the rooms are essential. Good natural-fibre door mats inscribed 'Salve' in Roman letters are still easy to obtain for the front entrance, too. For the interior, fluffy hand-knotted woollen mats or brightly coloured rag rugs are suitable and can be made by you, or better still by doting aunts, grannies or nannies.

The Arts and Crafts House

Many people's idea of the perfect floor for an old house—good quality timber of fine colour and patina lovingly polished—is largely a late nineteenth-century Arts and Crafts concept. The Arts and Crafts house will usually have excellent floors of good oak boards often invisibly fixed by wrought-iron clamps underneath, so that no screw or nail heads mar the surface. Wood-block or parquet floors were also popular in the late nineteenth century. Such floors just need wax-polishing and no other treatment. It is best not to cover them with a carpet but just to scatter as many old Persian or Eastern rugs around as you can afford. Such rugs should have felt underlays trimmed to fit exactly, partly to stop the rugs sliding about and tripping people up, and partly to cut down the wear on the rug which may in any case be rather thin and threadbare. (Such underlays will also make vacuuming rather easier, as without them thin rugs tend to be

sucked in by the more powerful machine.) These rugs are, of course, best if they are old. Modern 'Persian' rugs are horrible in colour and texture as well as being more expensive than 'worn-out' authentic rugs.

Oriental rugs are a distinguished and timeless floor-covering which add considerably to the beauty and dignity of interiors of all periods. Apart from being works of art in their own right, oriental rugs are surprisingly practical. The fact that they are hand-knotted (the more densely a rug is knotted, the better it is), means that oriental rugs are extremely hard-wearing. Many eighteenth-century examples still survive despite generations of wear. Most oriental rugs contain so many subtle variations of colour that they are a boon to the interior designer. Almost any rug can be relied upon to 'pick up' the predominant colours in a room without becoming unduly garish or obtrusive.

When choosing oriental rugs for your house there are several factors to be taken into consideration, apart from the obvious constraint of price. The most important of these is where the rug is to be sited, because although oriental rugs are hard-wearing there are limits to how much abuse they can take. Rugs in hallways, for example, look marvellous and add a welcoming warmth, but as very heavy traffic can be expected in this location do not use delicate antique examples here. Instead, save these for use in your bedrooms or, if the rugs are very fragile, suspend them from a pole as luxurious wall-hangings.

In the United States, narrow oriental rugs are often used as stair carpet. This practice is not to be encouraged as severe, uneven wear will result. In their countries of origin, oriental rugs were never intended for this purpose.

Where oriental rugs are used in drawing rooms and dining rooms there are two points to remember. In the first place, where it is possible always try to avoid placing very heavy pieces of furniture on your rugs,

Tower House, Melbury Road, Kensington, London. The mosaic floor in the entrance hall designed by William Burges. A splendid example of a type of floor treatment found in the halls of many Victorian houses.

Standen, Sussex. The drawing room showing the original Arts and Crafts decoration and fine carpet by Morris and Company.

such as pianos, large chests of drawers or grandfather clocks. After several months of this pressure the pile will be irrevocably dented and crushed. Placing some furniture on your rugs is unavoidable, but on important antique rugs try to disperse the pressure by placing the sharp feet of chairs, for example, in specially designed furniture cups.

The second thing to remember is that if you want a large rug to wear and fade evenly, you will have to put up with the chore of regularly rotating it.

Rooms in which oriental rugs should never be placed are bathrooms and kitchens. Water or dampness are immensely damaging to old textiles of any kind, and apart from rotting oriental rugs beyond hope of repair, there is always the likelihood that 'colour run' will occur in rugs with unstable red dyes.

When buying oriental rugs exercise extreme caution. The oriental rug trade is complex and ridden with vested interests, and apart from attending reputable auctions, the best way of buying rugs is to find a respectable dealer whose opinions and integrity you can trust. A good dealer will not push you into a sale but should let you 'borrow' several rugs to take home and see how they fit into your decor. Oriental rugs are usually very subtle objects and only by living with a rug for several days can you really begin to appreciate its qualities. If you borrow rugs you must be covered by domestic insurance against theft, however.

Another point in favour of buying rugs from a good dealer is the guarantee of his professional reputation. Always check to see whether he would 'buy back' the rug from you a few years hence (a sure sign of its value) and, of course, that if the rug should prove to be damaged, he will replace it for you.

One last point concerns the general appearance of the oriental rugs you buy. Always remember that a fully piled rug in good condition may not look any better in an old interior than a very worn rug which has worn thin and is virtually threadbare. Old rugs worn to a noble thinness look immensely distinguished and many discerning people prefer them for their look of worn grandeur. Whatever you buy, do not commit the error of placing an oriental rug on top of a wall-to-wall fitted carpet.

Modern mats and carpets with Arts and Craft patterns in greenery-yallery colours, or in kingfisher blues with stylised floral patterns, are still manufactured in reproduction by firms like Sanderson.

To get something of the right feel for an Arts and Crafts floorscape with rugs, browse through 'The small house of today' articles in early copies of *Country Life*. Standen, the National Trust house in Sussex, also has several good surviving examples of authentic floorcoverings, with its mixture of old rugs and Morris-designed Axminsters with borders by J. H. Dearle.

In the Arts and Crafts house it is also possible to have a range of hard floors made of materials such as red pantiles or hand-made bricks laid in herringbone patterns, especially in the hall, kitchen or dining room. And if your Arts and Crafts house has a strong Jacobethan flavour, rush matting is ideal. Genuine Norfolk rush matting woven to size is relatively expensive but there are many inexpensive and perfectly acceptable forms of rush matting imported from Taiwan and other places in the East which have cheap labour.

The Thirties Flat

This is in many ways the easiest interior for which to find authentic floorcoverings. The dowdier range of brown, beige, orange and green *Art Deco* linoleum and carpets can often be rescued from homes of relations, jumble sales or second-hand furniture shops.

A flat designed in the 1930s by Chermayeff. The wooden floor of narrow pale-coloured boards is covered with geometrically patterned rugs.

A drawing room decorated in the 1930s in Vogue Regency taste, with a white polar-bear rug.

The smarter type of 'blonde' (light-coloured) timber floor can easily be improvised by the imaginative amateur decorator. Pale beige, cream or white carpet is still 'fashionable' and is therefore easy to obtain almost anywhere. It can be fitted from wall to wall or confined to the middle. If the latter, the surrounding boards can be painted white, shining black or lacquered scarlet. A white carpet with a black surround, or a black carpet with a white surround, are both very smart. If the boarded floor is left bare, alternate planks can be painted black and white like a pedestrian crossing. If you wish to stain the floor-boards, a pale colour will be the most appropriate. Victorian mahogany shades or Arts and Crafts dark oak would not be right in this type of interior. But walnut or, even better, exotic 'bongo woods' from the Empire are exactly right. (If you have a big game hunter among your great-uncles, or you recently made a lucky coup at a house-sale, you could have a pale Walnut or African Wood floor strewn with lion skins and so on!)

If a Syrie Maugham white floor seems impractical, and you cannot aspire to zebra skins, it is still possible to create a perfectly decent effect out of standard, single-colour carpeting from good local department stores by giving it a border in a striking colour—say light brown carpet with a maroon border. Strips of coloured carpet can often be begged or acquired cheaply from carpet warehouses and used to make your own border by sewing them round the edge of the carpet or (and this is much easier), glueing them together with hessian bands and fabric glue.

It is usually a mistake to sand down the floors in old houses and to treat them with polyurethane unless you are going to have stripped pine furniture—and that is really the 1960s look, not to be dealt with here.

Flooring

Ordinary house paints can be used to create a stencilled floor. The best clear varnish for use over the paint is ship's varnish, which can be obtained from J. T. Keep & Sons, 15 Theobalds Road, London WC1, or in boat shops in most coastal towns. Ideas for stencil patterns, and for floor cloths, can be gleaned from John Gloag, *Early English Decorative Detail* (1965) and Nina Fletcher Little, *Floor Coverings in New England Before 1850* (USA 1967). The stencils can be made yourself out of stiff cards, or certain firms, such as Watts & Co, will make them for you to your design. Victorian tiles can be bought from several antique dealers, such as Jeremy Cooper Ltd, or straight from Shaw Hereford Tiles, Waterside, Darwen, Lancashire.

Linoleum is still manufactured in Britain by Nairn Ltd of Dundee, and Storey's Ltd of Lancaster, and can be ordered directly from them. Nairn's will make special linoleum floors to historic designs.

Tracking down appropriate carpets may be time-consuming, but is well worth the effort. Many reproductions of historic carpet patterns are still made by a range of British carpet manufacturers. Rose and Ribbon, or Tatton state couch patterns, can be obtained from Colefax and Fowler. Many variations of Victorian-type Turkey carpet are still made by Wilton Axminster carpets. Crossleys in Halifax also reproduce various Victorian carpet patterns and will do carpets to order.

The sale room is the best place to get old carpets and rugs. Christies in South Kensington, London, for instance, has frequent carpet sales and it is possible to get decent examples there very cheaply. And many of the rugs on sale in antique shops throughout the country are usually bought there.

For a good introduction to the purchasing, insuring, cleaning and repairing, of oriental rugs, Majid Amini's recent book *Oriental Rugs: Care and Repair* (1981) is the only oriental rug-book on the market with a practical consumer approach.

The Alpha Mosaic & Terrazzo Co

With its pre-War trained craftsmen and large stocks of marble mosaic from the Victorian period, this company is able to repair and extend old mosaic pavings.

This photograph was taken in 1957 and shows two of Alpha's craftsmen working on a mosaic floor in London's Battersea Town Hall.

The Alpha Mosaic & Terrazzo Co Ltd
Caversham Road
London
NW5 2EJ
Tel: (01) 485 7227/1010

Axminster Carpets

Axminster manufacture a range of Persian-style carpets and rugs. A Turkish-style carpet is also available.

Axminster Carpets Ltd
Axminster
Devon EX13 5PQ
Tel: (0297) 32244

Colefax & Fowler

Most of Colefax & Fowler's carpets are made to traditional designs, which include Rose and Ribbon, and Tatton Park state couch patterns.

Colefax & Fowler
39 Brook Street
London W1 1AU
Tel: (01) 493 2231

Crossley Carpets

The 'Sultana' range of ten carpets is based on traditional post-1850 designs. Traditional manufacturing methods are employed and even some of Crossley's original 19th century looms are still used.

Crossley Carpets Ltd
Dean Clough Mills
Halifax
West Yorkshire HX1 1XG
Tel: (0422) 65789

Minton Hollins

Minton Hollins were the largest manufacturer of ceramic tiles in Victorian England. Today they specialise in reproducing those tiles, using modern techniques of screen printing to provide a range of colours suitable for modern interiors. Minton Hollins also produce hand-painted and hand-decorated mural panels, using the same techniques as the Victorians and available in a variety of colours.

Minton Hollins
Highgate Tile Works
Tunstall
Stoke-on-Trent ST6 4JX
Tel: (0782) 85611

Nairn Floors

Nairn Floors manufacture a range of linoleum in four plain colours and 13 marbled patterns, and toughened linoleum tiles in 12 patterns. In 1981

Nairn provided three floors in 'Armourflor' toughened sheet linoleum made to Lutyen's design for the Hayward Gallery (*see* page 107).

Nairn Floors of Kirkcaldy Ltd
PO Box 1
Kirkcaldy
Fife
Scotland
Tel: (0592) 261111

Neofloors

This company specialises in the installation of all types of hard flooring finishes, including linoleum and wood-block flooring, and also ceramics.

Neofloors Ltd
98 Midland Road
Bedford
MK40 1QQ
Tel: (0234) 60217

Old Maw

The Old Maw Tileworks manufacture a range of 6″ × 6″ Victorian style decorative tiles. Much conservation work is undertaken by this company and customers' own original tiles can be reproduced.

Old Maw Tileworks
Jackfield
Shropshire
Tel: (0952) 882030

Watts & Co

Watts & Co provide a service of Victorian floor stencilling, using either customers' designs or those from their own archives.

Watts & Co Ltd
7 Tufton Street
Westminster
London SW1P 3QB
Tel: (01) 222 7169

Wicanders

Cork and wood are featured in two ranges of heavy duty flooring by Wicanders. 'Cork-o-Plast' vinyl-bonded cork flooring is available both in tile and plank form, while the 'Exclusive' range of vinyl-bonded wood flooring is available in planks.

Wicanders (GB) Ltd
Maxwell Way
Crawley
West Sussex RH10 2SE
Tel: (0293) 27700

Wilton Carpets

Wilton will manufacture to order any style or design of carpet for private individuals through a carpet retailer. They also have a stock of contract and domestic carpets available.

The Wilton Royal Carpet Factory Ltd
Wilton
Salisbury
Wiltshire
Tel: (072 274) 2441

Anna Wyner

Having trained originally as a painter, Anna Wyner now designs mosaic floors and walls, the insides of swimming pools, and any other interesting commissions; she can reproduce in mosaic virtually any design a customer wants. The materials used in her mosaics range from clay and slate to Italian 'smalti' with its limitless range of colours. Pre-cast mosaics executed in the studio can be shipped abroad to be slotted in on site, and in turn removed if necessary.

Anna Wyner designed, supplied and fixed this bathroom floor in a house in Surrey. Mosaic flooring was popular in England during the late 17th century.

Anna Wyner
Mosaic Artist
2 Ferry Road
London SW13
Tel: (01) 748 3940

Old floorboards, and wood-block and wood-strip flooring, can be obtained from the following architectural salvage firms:

Architectural Salvage

Hutton and Rostron
Netley House
Gomshall
nr Guildford
Surrey GU5 9QA
Tel: (048 641) 3221

T Crowther & Son Ltd

282 North End Road
Fulham
London SW6 1NH
Tel: (01) 385 1375/7

Glover & Stacey

Malt House Bungalow
Kingsley
nr Bordon
Hampshire
Tel: (042 03) 5754

Hale Farm Building Materials

32 Guildford Road
Farnham, Surrey
Tel: (0252) 726484

The London Architectural Salvage and Supply Co Ltd

Mark Street (off Paul Street)
London EC2A 4ER
Tel: (01) 739 0448/9

Solopark Ltd

The Old Railway Station
Station Road
nr Pampisford
Cambridgeshire
Tel: (0223) 834663

The following firms specialise in original Victorian and Edwardian tiles:

Jeremy Cooper

9 Galen Place
London WC1
Tel: (01) 242 5138

The Reject Tile Shop

178 Wandsworth Bridge Road
London SW6
Tel: (01) 731 6098

Townsends

1 Church Street
London NW8
Tel: (01) 724 3746

Plasterwork

laster is a wonderfully flexible building material. Most rooms in most houses have plastered walls and ceilings, and whether the wall is made of stone, brick, wood or breeze-block, the plaster covering makes it dust-proof and draught-proof and gives a smooth flat surface for paint or wallpaper. In the old days, plain plaster was applied over thin wooden laths nailed to the wall, or directly to the wall itself, but most modern plaster walls are formed of large pieces of plasterboard with a finishing top coat.

In one of its more durable forms, like stucco or cement, plaster is equally good for external work. In the early nineteenth century, stucco was often used to hide and weatherproof indifferent brickwork (as in the Regent's Park terraces) and to give a cheap approximation to the appearance of stone facing; the stucco was even tinted with stone dust to make the imitation more convincing. But the versatility of plaster is best seen in the infinite variety of the ornaments it was used to make.

The eighteenth century was a famous time for elaborate plaster decoration in the grandest houses, often carried out by specialists from abroad—usually from north Italy. In more modest houses plaster decoration was not common until after 1740. Before then walls were very often panelled in wood, with wooden cornices; when panelling fell out of fashion the wooden cornices went out as well to be replaced by plaster versions of the same thing.

The practical function of a cornice inside a building is to hide the junction of wall and ceiling, but the idea and the general forms derive from Classical architec-

Right: Ralph Gardiner was a suburban plasterer who built this house for himself in 1882. He used the outside of the building as a sort of trade sign and it still gives a good idea of the great variety of the kind of stucco ornaments which were used on the outside of nineteenth-century houses.

ture (Greek and Roman buildings). Just as in a correct Classical building, no part of the Classical order of architecture can properly be omitted, so for most of the eighteenth and nineteenth centuries it was unthinkable that a room in a decent house should be without a cornice of some kind.

The most common form of cornice has always been the plain continuous moulding, which occurs in varying forms right through to the present century. In the eighteenth century, cornices followed architectural examples fairly closely. The proper plain moulded cornice for the Tuscan order was often used, or a simplified version of it, but if the plasterer or his

client wanted a richer effect the cornices of the other orders could be followed. The three options were the mutule cornice of the Doric order, the dentil cornice of the Ionic or the modillion cornice of the Corinthian, all broadly similar but with slightly differing characters.

In the 1760s the architect Robert Adam started a fashion for lighter and more elegant plaster decoration. In his designs he used a large quantity of small-scale ornament on both walls and ceilings. The ornament was still Classical but took many different forms, including ox-skulls, vases, mythical beasts, leaves and the stylised honeysuckle flower called an

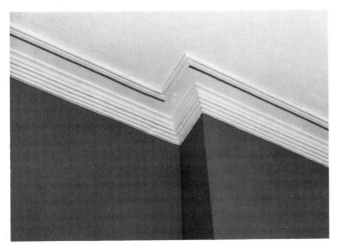

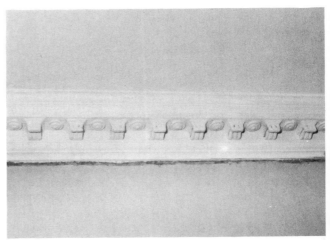

Above left: The simple continuously moulded cornice was a type often found in modest houses. This example dates from 1783, but could equally well be 1840, or 1930. The band of ornament on the ceiling side was to make the cornice look wider and would have been painted to match.

Above: A modillion cornice from a London terraced house of about 1770. The individual console brackets and small roundels called paterae *are simply stuck on to the body of the cornice, which is a continuous moulding.*

Left: This splendid ceiling, cornice and frieze in the Adam manner still exist in a house in Bedford Square in Bloomsbury, London, and show the very delicate effects which could be achieved with cast plaster ornament.

anthemion, which were all mixed together to make rich and varied patterns. The designs were usually cast in small pieces and then fitted together in the required combinations. This was a much quicker and cheaper method of producing delicate decoration than carving it by hand, and cast ornaments soon made their appearance in less fashionable houses. They were most commonly made into friezes along the top of the wall beneath the cornice, but also appear as wall panels, arch spandrels and overdoors. Cast ornaments were also used to decorate ceilings, although the great majority of eighteenth-century houses had completely plain ceilings.

The first decades of the nineteenth century were a time of architectural experiment, and houses were built in Greek, Gothic, Italian, Swiss and Tudor styles before settling down in the 1850s to be mainly Gothic. Plaster decoration was adapted to suit these styles as far as possible, with Tudor roses and Gothic pinnacles, and plaster was also used to imitate forms usually made of wood or stone because it was so much cheaper. But through all the experiments the idea of the cornice was never given up, even though there was no such thing as a Gothic or Swiss plaster cornice. As J. C. Loudon said in his famous *Encyclopaedia of Cottage, Farm and Villa Architecture*, 'Without a cornice, no room can have a finished appearance.'

The general tendency throughout the nineteenth century was for plaster decoration to become more elaborate, especially in the main rooms. One mid-century book of designs for quite modest houses directed that the cornices in the main rooms should be two feet three inches wide with two five-inch bands of enrichment. Lesser rooms might have smaller cornices: twelve inches wide in the best bedrooms, six inches in the lavatory. The 'enrichments' were the descendants of the simpler eighteenth-century cast ornament, but the original Classical forms were often abandoned in favour of stylised foliage, flowers or other patterns. A good idea of the great variety of current patterns can be gained from Owen Jones's famous book *The Grammar of Ornament* (1856), or from the Great Exhibition catalogue (1851).

The nineteenth century also saw the re-introduction of the ceiling rose (or ceiling flower as it was usually called). These can certainly be found in

Above: Two pieces of cast decoration from a house of about 1790, before and after cleaning. The notches on the sides of individual pieces enable them to be interlocked into a continuous strip.

Right: Late eighteenth-century plaster decoration in the hall of a less grand house. The mutule cornice is heavily clogged with paint, but the cast ornament of the hall arch is still quite crisp.

Many examples of Tudor and Jacobean-style plasterwork date from the early years of the nineteenth century. This example in a London pub is dated 1830.

earlier houses, but usually in the grander ones where the flower formed the centre of an elaborate ceiling decoration, or where provision had to be made for a chandelier. The arrival of cheap gas for household purposes made it possible for humbler houses to have a single powerful light in a room, instead of several oil lights or candles, and the obvious place for it was at the centre of the ceiling. A ceiling flower was the best way of giving elegance to the gas pipe, and larger flowers could be adapted to serve as inconspicuous ventilators to take away the 'vitiated air' that Victorians were so afraid of.

The increased demand for big cornices and elaborate ceiling flowers brought mass-production and new techniques. One innovation was fibrous plaster, patented in England in 1856 by a Frenchman named Desachy. In this process ordinary plaster was strengthened with a layer of coarse canvas, making it possible to cast whole lengths of cornice and other large items in one piece. The fibrous plaster technique was steadily improved and nowadays almost all plaster ornament is made in this way. But in the nineteenth century there was stiff competition from the makers of *papier mâché*, which was cheap, light, tough and suitable for very elaborate and delicate ornament that was difficult to cast in plaster. There must still be thousands of *papier mâché* ceiling flowers and miles of *papier mâché* cornice successfully masquerading as plasterwork.

Prefabrication and standardisation, as well as the fact that cornices and ceiling flowers were used to decorate even the meanest houses, lowered the status of plastering until, by the end of the nineteenth century, it had come to be considered wholly as a building trade, like bricklaying and plumbing. The products of the plaster factories which lacked the mark of the individual craftsman were heartily despised by supporters of the Arts and Crafts movement, who greatly influenced English taste at the end of Queen Victoria's reign. Under their influence a slight return was made, at least in more expensive houses, to viewing plasterwork as a craft. These disciples of William Morris also preferred English to foreign styles, and in plasterwork this meant the re-introduction of the bold and rather clumsy decoration of the Tudors and Jacobeans: ceilings covered with a net of thin ribs in the style of the 1530s, or with naturalistic flowers and animals in the style of the 1600s. Ornament of this kind was more suitable for large houses, but it soon influenced the makers of cast decoration and there are many examples of small-scale adaptations of *Olde Englishe* plasterwork. The simple Classical cornices of the eighteenth century

Right: Commercial illustrations of a few of the standard small mouldings or castings used in the nineteenth century.

Below: A page from Bielfeld's catalogue of papier mâché *ornaments, published in 1850, showing several types of ceiling flower. This firm was recommended by J. C. Loudon for the cheapness and strength of their products.*

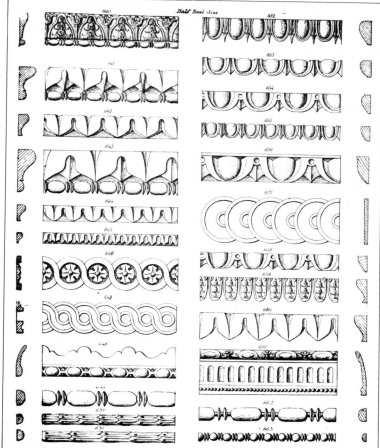

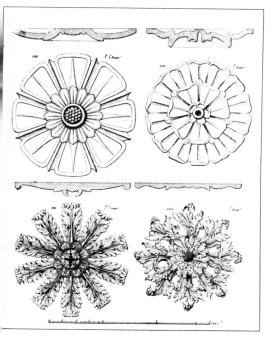

were also revived as part of the enthusiasm for the Queen Anne style. With the hearts and tendrils of *Art Nouveau* creeping in as well, the variety of plaster decoration available at the turn of the century was enormous.

After the First World War, plaster decoration went into a long and gradual decline. War veterans kept the hygienic short haircuts they had been given in the trenches, and the same hygienic tendency can be discerned in house decoration. The cornice gradually shrank to the minimum width necessary to cover the crack at the top of the wall, and the ceiling flower was diminished to a tiny nipple for the electric flex. The process of decline was long drawn-out, and there was a sudden vogue for plaster decoration in the Adam style of the 1920s; but by the end of the 1930s, plaster decoration was considered dead.

Nowadays it is easy to forget the attractive qualities of delicate plasterwork. In many houses, repeated painting over 100 years or more has completely obscured the details; modillions have become shape-less lumps and enrichments have turned into a string of meaningless blobs.

It is perfectly possible to clean off old paint and reveal the original decoration, but the process takes time and effort. Until recently ceilings and plaster-work were usually painted with water-based paints, and the simplest method of cleaning is to make the paint thoroughly damp and remove it with a sharp tool, a little at a time. The plaster itself is also water-based but is much harder than the paint. Where plasterwork has been painted with a modern vinyl emulsion, or even with gloss paint, cleaning is more difficult and a chemical stripper would probably be necessary. All traces of the stripper should be washed away before re-painting begins.

Cleaning may reveal that some of the more delicate decoration has been damaged. More serious damage is often found where large rooms have been divided up and the plaster decoration has been hacked away for the partitions. Damp is another danger and in a house that has been neglected and left damp for a long period the plain plaster may have lost its 'key', and come loose from the wall, while any cast decoration may simply drop off.

Repairing and patching old plasterwork is not unduly difficult. Any professional plasterer should be able to run a plain moulded cornice or cast a new length of cornice to match one already in place. 'Running', which means forming a moulding by

Opposite: Paint can completely obliterate a moulding, as this partly-cleaned section of a late eighteenth-century frieze shows.

Right: Modillions or console brackets from a late eighteenth-century ceiling before and after cleaning.

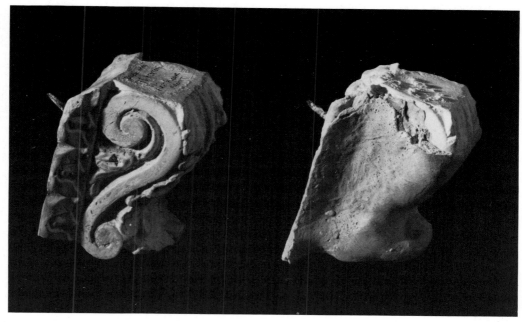

scraping a metal template across wet plaster to give the right shape, still forms part of a plasterer's training and it gives a crisper and sharper effect than cast work. Small ornaments, individual modillions and parts of large patterns can be replaced by casting plaster of Paris in a vinyl mould made from a surviving example. The vinyl compound needed to make the mould is fairly widely available. It is important to clean the original as much as possible to get a crisp cast. The finished casts can be set in place with more plaster of Paris.

Where the original plaster is beyond repair, or where new decorations are wanted, the simplest solution is to buy everything 'off-the-peg' from a manufacturer of fibrous plasterwork. There are several manufacturers who produce a range of cornices in different sizes and styles, as well as ceiling flowers and other ornaments. The casts can be fixed in position and the joints and corners made good in plaster of Paris. Good casts should look crisp; avoid any which look as though they have been made from badly cleaned originals. There are also various plastic imitations of plaster ornament which may be perfectly satisfactory, but since fibrous plaster is often the cheaper alternative it may be better to stick with a material whose behaviour is well-tried and predictable.

In ordinary eighteenth-century houses, ceilings and plaster cornices were usually painted white or grey, or in a similar plain colour. Gilding might be used to enrich ornaments. Robert Adam used delicate colours to pick out his delicate decorations, but plain colours remained the general rule until the early nineteenth century. The cornice was most often painted the same colour as the ceiling; in low rooms it might be painted with the wall to give an impression of greater height, or it might be given a transitional tint halfway between the colours used on the walls and the ceiling.

Bolder treatment was given to plasterwork in the nineteenth century. Plain moulded cornices might have their shape emphasised by being painted in lighter and darker shades of the same colour, and where wallpaper was used its background colour was often continued in the cornice. Enriched cornices were painted to harmonise with the walls in a similar fashion, but the ornaments were usually picked out, sometimes in gilding but more usually in a lighter shade of the main colour. Any broad flat surfaces in a cornice could be decorated with a simple flower or geometrical pattern, and it was fairly common to make a narrow cornice seem wider by painting lines on the ceiling side. The most elaborate ceiling flowers might also be picked out, but many were painted a plain colour, probably because ceilings in gas-lit rooms had to be re-painted every few years. The highly coloured cornice is characteristic of the mid-nineteenth century; by the 1890s plain colours were more usual.

Plasterwork

After woodwork, plasterwork suffers most from mutilation and damage in millions of modest 'period' houses. Layers of paint, accumulated over a hundred years or more, have often obscured attractive and delicate plasterwork details; or damp may have caused them to come away from the walls. Where large rooms have been divided up, plasterwork may simply have been torn down to make room for the partitions. Nowadays, there are many specialist craftsmen able to restore and replace decorative plasterwork.

All the suppliers and manufacturers listed here stock a range of fibrous plaster, including several different types of cornice, a variety of ceiling flowers and other ornaments. Most manufacturers will also make decorations to order and undertake their installation if desired.

William Birch & Sons

Established in 1874, this firm is well known in the field of building and civil engineering. They also undertake craft work in the field of plasterwork and brickwork. Recent commissions include the removal, restoration and re-siting of a Tudor ceiling in the King's Manor, York and the skilled restoration and re-siting of an ornate Georgian ceiling in Peasholme House, York.

William Birch & Sons
Spen Lane
York
YO1 2BT
Tel: (0904) 22185

Clark & Fen

A large manufacturer with a very wide range of good quality castings.

Clark & Fen Ltd
Mitcham House
681 Mitcham Road
Croydon
Surrey
Tel: (01) 689 2266

G J Green & Veronese

Created through the amalgamation in 1972 of two well known firms in the field of solid and fibrous plaster, Green and Veronese's recent contracts have included the refurbishment of the Dorchester Hotel. Services include glazing, murals, mirrors, gilding, etc., and a design team is also available. They keep a large stock of cornices, moulds, columns and other allied architectural details.

G J Green & Veronese
24 Edison Road
London N8 8AE
Tel: (01) 348 9262/4461/2

William Birch & Sons restored this ceiling from a Georgian house in York.

This example of Green and Veronese's work is of the recently refurbished Terrace Restaurant in London's Dorchester Hotel.

Hodkin & Jones

Hodkin & Jones have been manufacturing handmade fibrous plaster products since 1868. Their very large stock is produced by traditional methods and includes, for example, 25 different standard patterns of cornice. The 'Simply Elegant' range faithfully reproduces classical and traditional styles in the form of niches, 20 different styles of cornice, panel mouldings, ceiling centrepieces and other architectural details. They can also reproduce any pattern to a customer's own requirements.

Hodkin & Jones Ltd
515 Queen's Road
Sheffield
S2 4DS
Tel: (0742) 56121

G Jackson & Sons

A very old established firm, Jackson's still have some of the moulds for casts they

made for Robert Adam and their collection of moulds is probably the largest in the country. Specialist services include decoration and gilding, architectural mouldings in glass-fibre, composition enrichment, and the reinstatement and repair of decorative work as shown opposite, below right.

Jackson & Sons Ltd
Rathbone Works
Rainville Road
Hammersmith
London W6
Tel: (01) 385 6616

Jonathon James

This firm has specialists in solid and ornamental fibrous plasterwork, metal suspended ceilings, floor screeding and granolithic paving.

Jonathon James Ltd
New Road
Rainham
Essex RM13 8DJ
Tel: (76) 56921

J G McDonough

This firm provides a comprehensive service in both fibrous and solid plasterwork. They specialise in replacement decorative plaster details, including centrepieces, cornices, brackets and overdoors.

J G McDonough Ltd
347a New King's Road
Fulham
London SW6
Tel: (01) 736 5146

Moran & Wheatley

This company restores, matches and repairs original cornices and restores old ceilings. Where an ornate ceiling has become unsafe through rotting timbers and laths, they reinforce the back and can rehang the replacement timbers. Wherever possible it is their policy to retain original plasterwork. Fibrous plaster is also available.

Moran & Wheatley Ltd
Avondale Studio Workshops
Avondale Place
Batheaston
Bath
BA1 7RF
Tel: (0225) 859678

Plaster Decoration Co

The company normally acts as a subcontractor to a general contractor, but is frequently nominated so that the benefit of its experience and advice is available

A highly ornate ceiling rose of some 3 feet 8 inches in diameter, ready for installation at the workshops of the Plaster Decoration Co.

at a very early stage of design. The company has twice won the trophy awarded by the Worshipful Company of Plasterers for the best plastering in Great Britain. Services for both fibrous and solid plaster are available.

Plaster Decoration Co Ltd
30 Stannary Street
London SE11 4AE
Tel: (01) 735 8161

A Sanderson & Sons

Sanderson are well known for their fabrics and wallpaper, but they also have a small stock of ceiling mouldings at their Berners Street shop.

A Sanderson & Sons Ltd
53 Berners Street
London W1A 2JE
Tel: (01) 636 7800

L Stead & Son

Established in 1887, this firm are fibrous plaster manufacturers, specialising in the restoration of period plasterwork. Both

private and public commissions are undertaken.

L Stead & Son
Victoria Fibrous Plasterworks
Eccleshell
Bradford
West Yorkshire BD2 2DS
Tel: (0274) 637222

W J Wilson & Son

Specialists in ornamental fibrous plaster, Wilson & Son undertake both private and public works; recent commissions include the Theatre Royal, Nottingham and the Iranian Embassy, London. They also produce ornamental cement and glass-fibre work.

W J Wilson & Son
Elm Tree Street
Mansfield
Nottinghamshire
Tel: (0623) 23113

Woodwork

A front door can be the most interesting feature of a home. The way you restore or replace it will either make your house—or ruin it.

The great change, from oak to soft woods, began in building at the start of the eighteenth century. Oak had become scarce due to the amount of shipbuilding. Imported Scandinavian soft woods like pine and fir became the favourite material.

But oak was still used for high-class work like window joinery, staircases and more structural work. Mahogany from the West Indies came in a little later and was used mainly for staircase handrails, which became so popular for the next 200 years.

Design of external details like windows and doors was dictated by the Classical revival, from the start of the eighteenth century until about 1830.

The early eighteenth-century door case, when it survives in its original state, is a delight. Door cases of this period often had canopies supported by carved brackets. There might have been pediments, shell motifs, or simple flat canopies.

Designs varied from region to region. Generally door cases were made of soft wood, so great care should be taken when stripping intricate carved pieces. If you are unsure on stripping methods, seek expert advice.

Doors themselves had raised and fielded panels. Usually there were six or eight. The hinges were wrought iron and fixed with nails. The most common hinge was the 'T' hinge; cast-iron hinges were introduced in the late eighteenth century.

Fanlights were not always incorporated into the design at this stage. But when they were used, they were made simply, using the early thick glazing bar. Many fanlights were fitted later, and these are obvious due to the more delicate designs in cast lead which were popular in the late eighteenth century.

Pattern books containing designs for door cases were published up until about the 1760s. Many fine books are still available today, illustrating the

Left: Early eighteenth-century doorway in Abbey Square, Chester, with timber pediments and thick glazing bars in the fanlight, and ovolo moulding above.

Below: Cast-lead fanlight c 1791 from Hackney in London, showing the detail that was hidden by accumulated layers of paint. (In the Brooking Collection.)

amazing variety of Georgian doorways still to be seen. But it is worth pointing out some of the constructional points you should remember when restoring.

Up until 1700 most fanlights were made of wood. But the delicate designs of the late eighteenth century, like those of the Adam brothers, demanded stronger materials, and the cast-lead fanlight appeared. Wrought iron, cast iron and brass were also used. Wooden fanlights continued to be used for simple designs and cheaper work.

Lead fanlights were intended to be painted, but years of accumulated paint usually cover original detail. Stripping them down produces tremendous results. Most fanlights contain at least one or two panes of original Georgian Crown glass with its rippled surface, greenish tinge and sometimes air bubbles. Take great care to preserve this—it is extremely thin and easily broken.

Try and replace broken panes with salvaged Crown glass or old glass. Resist the temptation to use modern antique glass, as it is nothing like the original and looks quite wrong.

By the 1800s, the timber door case was being superseded by the circular headed door opening, or door void, which contained the fanlight and sometimes pilasters and sidelights. Most commonly there was the six-panelled door with a fanlight directly above, and no sidelights. But there were many regional variations.

In the late eighteenth century, carved ornament gave way to the mass-produced gesso. A cheaper alternative to a craftsman's carving, it was specially prepared plaster of Paris or gypsum. Gesso decoration was used in all kinds of situations, decorating door cases, fireplaces and architraves. When restoring a gesso-decorated capital from an 1812 door case in Chester, I removed about seventy coats of paint which had completely obscured the original design. The effect was shattering. But before doing any restoration work of gesso it is worth seeking advice about the best materials to use as it is very soft.

In the period 1800–25, reeded and fluted architraves became very popular. Door cases with reeded architraves often had lion masks or rosettes at the top two corners of the frame, made of lead, plaster or gesso.

During the Greek revival of the 1830s, many characteristic Victorian features appeared, including margin-light fanlights, twin and four-panelled front doors, and the use of coloured glass in fanlights.

Above top: Detail of fluted timber pilaster, c 1825, at 178 North Gower Street, London.

Above: 1820–30s doorway showing influence of Greek revival and use of four-panel front door in Lewes, Sussex. Notice the Venetian style sash windows.

Doorway designs in the early Victorian period were endless. The four-panelled door was perhaps the most common. More elaborate varieties had deep mouldings and an increasing use of decorative glass in the top panels from 1850 onwards. The glass might have been etched, cut, painted or coloured. Leaded panels came later, in the 1860s.

The Gothic revival brought innovations, including porches in front of the main house door and increased use of stained glass. By the 1870s all types of decorative glass were being manufactured on a large scale to meet the insatiable demand. Whole terraces sometimes used the same pattern of leaded light, while

Far left: Turned-wood porch and typical late Victorian/Edwardian casements, c 1897.

Left: Columbian pine front door with a very popular panel arrangement of the 1920s and 1930s which was manufactured on a large scale at this time. Found in a house built in 1931 in Guildford.

other rows of houses may have had individual designs. Sometimes the house number was set into the fanlight glass. Styles used in the decorative glass were mainly naturalistic themes, especially birds and plants. Clever geometrical designs were also popular.

With the Queen Anne revival of the 1870s (its exponents being architects such as Norman Shaw), the white-painted woodwork of the eighteenth century—with some stylistic changes—became popular again, and was adapted by many builders. An important development at that time was the turned wood porch, used with endless variations until the Edwardian period.

The Arts and Crafts movement, initiated in 1887, in which William Morris and Philip Webb played a large part, represented a move away from the general architecture of the period and a return to medieval vernacular craftsmanship and associated country crafts. Half-timbering and the use of oak for doors, staircases and windows were the direct results of this movement. Oak was left unpainted, front doors having fittings made by blacksmiths. On cheaper work in this style I have seen soft woods used, but this was always grained to look like oak.

Art Nouveau, a decorative movement of great vitality, was pioneered in England by Rennie Mackintosh. The designs were based on plants, the most distinctive being the tulip. *Art Nouveau* lasted from about 1892–1905, and by the mid-1890s, stained-glass windows were being strongly influenced by the movement.

By the end of the nineteenth century, many front doors (complete with stained glass) were mass-produced, mainly for terraced houses. You can see some front-door patterns all over Britain. From 1900 until the First World War, doors were solidly constructed, with leaded lights becoming less fussy and more influenced by *Art Nouveau* designs. A wealth of fascinating designs appeared. After the war, new homes were needed urgently and the mass-produced doors to standard designs came into their own. Styles which are familiar today appeared, like those with six panes of glass in the top half of the door and three vertical panels below. There were also the coloured-glass oval panels with the same panel arrangement below. Many of these doors were imported from the Scandinavian countries.

Half-timbered detached and semi-detached houses often had oak front doors, based on medieval designs, with imitation wrought-iron fittings. Leaded lights and coloured glass of this period were still slightly influenced by *Art Nouveau*, but simple naturalistic designs were more common.

Other popular coloured-glass patterns included ships, lighthouses and Dutch girls. They were mass-produced. The glass tended to be streaked with various colours, some very bright with moulded surface decoration.

Art Deco became popular after the Paris Exhibition of 1925, and it had begun to influence British designs by the 1930s, when patterns such as *chevrons* in frosted glass began to be incorporated into coloured-glass designs. In the later 1930s, front doors became plainer, often with a simple glazed panel. Doors of interior flats were often flush, with polished oak-veneered plywood or one single panel. The sunburst design also appeared at this time, and was widely used in front doors and gates.

Internal Doors

Doors to principal rooms in the early eighteenth century were panelled with simple mouldings, and the panels might have been raised and fielded. Two and six panels were most common, and in less important rooms the panels were unmoulded, a practice that continued well into this century. Architraves and skirting were based on Classical mouldings. In the latter part of the century four-panel doors became more common. Rim locks with brass drop handles or door knobs were used until the advent of the mortice lock in the late eighteenth century. Bow latches were often used on smaller rooms. Woodwork was nearly always painted, and graining (a paint finish) was often used to simulate the better woods like oak and mahogany. Four-panel doors remained the most popular design throughout the nineteenth century, mouldings and architraves becoming elaborate in the mid-Victorian period, which saw the start of mass-production of general joinery items. Battened and braced oak doors were widely used in the Arts and Crafts movement. Standardised designs again came into general use after the First World War. Plywood panels were used, and Columbian pine became a favourite for doors, door frames and architraves. Stained woodwork became very popular from the

mid-1920s until the Second World War. The flush door also made its appearance in the 1920s. Often it was veneered with hard wood. Architraves and skirting became much plainer towards the Second World War, reminiscent of designs of the post-war period. The lever handle became popular in the 1930s for internal doors.

If there is confusion over the date of period details it is worth consulting one of the expert advisory services listed at the end of this chapter.

Mouldings

Although most mouldings in the eighteenth and early nineteenth centuries were formed by a moulding plane, there were hand-carved and gesso-decorated types. This decoration may not be immediately obvious owing to layers of paint. Stripping should only be undertaken after advice has been sought. Dado rails were used up until the very early nineteenth century and the wall below was often panelled, or flush. In the early eighteenth century, box cornices were also made of wood, and were sometimes carved. If you have a panelled room of the early eighteenth century, the temptation to strip down and leave the

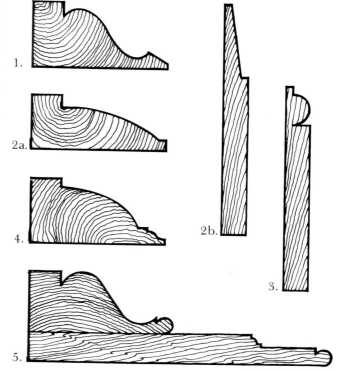

1. A very common architrave pattern of the Victorian/Edwardian periods. There were many variations of this design.

2. (a) Architrave and (b) skirting design of the 1930s.

3. A widely used skirting design of the nineteenth century.

4. Architrave sample from Unity House, Euston Road, designed in 1910 by John Newcomb. A popular design of the period.

5. Architrave sample from 49 Portland Place, London (the Chinese Embassy), built by the Adam brothers in 1785. A typical Georgian architrave design.

wood in its natural state should be resisted. These rooms were always painted, except in cases where oak was used. Skirting boards where often made out of two separate pieces, and in the early Victorian times could be as much as 12 inches high.

Windows

In the early 1700s, the four-light transom casement window with rectangular panes set in lead was the most widely used design of window. The opening casements have wrought-iron frames. But the sash window, thought to have come from Holland, was of a design that met demands of Classical architecture, and it immediately became immensely popular.

The first types were quite simple. They consisted of two sashes containing six panes, each set into a frame. The very early ones had fixed top sashes, with only the bottom sashes opening. Sash boxes containing the weight were hollowed out of solid timber, and the glazing bars were up to 2 inches thick, usually with ovolo mouldings inside. The sash boxes were set almost flush with the face of the brickwork, a practice outlawed in 1709 when an act stated that all woodwork be set back 4 inches from the face of the wall in case of fire. But this law was not always followed, or enforced. Crown glass was sometimes used, and every attempt should be made to preserve it when you carry out repairs.

The twelve-pane sash window remained the standard glazing pattern throughout the Georgian period. Most houses, except the smaller terraced

house, had inside folding shutters, secured by an iron bar when closed. These had moulded panels. Glazing bars became thinner as the eighteenth century wore on. By about 1730, sash boxes were made up rather than hollowed out of solid timber sections. Both oak and mahogany were used in construction. Many of the early eighteenth-century sashes with thick glazing bars were replaced with those of lighter designs at this time.

The Building Act of 1774 demanded that sash boxes should be hidden almost completely. This accentuated the slender lines of windows of the period.

Sometime in the mid-eighteenth century, the inside vertical sliding shutter working on the sash-window principle appeared, and remained in use until the 1890s. Another type of shutter slid horizontally into the surrounding wall when not in use. In the eighteenth century and early nineteenth centuries many ground-floor windows had outside shutters for security. This was very common in rural areas. Not many of them remain, so be careful to preserve any that do. These were panelled shutters often with flush panels, not to be confused with the later louvred-panel shutters seen on neo-Georgian houses.

Shutters should always be maintained in working order, and not nailed up as is so often the case these days.

The Venetian sash window became widely used in the later eighteenth century. It consisted of a large central sash window with two smaller, permanently fixed, versions either side. The sash cord for the central window ran over the top of the two side fixed

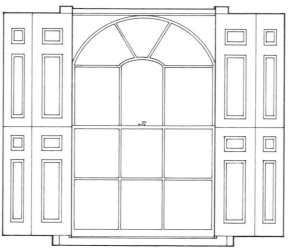

Far left: Early nineteenth-century sash window in Shrewsbury, Shropshire, with thick glazing bars and Crown glass.

Left: This sash window with its shutters open was rescued from a house in Warren Street, London, built in 1792. This example illustrates the typical joinery details of the period.

Right: Gothic-style house in Ely, Cambridgeshire, c 1825, with interesting Gothic windows.

Far right: Circular-headed sash window with Gothic glazing, North Gower Street, London, c 1825. When this window was examined after removal some original panes of Crown glass were found in the top sash. These houses were demolished in September 1978.

windows into the sash box, as there was no room for the weights in the mullions between the sashes.

In the early nineteenth century, the bow window became fashionable, particularly in seaside resorts. Most of them worked on the Venetian window principle, the central sash being the only opening part.

Margin lights also became widely used in the early nineteenth century. Often they contained amber, blue or ruby glass, or painted glass as in the example shown in the photograph of a house in Ely built *c*. 1825. Many pleasing glazing patterns were used in this period until the advent of plate glass, which became available in the 1840s owing to new production methods. At first it was only used in expensive houses.

Owners of older houses began to remove the glazing bars, or to replace the sashes with new frames containing plate glass. Another change greatly affecting the appearance of the sash window at that time was the introduction of a decorative moulding, creating a mortice and tenon joint at the corner joint of the outside meeting rail. This modification was probably to give added strength to take the weight of plate glass. It is not clear exactly when sash horns were first introduced. The earliest example I have seen was of the 1840s.

By the 1850s, one of the most common sash arrangements was the four-paned window. Houses had large paned windows in the main elevations, and cheaper small panes at the rear or on less important elevations. Small-pane windows were used in cheaper houses well into the 1860s. In the Victorian Gothic period, complicated sash window designs appeared, and the bay window became very popular. Cast-iron casements in timber frames, often with Gothic designs in their top panes, were widely used in many situations, including cottages. Shutters were used up

Window shutters showing storage recess and shutter bars.

until the 1880s, mainly in the ground- and first-floor rooms. Cellar windows had heavy shutters and burglar bars for security.

By mid-Victorian times, the sash window was most popular of all. In larger houses, particularly terraced

Detail of Gothic windows in 1825 house in Ely, Cambridgeshire, showing typical margin lights and painted-glass panels of the period.

houses, casement windows were mainly used for access on to first-floor balconies. Decorative coloured glass became increasingly used from the 1840s onwards, in the hall, landing and later sometimes even in lavatory windows. At first they were mainly margin-light windows with coloured glass in the margins, amber, blue and ruby being the favourite colours. Painted glass was also used. In better homes there might be acid-etched or cut-glass decoration. The use of a star motif in the corners of margin-light windows was a favourite.

As in the case of front doors, by the 1860s there were many decorative glass varieties, mostly with naturalistic themes. Leaded lights increased in the last forty years of the nineteenth century to become the most common form of decorative windows.

The Queen Anne revival brought the reintroduction of the leaded casement window which had been popular in the seventeenth century and in the early eighteenth century. Sash windows, with characteristic early eighteenth-century thick glazing bars, also came back into fashion.

The use of cottage-style casements became more popular with the Arts and Crafts movement. To meet demand for an improved casement window, which had to be made by a blacksmith in the eighteenth century, new firms like Crittalls sprang up, making casements of steel sections.

The use of the timber and metal casement window grew, and by late Victorian times houses used mixtures of both sash and casement windows. The revival brought the new concept of Georgian-style glazing in the top sashes, with plate glass used in the bottom sash—a favourite design of the Victorian and Edwardian periods. The use of sash windows in threes also became popular, often with decorative mullions. By late Edwardian times, the steel casement was mass-produced but not widely used. After the First World War, however, the need for cheap and quickly made building products encouraged the wide adoption of the standard metal window. Overnight the standard steel window became a feature of the many new housing estates.

Timber casement windows were also widely used, the bay or bow window, with simple leaded lights in its top frames, being a favourite. A large proportion of joinery was imported from Scandinavia, hence the recurring patterns found all over Britain.

Tudor-style properties, which were so popular between the wars, almost exclusively used steel casements with diamond or rectangular panes. Sometimes heraldic crests were incorporated in drawing room or hallway windows. The two leading manufacturers were Crittalls of Braintree and Thomas Hope of Lionel Street, Birmingham. There were many standard designs. A distinctive *Art Deco*-inspired design appeared in the 1930s. It had a very horizontal theme. The panes were long horizontal strips and there were many variations.

Steel windows were not galvanised but painted with red oxide or other paints for protection. Now many of them are corroding badly and need replacement. It is very important to maintain original glazing patterns, and Crittalls are worth contacting as they reproduce many of the old designs with modern protective finishes. Coloured glass was used sometimes in the top of dining, drawing and also bathroom windows, and in halls and landings.

Other Exterior Woodwork

In the early eighteenth century, eaves cornices were a prominent feature of the façade; many had carved details. In 1707 their use was abolished because they were seen as a fire risk. Of those that are left today, many have rotted and great care should be taken to follow the original style when replacing with new timber. The Gothic and Cottage style of the eighteenth and early nineteenth century produced many lively designs of bargeboards for dormer windows and gables. The Victorian Gothic revival increased this trend. Sometimes a row of villas had the same designs

Villa with hand-carved bargeboards, c 1853.

or a variation on a theme. Bargeboards were used throughout the Victorian and Edwardian years. The half-timbered gables in late Victorian buildings had oak, or painted soft wood sections nailed to the wall. In expensive work, real oak half-timbering was used. This trend continued in the 1920s, and 1930s, with the many Tudor-style houses being built.

When treating or repainting half-timbered work, the feet of the vertical members and horizontal sections below should be examined carefully, as rot often sets in here.

Late Victorian and Edwardian houses often had fine entrance gates, many with decorative woodwork and ironwork. These are always worth restoring, as they complement the original style of the house. Few now remain, but those that do are highly prized by the owners.

Staircases

Queen Anne and early Georgian staircases mostly had turned balusters, sometimes with delightfully carved barley-sugar twist designs. The wall side of the staircase was panelled up to handrail height, the newel posts often being miniature Corinthian columns complete with fluting and carved capitals. The ends of the risers on open-string staircases sometimes had carved brackets. Closed-string staircases also had Classical mouldings. Banisters became lighter as the century progressed. In the mid-eighteenth century, many staircases were stone with delicate wrought-iron balusters. The handrail was usually mahogany, which had come into use in the 1720s. In the 1770s the square section baluster, about half an inch or more

square, became very common. They were painted and the handrail polished. Later cast-iron balusters appeared, but were not widely used until the Regency period. The early designs were simple Classical motifs, but by the 1830s there were some quite florid designs used with various plant motifs. The simple staircase with square balusters was one of the most widely used designs of the late eighteenth century, and it continued to be popular up to the 1850s.

For most of the Victorian period, both cast-iron balusters and lathe-turned varieties were used. There were some extremely elaborate cast-iron designs produced, as a look at a contemporary ironmongery catalogue will verify. Handrails became heavier, and so did newel posts. In the 1870s and '80s, pitch pine became very popular, usually varnished. Newel posts and balusters of pitch-pine staircases tended to be very bulbous and heavy, a style much used in speculatively built houses. With the Arts and Craft movement, and later the influence of architects like Rennie Mackintosh and Charles Voysey, came the distinctive elegant staircases of the Victorian and Edwardian period. The slightly tapered tall newel posts and balusters, often pierced with a heart motif, became very popular. Many builders adopted these designs in the early 1900s. Oak was used in expensive work which might be stained or polished. After the First World War staircases became simpler. The use of turned balusters tended to die out in the 1920s.

Art Deco often made itself felt in a small way in the design of newel-post tops. Columbian pine was one of the most widely used woods of the period, and was usually stained.

After the Second World War, many staircases with balusters were boarded over with hardboard to modernise them. Many interesting discoveries are made by the removal of this unpleasant covering. Mahogany and oak handrails were often painted over too, and it is worth investigating to find out what is underneath the paint when you are re-decorating.

The replacement of any altered or removed joinery should only be undertaken when the original joinery features surviving have been closely examined so that they can be copied. When no original details exist, professional advice should be sought.

The restoration of sash windows, particularly those of the 1700–1835 period, demands great care. Proportions should be correct and small details like the moulding on glazing bars and the correct thickness of meeting rails and frame sections should be checked.

Woodwork

One of the most heart-breaking aspects of restoring an old house is the damage that has frequently been done to woodwork. Panelled doors are made 'flush' with hardboard; picture and chair rails ripped out; window shutters nailed in; and window joinery generally mutilated with nails and screws. Coats of paint and crude varnish have often been used to such an extent that decorative detailing is obscured.

For replacement and repair of woodwork, consult the following list of firms specialising in woodwork and joinery, listed alphabetically by county.

Co-Lignum Ltd
Atlas Street
St Philips
Bristol, Avon
BS2 0TG
Tel: (0272) 713679

McCurdy & Co Ltd
Manor Farm
Stanford Dingley
Reading
Berkshire RG7 6LS
Tel: (0734) 744866

Rattee & Kett
Purbeck Road
Cambridge
CB2 2PG
Tel: (0223) 248061

Bailey Brothers (Adlington) Ltd
Adlington
nr Macclesfield
Cheshire SK10 4NJ
Tel: (0257) 872227

Neville Balderston
Silverdale
Dent
Sedbergh
Cumbria
Tel: (0587) 20485

T N Hodgson & Sons
Sawmill
Kirkby Stephen
Cumbria
Tel: (0930) 71410

Herbert Read Ltd
St Sidwells Art Works
Odhams Wharf
Edford
Exeter
Devon EX3 0PB
Tel: (039 287) 4335

F Cuff & Sons
Aleveston
nr Sherborne
Dorset
Tel: (096 323) 219

Shelston
9 The Yews
Wimborne St Giles
Dorset
Tel: (072 54) 202

Brian Wakelin
c/o Portway Farm
Winfrith
Newburgh, Dorset
Tel: (0949) 462384

Hugh Loughborough
Panteg
Solva
Dyfed SA62 6TZ
Tel: (043 785) 294

J S R Joinery
Poole Street
Great Yeldham
Halstead
Essex
Tel: (0787) 237722

Phoenix Preservation Ltd
Ferry Lane
Rainham
Essex
Tel: (76) 53311

Capps & Capps Ltd
Hay Castle
Hay-on-Wye
Herefordshire
Tel: (0497) 820503

Waterhouse
Chipperfield
Kings Langley
Hertfordshire
Tel: (40) 67444

G E Wallis & Sons Ltd
Broadmead Works
Maidstone
Kent ME16 8RE
Tel: (0622) 54055

Shepherdson (Stockport) Ltd
Norwood Road
Great Moor
Stockport, Lancs
Tel: (061) 483 2638

E Bowman & Sons Ltd
Cherryholt Road
Stamford
Lincolnshire
Tel: (0780) 51015

J H Palin
The Old Manor House
Allington
Grantham
Lincolnshire
Tel: (0400) 81358

Dove Brothers
Cloudesley Place
London N1
Tel: (01) 837 8151

Caisley Contracts Ltd
Bray House
Breakspear Road
Ruislip
Middlesex HA4 7SE
Tel: (71) 31421

K W Joinery Ltd
Monks Eleigh
Ipswich
Suffolk

Howard Bros (of Battle) Ltd
Station Yard
Battle
East Sussex TN33 0DE
Tel: (042 46) 3272

J & W Lowry Ltd
64 Bath Lane
Newcastle-upon-Tyne
Tyne & Wear NE4 5TT
Tel: (0632) 323586

Robert Thompson's Craftsmen Ltd
Kilburn
York
YO6 4AH
Tel: (034 76) 218

Shepherd Construction Ltd
United House
Piccadilly
York
Tel: (0904) 53040

The
Kitchen

In this business of doing up houses, I firmly believe that one should adhere to the spirit, rather than the letter of historical periods. Many people, quite rightly, hanker after a Georgian or a Victorian terrace house; very few, I fancy would wish to reproduce, in all its labour-intensive detail, the cramped and ill-lit Georgian or Victorian kitchen.

The kitchen is, indeed, a special case. Other rooms in the house may be adapted without much strain to twentieth-century conditions. The use to which bedrooms and living rooms are put has not changed very markedly over the last 150 years. People do not spend very much more, or less, time in either than they used to, and the basic human needs to lie down, sit or study, and store clothes or books, remains constant. But the kitchen, in the days of the servantless household, has come up in the world. It is the most highly serviced, the most expensive and the most heavily maintained room in the house. And it is where the average family spends most of its time. The kitchen is where we bottle wine, clean shoes, delouse the cat. It is where children do their homework and where parents catch up with their correspondence. The kitchen in other words is now no longer simply a *machine à cuire*. It is at once a workshop, living room and dining room, and any discussion of the restoration of period homes must take this central fact into consideration.

When considering the Georgian house, or the coarser Victorian terraced house (which is where a large proportion of London families still live), one is immediately confronted by the problem of basement kitchens. These houses were all planned on the peculiarly British concept of vertical living, with two rooms on each floor stacked alongside a circulation space. The meanest of the spaces—the basement and the attic—were assigned to the servants, while the family, like the meat in a sandwich, dwelt in the middle. Typically, the basement kitchen enjoyed no view, was meaner in scale, bereft of ornament and short of natural light; scarcely a promising environment for the nerve centre of the modern home. The

With its draught-excluding valance and curtain this Hampshire kitchen hearth (c 1800) resembles a proscenium stage. Sporting pieces on the wall above suggest an establishment of some substance. Note also the wall-mounted 'units', forerunners of the fitted kitchen of today.

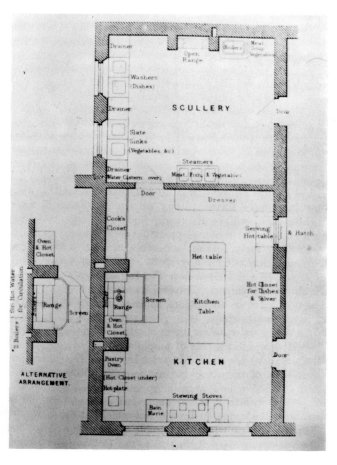

first decision that has to be made therefore concer
the siting of the kitchen.

There are undoubtedly strong arguments in favou
of keeping it in its natural place. An enlarge
basement with an opening in the dividing wall an
carefully detailed double doors makes an exceller
kitchen, dining and living space. On one side there
easy access to the street, and on the other a view of th
garden. Kitchen waste material can pass in eithe
direction: to dustbins on the street side or to th
compost heap on the other. Furthermore, by assignin
the entire floor area to kitchen and kitchen-relate
activities, skilful use can be made of subsidiary space
beneath the stairs or below the area steps (a natura
cellar or larder). There is usually space for a toilet, fo
washing machines and ironing boards, and for storin
wine and frozen food away from the kitchen spac
itself. It is thus possible to achieve a kind of twentiet
century version of the Georgian kitchen, with i
pantries, sculleries, china closets and wash houses, ye
free from the noisome by-products—principall
fumes, heat and smell— which in the nineteent
century made segregated living quarters so necessar
and desirable.

In the basement there will be less to 'preserve'—n
money would ordinarily have been lavished o
mouldings or other forms of ornamentation. Pro
portions of the spaces are meaner than the livin
quarters on the floor above; this means that ver

*Above: Plan of a substantial
Victorian kitchen and scullery,
designed to cope with the division of
labour. Those condemned to
washing dishes or preparing
vegetables at the double sinks would
at least enjoy a view through the
window.*

*Left: The scullery at Lanhydrock
House in Cornwall, dominated by a
steaming range and a majestic plate-
drying cabinet.*

careful thought must be given to lighting and to ventilation. If by placing the kitchen in the basement the family finds that most of the household duties have to be carried on under artificial light, then in my view serious consideration should be given to positioning the kitchen elsewhere.

Indeed, it seems to me logical that if the kitchen is acknowledged to be the most important room in the house, it should also occupy space at the house's centre of gravity. This, in the Georgian or Victorian terraced house, is the ground floor, which may in fact be as much as 10 feet above true ground, or garden level. As a rule there are three rooms at this level. The front parlour and the rear living room (usually interconnected); and a smaller room, often added on in a later extension giving access to the garden. There are too many variations on this pattern to permit one to generalise; and in any case the small rear extension has often been introduced with the specific intention of providing a kitchen at ground-floor level. It is really for the household to decide whether it requires a small space for preparing food or a much larger multipurpose family room. This is quite often a matter of temperament. Miracles of *haute cuisine* have been performed in confined spaces; and it should be pointed out that the nineteenth-century pioneer of kitchen reform, Catherine Beecher, drew her inspiration from the layout of galleys on ships and railway carriages.

If, however, the family decides on a larger living space, then it is worth giving serious thought to the front room adjoining the front door. There are obvious advantages in placing the kitchen here. The distance which heavy shopping loads have to be carried is cut to a minimum, and answering the doorbell does not entail a long upstairs journey from the lower regions. I speak from experience. My wife and I have lived in three nineteenth-century terraced houses. In the first, the kitchen was situated in the basement at the end of a corridor—inconvenient and remote. In the other two houses, both of which were partial if inadequate conversions, we positioned the kitchen next to the front door. I do not claim that the solution is perfect; but it is as good a compromise as any.

Wherever you decide to put the kitchen, there are basic principles which hold good for all forms of conversion. These are, that you should attempt to respect the proportions of the existing space into which you intend inserting your kitchen; and that wherever possible you should try and retain, and perhaps even replace, as many of the existing features as possible. The proportions of the room will be greatly affected by the proportions of cupboards, shelves, and kitchen appliances—many of which are standardised. You will naturally be tempted when planning your new kitchen to install a 'fitted' kitchen. This in my view is a temptation which should be strenuously resisted. The paradox of the fitted kitchen is that it seldom fits. Unless you go to the trouble of remodelling the proportions of your kitchen to accommodate them (by lowering ceilings and so on), the factory-built units of the fitted kitchen invariably look ill at ease. A fitted kitchen in a period home is rather like a modern office block inserted into an English market town. The hard boxy outlines and

The range at Saltram House in Devon is a fine example of the Victorian iron-founder's art. Behind it, an equally characteristic batterie de cuisine.

Left: *The kitchen at Minley Manor in Hampshire. By 1903, when this photograph was taken, electric light had arrived to supplement natural light from the dormer window. High-level windows were common in Victorian and Edwardian kitchens: the owners had no wish to be overlooked, and the staff, too, were entitled to their privacy. Despite the sawdust on the floor this is a relatively opulent kitchen.*

Right: *With his mania for designing everything—even rolling pins and pastry boards—Lutyens produced at Castle Drogo one of the finest examples of the architect-designed kitchen. Note the absence of projections: kitchen range, coal chutes and dresser have all been recessed from the wall plane. The clumsy and intrusive light socket must be a later addition.*

A cast-iron kitchen range, properly integrated, with tiled surround and architrave. This was no place for the faint-hearted. The size and weight of kitchen utensils necessary for feeding a large Victorian household were calculated to develop the forearms and fray the nerves

lossy surfaces not only lack character and variety—
they jar with their surroundings. In recent years, it is
quite true, most kitchen manufacturers have gone all
revivalist and retrospective with their joke oak and
dust-collecting fielded panels and exposed brass
hinges—the fitted 'kitschen'—but no amount of added
texture can alter the fact that the units have been
mass-produced and have not been designed for the
spaces into which they have fitted.

So what, then, is the solution? In my opinion
individual pieces of furniture are far more appropriate
than serried ranks of fitted cabinets. The precise
'period' as such is relatively unimportant. But the
advantage of furniture over fixtures and fittings, apart
from the fact that it will appreciate in value and is
easier to take with you when you move house, is that it
protrudes far less into the volume of the room. On the
whole I would suggest a mixture of furniture and
joinery. Fixed storage units, say below work-surface
level, and glass-fronted cabinets or open shelves
above. Kitchens invariably contain a large number of

items you wish to hide, and others, such as copper pans
and decorated plates, which deserve to be displayed.
As a general principle, fittings and furniture should be
heavy and enclosed towards the bottom, becoming
thinner and lighter and more exposed towards the top.
The Welsh dresser is a perfect example of this
principle in action; and it illustrates a very important
rule in storage design: that no shelf should be more
than one item deep.

If you are installing your kitchen at basement level,
or if you have the space in a much larger detached or
semi-detached Victorian villa, a larder is well worth
installing. Many families quite erroneously use their
fridges for storing all perishable food, when in fact all
that is required is a relatively cool cupboard, which it
is not even necessary to ventilate unless ventilation is
the only means of keeping it cool. A larder ventilated
by a vent to the outside is difficult to install in terraced
houses, but in a larger establishment where the
kitchen leads directly onto the garden, it would be
well worth considering. It could also contain the

freezer, wine, bottled fruit, bulk purchases and other items of long-term storage best kept away from the kitchen itself.

Storage apart, the two other key components of a well-planned kitchen are the positioning of the sink and the cooker. Much has been written elsewhere about the mystique of work triangles and of the correct relationship between food preparation, washing up, and cooking. The kitchen planning manuals offer all kinds of possible configurations. I am convinced, however, that the food preparation area and the sink should adjoin a window. Cooks spend most of their time at the sink or at an adjoining work surface, and like everyone else they do not wish to be condemned to stare for long periods at a blank wall.

The placing of the cooker is more complex, depending on whether you have separate hobs and oven or some kind of free-standing appliance. If the latter, then it should look good enough to stand on it own; and this effectively means that it should be either a period-piece gas or electric cooker, or a solid fuel, gas or oil-fired range of the Aga or Raeburn type. The best position for these is in the chimney breast, with tile surround and a powerful air extractor ducted discreetly to the outside wall. Wherever you place your cooker, try to avoid if possible the flat extractor hoods which float over the hobs like the testers of medieval pulpits; they are unsightly and not very efficient.

If you decide to install your hobs on the work surface, and mount your oven on the wall, you are then free to use the fireplace for its proper purpose. Even a tiny coal fire can turn a kitchen from a forbidding laboratory into a delightfully informal living room.

It goes without saying that you should respect the

existing features of the room itself. It is a major crime to cut into mouldings or architraves when trying to accommodate cupboards or work surfaces. Nothing looks worse than a sink unit slicing across the lower third of a large window, or butting rudely into an architrave. Corners should be rounded or splayed where necessary. You may find you are compelled, in a room with large window and door openings, to install an 'island' unit. Properly designed, this is perfectly acceptable. Besides saving wall space, it has the added advantage of separating the cooking zone from the living and eating space.

All these general principles apply also to the Arts and Crafts house. The seminal importance of the kitchen in the Arts and Crafts movement was identified by Hermann Muthesius in his study of the development of the English house. 'The leading sector of the people in intellectual, spiritual matters is in particular given to the country life', he wrote. 'Great emphasis was placed on untreated wooden surfaces. Primitive peasant forms were revived, construction details were always apparent (often in a most obtrusive fashion), and little heed was paid to comfort or refined modes of life. The thinking behind this was that one must go back and start at the beginning in order to get over the degenerate state of culture which the nineteenth centuty had brought about. The only room in the house to which the so-called artistic strivings of the time had not penetrated was the kitchen. So they went back to kitchen furniture: kitchen chairs gave them ideas for new forms of chair, kitchen cupboards for new forms of cupboard. This new furniture differed from the genuine kitchen pieces in that it was ten times more expensive because it was produced under the uneconomic conditions of 'works of art'.'

Left: The country kitchen upgraded into a setting for a dinner party. The original range, replaced by a unit in front of the window, assumes a decorative role. Only the chairs and the downlighters seem seriously out of place.

This page: A traditional chair of the type produced during the Second World War as part of the range of utility furniture. It has a pleasing simplicity that allows it to fit in with many twentieth-century kitchen styles.

That the kitchen was the repository of Arts and Crafts values seems also to have been confirmed by M. H. Baillie Scott. In an article on 'An Ideal Suburban House' (*Studio*, vol 4, 1894–5) he wrote: 'The kitchen of the average suburban house does not present so much room for improvements as the family rooms. Here at least, where things are for use and not for show, some approximation is made to a successful interior effect.' Scott does not appear to have grasped that objects for use may also be objects for show—a concept which Terence Conran and others have marketed with brilliant success. It is axiomatic in kitchen design that you should try and strike a balance between the conspicuously labour-intensive and the discreetly labour-saving, and the success of your kitchen will largely depend on a harmonious mixture of the two.

The Kitchen

You would have to be rather dotty to want a totally 'authentic' Georgian or Victorian kitchen. In those days, a kitchen was purely the domain of the cook and other hard-pressed servants, and little thought was given to its lighting, use of space, ventilation or general comfort. But today, the purpose of the kitchen has changed, and it has become the hub of family life. To make your kitchen strike a balance between historic charm and modern convenience, consult the following list, which mentions suppliers of high-quality domestic equipment designed on traditional lines. For flooring tiles, brass taps, stoves, etc., consult the Architectural Salvage and Metalware sections.

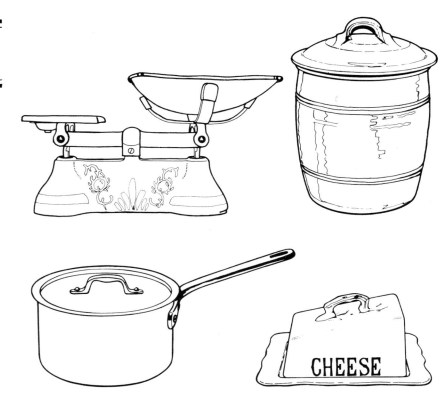

A selection of traditional items from David Mellor. As well as being practical, items such as these provide the finishing touch to a period kitchen.

Elizabeth David

Elizabeth David Ltd was founded in 1965 and was the first of the kitchen shops, stocking a full range of utensils. Every type of high quality kitchen utensil is stocked, the polished copper baking moulds being particularly attractive. These are available in a number of different designs, including lobsters, fish, pineapples and hearts.

Elizabeth David Ltd
46 Bourne Street
London SW1
Tel: (01) 730 3123
and
Covent Garden Kitchen Supplies
3 North Row
The Market
Covent Garden
London WC2
Tel: (01) 836 9167)

Divertimenti

Divertimenti stock a huge range covering every conceivable item of kitchen equipment from wooden spoons to asparagus kettles.

Divertimenti
68–70 Marylebone Lane
London W1
Tel: (01) 935 0689

David Mellor

David Mellor, silversmith and Royal Designer for Industry, set up his first shop in London ten years ago. Today there are shops in Sloane Square and Covent Garden in London, and in Manchester and Sheffield. All these shops offer a comprehensive selection of fine quality cooking equipment which is chosen, as far as possible, for both its functional and aesthetic qualities.

David Mellor
4 Sloane Square
London SW1W 8EE
Tel: (01) 730 4259
and
26 James Street
Covent Garden
London WC2E 8PA
Tel: (01) 379 6947
and
66 King Street
Manchester
M2 4NP
Tel: (061) 834 7023

and
1 Park Lane
Sheffield
S10 2DU
Tel: (0742) 664124

The Olive Tree Trading Company

This firm, better known in the field of terracotta garden ornaments, imports attractive earthenware and stoneware from Italy and France. The range is both traditional and functional. The 'Vulcania' range of earthenware cooking pots from Italy, for example, has been in production since the beginning of the century.

The Olive Tree Trading Company Ltd
Church Wharf
Pumping Station Road
Chiswick
London W4 2SN
Tel: (01) 995 5281/2/3

The Bathroom

When people took a bath in the eighteenth century it was normally in a portable bath in front of a good fire. The object was not so much to get clean as to cure an ill or to recover from a fatiguing activity. The hypochondria allowed by the increasing wealth of the nation had led not to hygiene, but hydrotherapy. Baths were used in bedrooms and dressing rooms, in kitchens or sculleries. The advantage of taking a bath below stairs was that it was usually the only floor supplied with water and near the only place it could be heated—the kitchen range.

Every bedroom had a wash-stand with a basin and jug. It was usual to wash the face and hands every day and the neck and feet on Saturday nights (if it was not too cold), a custom that originated with the ritual washing away of sins before the Sabbath. Fuel was expensive and hot water something of a luxury. The poor hardly washed at all, firm in the belief that they might die of cold if they did.

Drainage was also limited to the lowest floor. Since the available designs for closets failed to check smells, these were usually outside in the yard. In towns with main drainage, primitive water-closets were used, conveying the soil to the rivers. In country areas, pits were dug to collect the waste for re-distribution on the land. This was the method that had been used from time immemorial, and it had the dual benefit of not only improving the land but also keeping the rivers clean. The desire for privacy for either bathing or relieving oneself had yet to materialise, so many of these simple closets were built for several people to use at once, to prevent a queue before and after work. Inside the house chamber-pots were used, kept in 'night commodes' in the bedrooms. Other chamber-pots were kept in more decorative cupboards in the main rooms. These are sometimes sold today as wine-coolers. They were used by men at dinner, after the ladies had risen.

Designs for baths varied greatly. Basically, they were conceived as pieces of furniture and could look like sofas or chairs filled with water. Plainer, metal baths were much more practical They were soldered together from separate sections, and to make them more comfortable a piece of fabric was laid in them. The most expensive were made of copper, which has the property of spreading heat evenly, as in saucepans. Most people used tinned sheet-iron baths. Zinc baths were seldom used in England, though they were popular in France and Scotland. They looked fine

The early Victorians enjoyed the luxury of bathing in front of the fire in their own bedrooms. Upstairs, water was a luxury as there was no plumbing. It had to be brought all the way up in cans from the kitchen in the basement and then taken all the way down again in pails. Small hip baths, made of iron and painted, like the one shown here, were a popular design of the 1840s.

when polished, but this took a great deal of time. Copper and sheet-iron baths were given several coats of heat-resisting paint (first introduced in 1770), often simulating marble inside with a plain colour outside. This paint was easily chipped and had to be touched up frequently.

The two most popular bath shapes were the reclining and the hip. Reclining baths were full-size, tapered to save hot water, with either straight or sloping sides and foot. Sometimes the head of the bath was sloped for the back, with sides curved up to take a cushion. The hip bath was much smaller, used far less water and did not involve fully undressing. The bathers, or patients as they were usually called, simply sat in it. Hip baths had a high back and sometimes a removable wooden seat. Sitz baths were very similar. Rectangular versions, designed for building-in, are still made today. Sponge baths, like the medieval head bath, used very little water and were simply large shallow basins placed on the floor to wash over. Some shower trays today have the same function. Other baths were made for bathing just a foot or a leg. The very cheapest baths were oak tubs, following the medieval tradition, but usually painted on the inside. Although they were warm to use, they were difficult to clean.

Fixed baths were not unknown, but they needed a bathroom or bath house, something that only the largest houses had. Some had piped hot and cold water, but generally they were just large cold plunge baths, to be used after hunting. The most extravagant

were hewn from solid marble, while others were made from slabs of marble or painted local slate, held together with iron bars and sealed with Roman cement. Cheaper baths were made of oak or walnut, lined with copper or lead. The cheapest were brick cisterns dug into the ground and faced with cement.

The most difficult problem in modernising houses of this period is to find the space for a bathroom for which no provision was originally made. What makes it doubly difficult is that very often these houses have already been converted, often at a time when their architectural values were not fully appreciated. In terraced houses, back extensions often mar the staircase, blocking the light that was designed to show its elegant design. The purest solution is to demolish the additions and restore the basic form of the house, for nothing will be lost visually by returning to the original design of houses for this period. But a house that is two hundred years old has seen a series of technological revolutions, the products of many of which we find indispensable today. The most sensible course to take is to recognise this history and to add in new developments in the best way that they occurred. Some devices, like late nineteenth-century Geysers, might be fun as sculpture, but are appropriate neither to the date of the house, nor to today's life style.

We still have some things in common with the late eighteenth century. Baths are taken to relax in, bath salts are still used to ease an aching back. An outside WC is still useful for anyone in the garden. But some parts of the house may be anachronistic, like a large cellar for coal and wine or a wash house. Today, there may be a basic design problem involved in replacing the servants' quarters in the basement with a separate flat. There will certainly be the problem of how to fit soil pipes down through a house where there has been none before, since new outside soil pipes are a mistake, both functionally and visually.

With these thoughts in mind, a typical London terraced house, with two rooms on each floor, might be converted as follows. The bathroom for the principal bedroom on the second floor would go in the back room; very often this was a dressing room and has or had an inter-connecting door. The bath should be on the wall opposite the fireplace, standing clear of the walls by some 1 foot to 1 foot 6 inches. It should not be built-in, but stand on its own. It could be

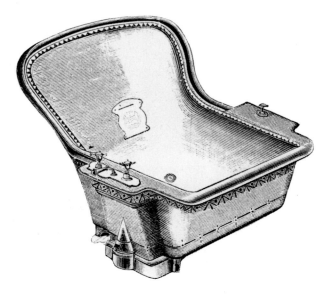

A fixed sitz bath of 1890, sold complete with fittings to save plumber's work.

one of the new Italian sealed-wood tub baths (now easy to clean), a plastic bath with a marble finish, or a plain old white cast-iron bath of the type that might have been put in during the 1920s. The advantage of standing the bath free from the walls is that there will be no differential movement between the wall and bath top to be sealed, and the walls do not have to be tiled but can be finished in a traditional wallpaper, or painted. Since the eighteenth century rarely used solid colours, and did not have gloss paint, a possible scheme would be to paint the room with white eggshell and then put a very thin coat of colour on as evenly as possible, followed by a coat of matt varnish. The basin could be a converted mahogany wash-stand from the 1840s with a practical marble top. This would be more useful than a wash-stand of the exact period.

There is no easy solution to adding a WC and bidet. Perhaps the simplest answer is to choose very neat wall-hung designs, choosing not white but a colour to blend with the room. The best position would be against the recess between the fireplace and the window wall. The soil pipe, in sound-proofed cast iron, could then run straight down to the basement in the corner against the wall. Where this passes through the room below, the reveal at the side of the fireplace may have to be made into a cupboard, or shelved with a small duct (run the cornice from the front of the fireplace to the window wall in a straight line). The flushing cistern could easily be hidden in a wall cupboard behind. The floor could be painted boards or natural cork tiles, a quiet colour that could take an old Persian rug. It should be easy to find contemporary prints for the walls. There is one great advantage that this bathroom has over the past; it can have thermostatic mixers that do not make steam and spoil the decorations.

The problem remains of fitting a second bathroom on the floor above. Losing another room as a bathroom is usually uneconomic. One solution is to build a very small bathroom at the back of the rear room. It should have a lobby outside, so that access can be made to the now smaller bedroom at the back. The walls should be sandwiches of sound-proofing glass fibre or mineral wool. For the bedroom, the new doorway and skirting should be made to match the existing, so that they look original. The door can be the one from the staircase re-used. The bathroom, suitable for children, can be very neat and modern. It need not be larger than 5 feet 6 inches square to take a standard 5 feet 6 inch bath, a WC and large corner basin. The door need not be larger than 1 foot 6 inches wide. The bath should be designed to incorporate a shower. Alternatively, even smaller bathrooms are possible, down to 4 feet 6 inches × 3 foot 6 inches, using a shower tray or sitz bath instead of a normal bath. If it is difficult to fit a 4-inch soil pipe through the floor or across the fireplace, there is now a sanitary shredder, the Saniflo, that uses a pipe of only 1 inch. Small bathrooms need plenty of mirrors to prevent them from seeming too much like cupboards. Queen Elizabeth I had her bathroom lined with looking-glass above the wainscot. Downstairs, the problem of fitting in some kind of WC for the ground floor is best solved by putting it under or by the stairs, fitted with an extractor fan. For the basement, another small bathroom like the one described need not take away valuable natural light from the main rooms. It could be in the centre of the house, under the front-door steps or in an old coal-cellar. To make a laundry area upstairs, a small combined washer and dryer which condenses its extract air makes an external vent unnecessary, and can usually be fitted in one of the top bathrooms, as long as the machine and sockets are enclosed in a cupboard.

The Nineteenth Century

Eighteenth-century methods of bathing were labour intensive. Carrying hot and cold water up to each of the bedrooms, filling baths and carrying the slops down again took a geat deal of time. It is not strange that our ancestors thought washing a luxury. The gradual move towards having a plumbed bathroom was generated by a desire to save labour, not to be cleaner. Early in the nineteenth century some of the larger houses in London had started to use the head of water supplied by the water companies to drive water up to the roof, where it could fill storage cisterns. Cisterns had long been in use in kitchens, because the water supplies were not constant, coming on for a few hours a day only when the water pumps worked. Another system was to pump up the water by hand, though this was laborious. These developments meant that cold water could be supplied to the dressing rooms and also to a WC for visitors on the ground floor. Small terraced houses often had a corner sink placed on the second-floor half-landing, for filling cans and emptying slops.

It became common practice to fit baths which had

their own small coal-fired heaters at one end with a flue taken into a nearby fireplace. Gas was also becoming available, and baths with numerous small gas jets under them, like huge kettles, could be warmed up in half-an-hour. The pattern of house planning began to change. In 1850 many houses began to have small, separate dressing rooms in addition to the standard two rooms per floor of the previous century. These could be used for bathing, though many did not have a fireplace. They were to become the prototype for the bathrooms fitted in most middle-class houses in the second half of the century.

The design of WCs took a great step forward with Joseph Bramah's valve closet of 1778, a development of Cumming's patent of 1775. Basically it consisted of an earthenware bowl fitted with a flap at the bottom, normally held tight shut. A certain amount of water remained in the bowl to ensure that no smells came up from the drain below. To flush the pan, a complicated set of cranks was set in motion on pulling up a handle in the seat. This automatically opened the valve and flushed the bowl from an overhead cistern and, on closing the valve, re-filled the bowl. When well looked after, the Bramah closet was quiet and efficient. Although more expensive than its competitors, it remained in production from the end of the eighteenth century till the 1890s in a modified form. There are one or two Bramah pattern pans still working today.

Outwardly, all closets looked basically the same. They had a broad bench top, often running from wall to wall. This provided a useful support on rising. Below, a panel covered the various mechanisms for waste disposal, including the complicated apparatus of levers in the Bramah; the cheaper, more popular but less effective 'pan' WC; the old 'plug' closet, where the hole in the bowl was simply closed with a plunger; and the non-mechanical short and long hopper pans, which depended on trapped water for sealing as today. Privies, over cesspits or using pails and earth closets, all looked similar to the user. The only difference was in the materials. Superior closets were made of polished Spanish mahogany, with skirtings to match. The bowls were often coloured or had printed patterns. The cheaper closets, for servants, were made from pine. WCs often had tanks made in wood to match, lined with lead.

The early Victorians liked showers in their rooms. For one thing, they required far less water, which had to be carried upstairs. These early showers looked like

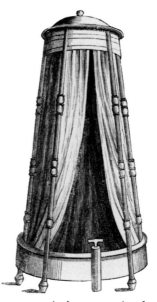

A commonly used shower-bath of the 1840s. The water was forced up into a cistern in the top by a syringe through a hollow support. The user pulled a string to open a valve, 'causing the water to descend suddenly in a shower' and run through the perforated bottom into a receptacle in the base. Made of tin plate and painted, they were sold by most ironmongers.

tents at Agincourt. At the top a cistern was filled by hand. The user then pulled a string and the whole contents fell on their head with a roar, to be caught in the basin below.

An early method of sending hot water to the upper floors, used in hotels and residential clubs, was to boil it on the kitchen range. The fire needed constant attention and steam often came out of the tap instead of water. In houses, the eighteenth-century system had been to boil water in an open-topped cast-iron boiler with a tap. The cook filled the boiler as required, but sometimes she forgot. The next step was to provide cold water for a shower by adding a feed-cistern at the same level, fed by the house supply through a ball valve. The hot water could be pumped upstairs if necessary. No doubt the hot water in the range, on expanding, could find its way back into the supply tank.

It was not long before circulatory systems came into use. The range kept its boiler, with its temperature controlled by a series of flue dampers. The hot water passed up to the hot-water tank, supplying taps in various parts of the house as it went. A return pipe led back to the kitchen range. The system was topped up from a cold-water storage tank in the roof. With hot and cold water and a waste-disposal system, the concept of the portable bath began to fade. The revolution was quick. Thomas Webster, in his *Encyclopaedia of Domestic Economy* (1844), suggested cold baths lasting from ten to twenty minutes for healthy people every morning. He wrote

'It would be desirable that a room for bathing should be constructed in every house, though this is scarcely possible in the present condition of society, yet a bath should be considered indispensible in every mansion of considerable size.' But by 1865, Robert Kerr was able to write in *The Gentleman's House*: 'No house of any pretensions will be devoid of a general bathroom; and in a large house there must be several of these.' Kerr says that the hot water must be supplied from the house supply or the water should be heated in a fireplace boiler in the bathroom. The bathroom must be large enough for a reclining bath, a wash-basin and the fireplace, with space for dressing and possibly a shower-bath, though this could be fitted over the bath. An alternative arrangement was to have a separate dressing room with the wash-basin in it. If the dressing room had a fire, but the bathroom was too small for one, the bathroom door should face the fire. He suggested that the WC could be either in an adjoining room or in the bathroom. A separate WC came to be known as the English system, strongly recommended by most writers on the grounds of hygiene and its convenience for family use. The Americans, with perhaps better sanitary ware and more bathrooms, argued that it was much more convenient for the user to house the WC in the bathroom. The battle was finally decided by plumbers, who found the American system cheaper.

Once baths no longer had to be strong enough to be portable, they began to be made of thinner metal to save cost and had to be supported on wooden cradles. They followed the general pattern of closets; a receptacle in an easily cleaned material built under a top and panelled all round to hide the plumbing. But there were objections to this, on the grounds of hygiene. Successive outbreaks of cholera between 1832 and 1866 had forced the attention of the public on hygiene for the first time. As an alternative to the cased bath, glazed ceramic baths were made, smooth and easy to clean both inside and out. In 1880, the first cast-iron baths began to be made. Just as smooth inside, their surface at first was not so durable as that of the glazed ceramic baths, but they took less heat to warm up, an important factor when hot-water systems were still primitive by modern standards. Free-standing uncased baths were called 'Roman'. Doubts about plumbers' joints, and fears about rot, meant that baths and WCs were usually placed in a lead tray, or 'safe', with its own waste-disposal system fitted with a copper flap to stop the outside wind blowing in. Although these trays could be painted, they were an eyesore. Towards the end of the century they were replaced with marble slabs wherever they could be afforded.

The most majestic bath ever produced in the nineteenth century was a full-length model with a hood at one end, tall enough to stand up in. A series of taps produced a normal shower, a needle spray, a douche from above, a sitz spray or a wave spray at will. The Victorians were also keen on home Turkish

A comfortable bathroom of the 1890s, with a panelled porcelain-enamelled heavy cast-iron bath, Bramah WC, china basin and fireplace.

A grand bathroom built about 1900 that could also be used as a Turkish bath. It has a very heavy 'Roman' fireclay bath, needle-spray bath, an American-type syphonic low-down WC suite, free-standing fireclay basin and a marble slab for 'shampooing' or massage. After a Turkish bath, one cooled off in the adjacent bedroom.

baths, converting their tiled bathrooms into a steamy hot space with a small stove, just for the day, and cooling down in the bedroom. But some of these home baths were complete reproductions in miniature of a public bath. They were forerunners of today's Finnish sauna. With a Victorian house, it might be worth investigating the possibilities of a tiled steam or hot-air bath, instead of the ordinary prefabricated timber structures sold today, which often look out of place.

The design of basins passed through several distinct stages. About 1830, large wash-stands to hold a growing multiplicity of toilet aids replaced the little basin holders of the past. Marble was introduced for the tops since its finish was so much more durable than polished or painted wood. They had either a hole in the top for the basin or were flat, so that they could be used as dressing tables. Some were made for double basins. These stands were normally designed to hold a basin, a ewer either in the basin or on a shelf below, a carafe of spring water with several glasses, a can for hot water, soap and sponge basins and shaving equipment. There were small drawers and possibly a cupboard for the chamber-pot. Some had a mirror in a fold-down top for use in the library or the cloakroom by the front entrance. The next stage was to plumb in the wash-stand, using a glazed earthenware top in one piece. Sometimes the soap dishes were also combined,

with their own little waste-disposal systems. An alternative to the fixed basin was a curious compromise between a separate basin and a fixed one, known as the 'tip-up'. It was fixed on a pivot system known as a gimbal. For washing it presented a clean bowl without a waste-disposal system to break the surface. To empty, the contents could very quickly be tipped into a receptacle below, which was connected to the drain. From the servant's point of view, there was the extra burden of cleaning the receptacle as well as the basin.

The chief problem encountered with the new hot-water supply was the effect of steam on the decorations. The new bathrooms were small compared to a bedroom, and jugs of hot water do not produce steam. The solution seemed at first to be to make all the surfaces hard and non-absorbent—an idea that fitted in with the new desire for hygiene. They used marble, slate and tiles on the floors and walls, with cement ceilings. Cheaper bathrooms had varnished wallpaper on the walls and wood floors, carefully filled and painted. Cotton mats were laid where bare feet would touch the floor. Oil-cloth and similar materials were not recommended, since they were subject to mildew. Although there was usually a fireplace, these bathrooms were notoriously cold.

In fact, the suggested surfaces were just the ones

hat were least suitable to counteract steam in the atmosphere. Other methods of counteracting steam were tried. Shelves were put at the foot of the bath to keep in the steam, or the water was supplied at low level, below the surface. The real answer was the mixer tap, which appeared towards the end of the century.

There were objections to the 'general bathroom', specially by ladies who felt they did not wish to use a bath that someone else had been in. They much preferred the comfort of bathing by the fireside in their own bedrooms. There were also problems with WCs. Now that they were indoors and near the bedrooms, any smell or noise became much more disturbing. A number of people objected to the idea of a WC in the house and much preferred to keep the outside privy. The chamber-pot was silent, convenient and easily cleaned by others. In 1870, the eventual successor to the old valve closet appeared from America: the new siphonic closet, which acted fast and almost silently. It is still the best today. There remained the problem of noise from the flushing cistern. Traditionally, the cistern had been put up high, to increase the pressure of water into the bowl, but this caused a loud rushing sound. To cure the noise, in 1895 the 'lowdown' WC suite was introduced in which the cistern was lowered to the top of the pan and increased in capacity from a standard 2 to 3 gallons to make up for the loss of pressure. The pipe into the pan was also increased in size, and the feed pipe into the cistern was taken down to the bottom, to stop it splashing. There were objections at the time from the water companies that siphonic pans used too much water, and for similar reasons they still limit the use of the flushing valve, which uses no cistern.

There was another piece of equipment to be found in many late Victorian bathrooms; the Geyser, first introduced in 1868. It was usually fired by gas, but it could use oil, coal, coke or wood. They were (and still are) used instead of a circulating hot-water system. Made of polished copper and brass, or more often painted copper with brass fittings, it must have been like keeping one's own private steam engine at home.

Mrs. Panton, writing in *From Kitchen to Garret*

Above: A portable mahogany wash-stand for the 'gentleman's room or library' of the 1840s. The lid closes down to hide the basin and ewer.

The Sanitas valve WC of the 1870s. Made in white porcelain, with the trap below raised above the floor for easy access.

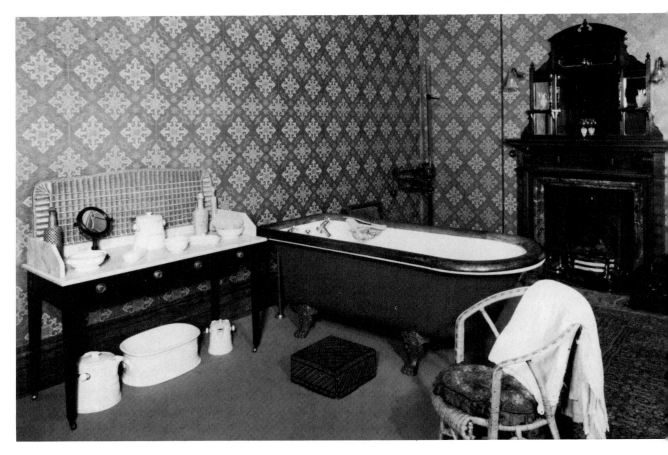

A bathroom of the 1880s, with a fine marble-topped mahogany wash-stand, a free-standing lion-footed cast-iron bath with a teak rim to protect the fragile enamel of the time, a weighing machine and a fireplace. A small china foot bath is placed below the wash-stand.

(1888), described the washing facilities she would prefer in her ideal bedroom. Two wash-stands with marble tops and tiled backs; a basin, a jug with a double lip, soap and sponge basins with drainers, all in white rope-pattern handled Beaufort ware; tooth and nail brushes in a tall spill holder; and a green glass carafe and glasses, with gas-lighting globes to match. Also essential were a brass hot-water can, with the name of the room on the label, a white china foot-bath, and a slop pail. For re-filling foot baths, the house-maid needed an oak-painted hot-water can. She mentions that even then there was a lack of bathrooms in old houses. If the bath had to be in the dressing room, it should stand on a large piece of oil-cloth, covered by a bath mat made up from gold and dark brown blanket material.

At the end of the period, H. C. Davidson, in the *Book of the Home* (1902), wrote about the decoration of the bathroom of the time. He advises that it should be 8 feet wide by 10 to 11 feet long, with a fireplace not so much for heating as for ventilation. The hot-water tank should be in an airing cupboard in the bathroom. He suggests using the then popular blue-and-white geometric or pictorial pattern tiles on the walls. He is against the matting or wallpaper often used, unless the bath and basin are in their own tiled recess. Another wall could then have a pair of heated airing cupboards with lattice doors and a dressing table with a mirror between. The floor, if not tiled, should be lino or cork carpet, either plain or with a very neat and unobtrusive mosaic or tile pattern. As an alternative, he suggests Indian, Chinese or Japanese matting, bound with American cloth. He advises that a wallpaper should not be plain, otherwise it will show trickles from condensation. It should have a graceful, simple design in light, soft colours and be varnished. Instead of paper, one could have lincrusta, well painted. In a small room he suggests a tiled dado all round. As furniture, he mentions a high-backed, wide-seated chair, a good-sized rush-topped footstool, and perhaps a light wood-framed screen covered in fluted cretonne or sateen. Or one made of bamboo, with panels of linen embroidered with designs of aquatic plants with flax-thread. For windows, linen curtains; for splash curtains behind the bath and basin, kus-kus matting, lincrusta, washing linen or fine Japanese matting. He does not like art muslin, pongee silk or cotton crepe here. The most practical bath mats, he thinks, are cork, the prettiest an art-blanket embroidered with thick wool or rope flax. He also likes blue-and-white Japanese rugs. He makes the following suggestions for colour schemes:

Dado of plain, pale green tiles; leaf-pattern wallpaper in greens with a white ground; white or deeper green paintwork; green cork carpet.

Dado of lincrusta painted ivory; blue-and-white paper above; blue paintwork; ivory coloured Indian matting with a blue-and-white Japanese rug.

Paper in shades of green; frieze with design of aquatic plants and reeds in soft blue-and-green; ivory paintwork; green Japanese matting on the floor, blue-and-white Japanese rug.

Dado of white tiles; pink-and-white paper above; pale green or white paint; green cork carpet.

Dado of anaglypta painted cream; deep-yellow paper above; woodwork stained brown or painted cream; brown linoleum.

The Twentieth Century

With the sophisticated wash-down and siphonic closets made at the end of the nineteenth century, and the much improved cast-iron baths of the period, the style of the bathroom began to change again at the beginning of the twentieth century, to become a bleaker but more functional space. Baths and WCs were no longer to be cased, on hygienic grounds, and basins had to be wall-hung, on legs or pedestals. Only in the last resort were they to have cupboards below them. C. H. B. Quennell, writing in 1912, could declare that 'For sheer unadulterated luxury, nothing can be compared to the enjoyment of jumping out

A 1905 Doulton bathroom for a 'house of moderate size'. Everything is in white with gold lines.

from a cold bath and dressing in front of a good fire'. He thought that WCs should never be put in the bathroom, and that it was essential to have a separate boiler for water heating, so the range had only to be lit for cooking. He suggested that the bath, of vitreous cast iron with a wide roll edge, should be parallel-sided, set on a pedestal and stand out into the room. Sometimes sitz and footbaths or separate showers are added 'if one just wants a shower after tennis'. A bathroom should be large enough for physical exercise. Although marble was readily available for wall and floorcovering, he felt it should be used with restraint, otherwise the bathroom will be 'reminiscent of a cheap restaurant'. The towel rail should be used for heating small bathrooms, while larger bathrooms called for a radiator or fire. He was in favour of everything being white, with ideally a well-waxed warm-red tile floor. For easier cleaning, the tiles should have a little round where they meet the wall tiles. Tiled walls should be white, 'so one's body appears ruddy with health' and could go up to 14 feet 6 inches with Keene's cement painted white above, or right to the ceiling if one could afford it. He described

Left: A bathroom for a rather more opulent household by Beaven's in 1900, with white porcelain-enamelled fire-clay baths and basin, shower for 'hot, cold and tepid' water and shampoo fittings.

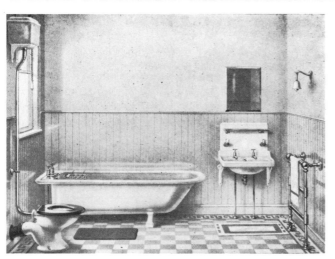

A simple Shank's bathroom of 1927, with a 'Roman' cast-iron bath and a cheap but noisy wash-down WC pan, high-level cistern and wash basin all in vitreous china. For economy they are placed together in one room.

a bath by Lutyens with a marble top, taps set at one end, and sides framed in a trellis of ebony with chintz hanging behind—not recommended by Quennell for general use. Basins should be large, white glazed with marble tops and backs. He mentions a 'Luxurious new fitting': a hot and cold shampooing mixer which could also be used for 'spraying the face after the heat of the summer's day'. He concludes: 'In all cases, be it bathroom for peasant or millionaire, the effect must be obtained in simple fashion.'

Meanwhile, the peasants were being introduced, often unwillingly, to the joys of having a bath downstairs. The scullery or wash house was usually transformed, once a week, into the new bathroom. Since there was little room, a number of contrivances were developed to save space. Baths could have removable wooden tops and be used as tables, be sunk in the floor with a panel over them, hinged-up into a wall-cupboard or pivoted on their wastes to slide into a fitment. Some of these ideas could be useful today.

The Bathroom

The bathroom often presents serious problems in an old house. In houses built before the middle of the 19th century, no provision would originally have been made for a bathroom, and the first job is to find a suitable space for one. The next job is to decorate it suitably, finding the best way to marry period bathroom fittings to basic modern plumbing.

In the following listings you will find a selection of suppliers of high quality antique or traditionally inspired bathroom fittings and accessories.

Albion Hardware

This firm manufactures an attractive range of traditionally inspired co-ordinated bathroom accessories. Hand-

Below: Bathroom accessories from Albion in the Meadow Flower (Porcelain) range. The flower patterns give a traditional flavour to a modern bathroom. Right: Bathroom fittings from Albion. These traditionally inspired designs combine the advantages of modern manufacture with period appeal.

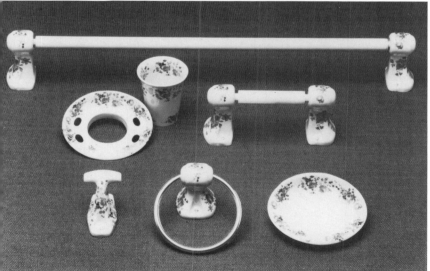

made porcelain basins, bidets, baths and handles are all decorated with delicate floral patterns. Metal taps and rails are available in either solid brass or chrome.

Albion Hardware Ltd
Simon House
Sunderland Road
Sandy
SG19 1QY
Tel: (0767) 80330

Anderson Ceramics

The 'Victoriana' range is hand-worked from fireclay and is available in either a floral *Art Nouveau* design, available in various colour combinations, or plain colours. The bathroom suite is available with a mahogany toilet seat and gold plated taps for the basin and bidet

Anderson Ceramics Ltd
Dukesway

Team Valley
Gateshead
Tyne & Wear NE11 0SW
Tel: (0632) 874511

Architectural Heritage of Cheltenham

A selection of Victorian and Edwardian bathroom fittings is available, including complete bathrooms, hand-basins, painted toilet pans, rolled-top baths and vanity units.

Architectural Heritage of Cheltenham
Boddington Manor
Boddington
nr Cheltenham
Gloucestershire
Tel: (024 268) 741
(0242) 22191

Atkinson & Kirby

Britain's leading specialist in beautifully finished wooden toilet seats. All the hinges are brass.

Atkinson & Kirby Ltd
Wigan Road
Ormskirk
Lancashire L39 2AP
Tel: (0695) 73234

Chiltenhurst

Chiltenhurst specialise in wooden bathroom fittings. The 'Classic' range is made from solid mahogany or pine finished with brass or chrome fittings, and includes toilet-roll holder, towel ring, towel rail, shelf, soap dish, tumbler and toothbrush holder, robe hook and toilet seat.

Chiltenhurst Ltd
48 Coldharbour Lane
Harpenden
Hertfordshire AL5 4NF
Tel: (058 27) 60281

Czech & Speake

The 'Edwardian' range consists of fine 19th century-style bathroom fittings, made with the original tools, and available in polished brass in varying finishes, nickel plate, or lacquer. The range also includes similar bathroom accessories such as towel rails, bath hooks, and sponge and soap baskets. This charming shop also stocks a fine selection of ladies' toiletries, sponges, and gentlemen's 'aromatics'.

Czech & Speake Ltd
88 Jermyn Street
London SW1Y 6JD
Tel: (01) 839 6868/9

C P Hart & Sons

C P Hart distribute the imported 'Leonardo' and 'Montmartre' ranges. These are fine quality traditional-style brass bathroom fittings, the 'Leonardo'

Leonardo range from C P Hart

Nostalgia range from C P Hart

range being in polished brass with matching accessories, and the 'Montmartre' available in either polished brass, nickel plate or a range of colours, including red, blue, green, yellow, and ivory. The 'Nostalgia' range, made of solid brass with decorated ceramic bases and hand wells, is also available.

C P Hart & Sons
Newnham Terrace
Hercules Road
London SE1
Tel: (01) 928 5866

The London Architectural Salvage and Supply Co

Items for sale include: original cast iron baths with claw or plain feet, panelled baths with surrounds, basins, taps and shower fittings, towel rails, toilet pans and seats, cisterns, and occasionally old massage tables.

The London Architectural Salvage and Supply Co Ltd
Mark Street (off Paul Street)
London EC2A 4ER
Tel: (01) 739 0448/9

S Polliack

S Polliack have a large choice of traditionally inspired bathroom suites. A large selection of fittings and accessories is also available.

S Polliack Ltd
Railway Street
Slingsby
York YO6 7AN
Tel: (065 382) 347

Sitting Pretty

Sitting Pretty is an antique shop stocking a comprehensive range of both genuine and reproduction period bathroom items. These include wooden cisterns, porcelain pull handles, cast iron baths, brass taps, stained glass mirrors and lights, and original Victorian and Edwardian decorated toilets. They have a large stock of handmade wooden toilet seats available in either solid mahogany or obeche; they specialise particularly in monogrammed toilet seats.

A hand basin complete with original taps. Decorated in dark blue.

A beautifully decorated Victorian lavatory pan which uses a floral design in blue.

Sitting Pretty
131 Dawes Road
London SW6
Tel: (01) 381 0049

Walcot Reclamation

This architectural salvage firm has a large stock of original 19th century bathroom furniture. Period and modern cast baths, basins and taps, toilet pans and cisterns are all available.

Walcot Reclamation
108 Walcot Street
Bath
BA1 5BG
Tel: (0225) 310182

Colour

The question of colour is much disputed by experts on historic buildings. Perfectly preserved colour schemes are very rare, and exist mostly in houses which are too grand to be typical. The colour schemes of smaller houses can be reconstructed only from literary sources and from the colour pictures in books. There is always the complication of later colour schemes being superimposed on the original, and an existing scheme, even if not original, may in itself be interesting enough to merit preservation and be more valuable in its authenticity than a speculative attempt to return to a lost original state.

Personal taste also figures largely in matters of colour, and it is ultimately the trained eye of a decorator which will decide whether a restored colour scheme in an historic building is 'right' or not. Houses which were restored thirty years ago in the belief that they were 'accurate' already look dated, and it is possible that taste directs what we want to find out about historic colour. If the choice of colour is ultimately subjective, it can be reinforced by reference to all the artefacts of a period, and its literature. This will help to create an understanding of the ideals and aspirations of past ages.

In the face of these difficulties, the ordinary house-owner should not be afraid to experiment, as colour is one area of restoration which is neither irrevocable nor very expensive. Colour in terms of paint, as discussed here, is only one part of the general effect achieved in a house with upholstery, curtains, floor-coverings and wallpaper, all of which have to be considered in relation to each other.

Pre-Eighteenth Century

The plastered walls in farmhouses and cottages were treated with whitewash—the simplest form of paint, made of burnt lime mixed with size and water. Whitewash and distemper are essentially the same, and although they are not long lasting they can easily

A stencil decoration revived in the Arts and Crafts period by M. H. Baillie Scott at Blackwell, Windermere, in 1900. Its flatly coloured plant form follows the tradition of William Morris.

be renewed. Modern emulsion paint which has replaced them is washable, but does not have the pleasing powdery texture of distemper. A few houses preserve fragments of painted decoration, often in the form of stencilled patterns imitating the fabrics which were hung in the great houses. A popular pattern was the pineapple, which can easily be reconstructed. Some houses retain traces of crudely painted murals done in imitation of tapestry subjects, simply painted in black and red tempera (pigment bound in egg yolk). Boarded partitions and beams were often painted with flowing paint designs, interwoven with mottoes and texts, and a sophisticated tradition of decorative painting of this kind survived in Scotland through the seventeenth century.

The exteriors of plaster-covered, timber-framed houses, and of the harled and rough-cast houses of the north and west, were also whitewashed regularly, and variations of colour were achieved by using natural earth pigments like ochre and burned earth. The famous Suffolk pink should thus have a brownish tint which is seldom achieved in modern exterior paints.

The wooden window shutters of cottages hardly ever survive, and the wooden sashes and casements or iron-framed casements with lead cames should be treated according to the prevailing style of the period in which they were introduced.

The Eighteenth Century

The later years of the seventeenth century saw a large number of modest houses in which there was a surprisingly large expenditure on panelling and decoration. Rich and heavy effects were preferred, and elaborate marbling and graining was carried out by professional painter-decorators, who also specialised in glazed effects on walls, achieved by applying thin washes of transparent colour over a white ground. The Palladian period introduced a preference for uniform, flatly painted surfaces, which coincided with

Grecian taste in the Jane Austen period: 'A Saloon' from Ackermann's Repository 1816. Marbled dado, pale blue walls, pink ceiling and panels with gilt ornaments. Elegant crimson draperies.

the manufacture of ready-mixed paint. It was now possible for ordinary house servants to undertake painting to a satisfactory standard, causing much resentment among professionals. A further important change was the introduction of deal (pine and fir) in place of native hard wood for interior and exterior woodwork. Externally, deal has to be painted to preserve it from damp, and it seems that pure white lead paint was favoured as it gave the maximum protection, as well as a conspicuous smartness. A variation, recorded from the 1730s onwards, was to throw sand on the wet paint (sometimes twice over) to give added protection against weather, and to simulate stone.

The two main colours for interiors were stone colour and pea green. Neither of these was a uniform colour, but they would be modified by the types of pigment used. Stone colour was made with lead white and sienna or umber, while pea colour was mostly made with Prussian blue and a natural yellow pigment. They were ground in nut-oil, and applied to walls and woodwork in several coats. Other colours available in the 1730s included (in ascending order of expense) olive, sky blue, orange, lemon, straw, pink, blossom and 'Fine deep green' made from verdigris (green copper oxide). It is possible to scrape down layers of paint in an attempt to find traces of original colour, or otherwise to have a cross-section of paint analysed, although between undercoats and later layers, it is easy to miss the vital clue. Only a perfectionist would wish to mix his own colours today, and it should be possible to create reasonably authentic effects with manufacturers' colours provided these are carefully chosen and modified where necessary. Colours like Prussian blue and the earths are available in the form of artist's oil paint, and could be used to colour a white base. Eggshell comes closer in effect to eighteenth-century oil paint than full gloss. Within the limited range that was available, the eighteenth century treated room colours as a matter of taste much as we do today, and there are no strict rules for the colours of different rooms.

One rule which does exist, however, is that deal woodwork should never be left in its 'stripped' state, as this was never intended. The poor quality of the wood must make this obvious. Window frames and mould-

Bolder and heavier colours appear in the 'Etruscan' room from Smith's Cabinet Maker and Upholsterer's Guide *1826. This elaborate scheme includes marbling, graining and mural painting, suitable for the dining room of a stuccoed villa.*

Yellow sienna marble and light oak graining reconstructed at Keats's house, Hampstead, London. Sham materials suited the sensibility of the Romantic period, and these effects can be produced with practice by home decorators today.

ings would probably be white, and doors were frequently black or dark brown. Graining returned to favour in the later eighteenth century, together with marbling, and these remained through all the fluctuations in taste until the twentieth century, when they have mainly been practised in public houses. Graining is easy to learn, and enjoyable to do. It is also very practical and hard-wearing. Marbling is slightly more difficult, but simple effects can be achieved with very little practice. Real wood and real marble were not intended to be mimicked exactly; the main intention was rather to create a pleasing decorative effect. These processes are now undergoing such a revival that it may be necessary to add a note of caution against carrying effects further than may be suitable for the period of the house.

The later years of the eighteenth century, and the Regency period, saw an increasing richness in effects of colour and furnishings, combined with a search for simplicity of outline. New discoveries were made in colours, and fashions changed faster than before. The beautiful colours of the Adam brothers, so much misunderstood by decorators of the past, were intended to evoke the richness and contrasts both of nature and of ancient Rome, while the Etruscan rooms of the time were based on the deep reds of Greek vases set off against a pale green or blue background. The delicate mouldings of the period were intended to appear against a darker background, but these colours should be soft and rather thin. The effect of shallow mouldings was accentuated by the shadows cast from candles, and is often lost with modern lighting.

The Wedgwood Room at Broadlands, Hampshire was created in 1769. The delicate neo-Classical style uses colour to create mood and contrast, not always in these pastel shades. Painted furniture often complemented the architectural arrangements.

The effect of colour in a Regency town house may be studied in the Soane Museum in Lincoln's Inn Fields, London, where the dramatic contrasts of the age of Sensibility and Taste may be observed in all aspects of the architecture and furnishings. The Soane Museum contains examples of graining and marbling. Ceilings with simple clouds against a blue sky can be seen at the Brighton Pavilion, which could be modified and appropriately introduced into smaller houses.

The discoveries at Pompeii and Herculaneum which had excited connoisseurs in the 1780s were affecting the decoration of ordinary houses by the time of the battle of Waterloo in 1815. The colouring of

ordinary houses may be seen in works like Pierce Egan's *Life in London* (1821), and in Ackermann's *Repository* (1816). In a house of the period, the stair hall should be marbled and grained, and other rooms treated with contrasting colours in walls and furnishings.

The exteriors of houses after the 1780s were increasingly covered with stucco (alias Roman cement or plaster rendering). This was meant to imitate stone, and the Nash terraces in Regent's Park were originally painted in 'fresco', which for this purpose meant an uneven brown applied with the intention of imitating Bath stone, complete with scored and painted joints. The ironwork was painted in imitation of bronze, and the windows and doors grained. Thus the houses were meant to blend with their natural surroundings, unlike their crisply pointed and painted mid-Georgian predecessors. The now universal cream paint of stucco is a later invention, in response to the Victorian hatred of shams. White window frames did not return to favour until the Queen Anne movement of the 1870s, when they contrasted with red brick. Stucco and stock brick houses after 1800 should have brown, grey or even black exterior woodwork.

The Victorian Period

In most aspects of furnishing, the early Victorian period was a richer and heavier version of what had gone before. This is equally true of colour, where chocolate brown paintwork, maroon and deep blue were favoured, although they were not unrelieved by lighter touches. The published restorations of ancient Greek temples showing their original bright colouring had a widespread influence from the 1830s, as can be seen, for example, in Charles Barry's Reform Club in Pall Mall, London. At the same time there was a lighter, more feminine side to early Victorian furnishing, mainly expressed in wallpapers and fabrics. The newly discovered aniline dyes, which gave a range of yellows, purples and viridians to the Victorian palette, seem also to have been used more in furnishing and dress fabrics than in paint, although a fashion for graining drawing rooms gave painter-decorators some scope.

The Great Exhibition of 1851 provides a useful point of reference, and it is interesting to note that the Crystal Palace was painted inside with pure red, blue and yellow according to an optical mixture devised by Turner and carried out by Owen Jones, to give an effect of sparkling light over its great length. The use of small lines and patterns of bright colour against a uniform background is characteristic of early and mid-Victorian decoration, and a whole range of combinations of colour and form can be studied in Owen Jones's *Grammar of Ornament* (1856).

In the aftermath of the Great Exhibition came the attempt to 'reform' Victorian taste, by a return to the Middle Ages and to supposed 'natural' and 'rational' sources of ornament and decoration. This was cross-fertilised with the discovery of Japan in the 1860s to produce the Aesthetic movement of the 1870s, as satirised by George du Maurier and W. S. Gilbert. In colour and decoration, the effect was a general lightening, although much respectable gloom remained. The prevailing principle was to choose neutral tertiary colours as a background for small patches and ornaments in brighter primary colours.

In the arrangement of walls, the tripartite division of walls with dado and frieze was an Aesthetic principle (apparently introduced by Lady Fitzhardinge in 1875) which became universal within ten years. Green was considered an Aesthetic colour, possibly in response to William Morris's aversion to the use of pure colour; but he cautioned: 'on the other hand do not fall into the trap of a dingy bilious yellow green, a colour for which I have a special hatred because I have been supposed to have somewhat brought it into vogue.' A book of 1876 recommends a drawing room of 'warm apple-green' and a contrasting dining room of reddish grey or Pompeian red. In spite of the hatred of sham effects expressed by Ruskin and Morris, graining and marbling continued in popularity in all but the most artistic houses. In fact, outside the specialist confines of the artists' colonies of Chelsea, Bedford Park and Hampstead, the Aesthetic movement was a licence to an eclecticism even greater than that of the early Victorians. Most of the decorative effect was achieved through wallpapers and fabrics, but there was a steady growth in stencilling patterns, which was considered a suitable occupation for the amateur artist. Patterns were based on medieval tiles, Japanese birds and flowers, and the Moorish work of Spain. They would have mainly been used for dados. A lady writer in *Queen* magazine runs through the colour scheme of an Aesthetic 'house beautiful' of *c.* 1876 thus:

Hall and Staircase: sober yellowish drab and high red dado with two lines of white.
Dining Room: walls dark drab, with high dado of mauve and drab in alternate colours (curtains dark bluish green, bands of pale yellow and black velvet, embroidered peacock feathers).
Boudoir: pale blue, sage green, woodwork ebonised oak, wallpapers, ceiling lemon yellow, with apple leaves and nesting birds.
Drawing Room: deep maroon velvet, dark green walls, ceiling decorated with leaves and pomegranates. Woodwork black.

Some parts of this description inescapably recall W. S. Gilbert's 'cobwebby grey velvet with a tender bloom like cold gravy', but mixed in with the Aesthetic movement was a renewed interest in the Adam and Empire styles, even if these were very freely treated at first. This influence helped to keep some brighter and sharper colours in rooms, while Morris himself used very light colours in many of his patterns which could be used as a basis for painted decoration (although it would be hard to match the beautiful natural dyes of original Morris chintzes). The use of black woodwork was a Japanese influence, promoted by D. G. Rossetti in the work of Morris and Co., and in the furniture of E. W. Godwin. In his *Hints on Household Taste* (1868), Charles Eastlake recommends the use of flatted colour (that is, matt oil paint) for deal, and, in particular, Indian red and bluish green; the latter being perhaps the colour which *Punch* referred to in 1879 as 'no tint which common blue and yellow mingled make, but greeny wrought of sepia without stint, with indigo and lake'.

Late Victorian and Edwardian

After an initial period of mockery, 'Art Furnishing' spread down to the lower middle classes, and provided the basis for interiors until the First World War. In the sphere of decorative painting, the stencilled frieze wa the major innovation of the 1890s, and many pattern were held by trade decorators which are mostly distant echo of the continental *Art Nouveau*. C. R Mackintosh and M. H. Baillie Scott also mad effective use of stencilling on walls and furniture, an their work provides better, if less typical, examples t follow than the trade decorator's frieze. In the work c Voysey a strict simplicity of colour was achieved wit white and green. The outside details of Voysey house were painted with Brunswick green, which weather to a beautiful indigo.

Away from the refinement of these architects, th Edwardian house was often the scene of experiment with newly formulated high-gloss enamel paint which were used for walls and woodwork. The mai areas were treated with 'pastel shades' but ornament and details were picked out in the brightest colours, speciality being black woodwork with lines of alumin

Lutyens loved strong colours for his highly architectural interiors. The Arts Council Lutyens Exhibition 1981–2 reconstructed the effect of his geometrical black and white floors and Gibbs-surround doorways standing out against a field of brilliant red. He also favoured black as a decorating colour. Paint manufacturers in the Edwardian period perfected gloss surfaces and primary colours. The prevailing key of colour was high compared to late Victorian richness and mysterious gloom.

Left: An Aesthetic interior of the 1870s at 16 Stafford Terrace, London W8, the home of Punch *artist Linley Sambourne, constructed in an ordinary Kensington Italianate house. The dado is modestly low, but a frieze has been introduced to allow the use of two Morris wallpapers, including the early* Pomegranate design. *Note the painting on the door and the prevailing sage-green colour. Darkness and complexity (enhanced by convex mirrors) made such late-Victorian homes worlds of private fantasy in which every surface was lovingly decorated. This house, now open to the public, is the best surviving example of a complete house of its time.*

ium silver paint. It may be recalled that Mr. Pooter in *The Diary of a Nobody* (1892) worked wonders with 'new Pinkford's enamel' until his unfortunate experience with the red bath.

Among architects and artists who were not followers of the Arts and Crafts movement, there was a preference for strong uniform colours. Lutyens favoured black ceilings, red walls and green floors, colours which also dominate the paintings of his friend William Nicholson. In Liverpool in 1905, C. H. Reilly had a dining room ceiling of pillar box red, a varnished black cornice, and walls covered with brown wrapping paper. Later, in Mortlake, his friend S. D. Adshead had royal blue walls with a gold fret, and red upholstery. These colour schemes were influential in the 1920s on architects like Clough

Williams-Ellis and Philip Tilden, who also picked up the bright colours of Claud Lovat Fraser's sets for the *Beggars' Opera* of 1921.

The 1920s and 1930s

With the exception of the few architect-decorators mentioned above, the 1920s were concerned with a search for 'good taste' in furnishing, in which nothing was over-assertive. Cream, buff, white and yellow were favourite colours, and effects of paint were generally flat and slightly glossy. Decorators like Basil Ionides were more concerned with the repainting of old houses than with new ones, but their preference for strong overall colours may have filtered down into popular taste. It was a period of some confusion in decoration, as shown in a verse by H. S. Goodhart-Rendel of about 1924, in which an experienced decorator addresses a novice:

For the fashionable status of the folk for whom one
   caters
You must study or their custom one may lose,
For Mayfair will seldom vary far from William and
   Mary
While in Chelsea later Regency they choose.
Louis Seize may prove the saviour of poor out of date
   Belgravia,
William Morris still survives on Campden Hill;
Dear old Pont Street clings to Tudor,
Rutland Gate is even cruder,
And the suburbs are Elizabethan still.

From the mid-1920s a number of architects and decorators succeeded in bringing more colour into English rooms. Reflecting surfaces of glass or silver paper were popular, and various forms of metallic painting, stippling and mottling were carried out by professional decorators in houses built by building societies for speculation. Pastel colours were dominant, and could either be used as complementaries, as in the mauve and lemon yellow drawing room in Edward Maufe's Yaffle Hill, or in graded schemes of cream and brown. The famous white interiors of Syrie Maugham were a matter of furnishings as much as paint. A more typical decorator's scheme might be the early 1930s interior by Betty Joel: real silver walls, matt grey paintwork, dark blue curtains lined with yellow, grey beige carpet, coral and white rug, white silk upholstery.

Colours like these were used by early 'modern' architects such as Chermayeff and Raymond McGrath, and it was not until the very end of the '30s that le Corbusier's primaries were adopted, although they later gained in popularity and formed one of the bases of '50s colour schemes. A unifying link between traditional and modern design in the '30s was the taste for natural wood surfaces, even if these were only veneered plywood. This taste unfortunately led to the stripping of paint from earlier woodwork, a menace which is not yet over.

Houses of the 1930s are only just becoming 'historical', but it would be an extremely interesting exercise to restore the original colour schemes, wallpaper, and all other fittings, even in a relatively humble suburban 'semi'.

Bibliography

Bristow, Ian 'Ready Mixed Paint in the Eighteenth Century' in *The Architectural Review* CLXI (April 1977)

Cornforth, John *English Interiors 1790–1848, The Quest for Comfort* (1978)

Cornforth, John and Fowler, John *English Decoration in the Eighteenth Century* (1974)

Cowtan Cowtan, Mawer *Reminiscences and Changes in Taste in House Decoration* (1914) (Victoria & Albert Museum Library, London)

The Decorator's Assistant (1847)

Emerton, Joseph *Directions for Painting* (c 1744) (British Museum, Heal Collection)

Innes, Jocasta *Paint Magic* Useful practical information on different techniques and lists of suppliers (1981)

Ionides, Basil *Colour and Interior Decoration* (1926)

The Paper Hanger, Painter, Grainer and Decorator's Assistant (1876)

Parsons, Thomas and Sons *A Few Suggestions for Ornamental Decoration in Painters' and Decorators' Work* (1909) (Victoria & Albert Museum Library, London)

Patmore, Derek *Colour in the Modern Home*

Salmon, William *Palladio Londiniensis* (1734)

Smith, John *The Art of Painting in Oil* (1687)

Vanherman, T. H. *Every Man his own House-Painter and Colourman* (1829)

Colour

Like lighting, colour is one of the most ephemeral aspects of interior design, and a subject on which many historical experts violently disagree. To establish precisely what colours were used at a given period is an extremely difficult matter, and one in which contemporary preferences can easily and subtly cloud our historical judgement. Whether you adopt the archaeological approach, and have scrapings of paint from layers of past decoration analysed, or whether you simply look at colour plates in books of the period to establish period colours, you will benefit from contacting any of the following suppliers to obtain a more varied selection of paints and materials than is normally stocked.

Older buildings or modest rural structures of almost any period up to 1945 will often have plastered walls and will have been decorated in limewash. It is important to continue this tradition in order to allow the plaster to 'breathe'. Appropriate lime can be obtained from:

H J Chard & Sons
Feeder Road
Bristol
BS2 0TJ
Tel: (0272) 777681

Chichester Cathedral Workshop
The Cathedral
Chichester
Sussex
Tel: (0234) 784225

Lime can also be bought or ordered in other areas at the depots of **Tilcon Ltd.** Inquiries should be directed to:

Tilcon Ltd
171 Boundary Road
London SW19
Tel: (01) 542 1191

Totternhoe Lime & Stone Co Ltd
Totternhoe
nr Dunstable
Bedfordshire
Tel: (0525) 220300

Colouring for limewash is obtained by the addition of pigments. The most common colours for limewash are the different shades of ochre. Suitable powder pigments can be bought at most theatrical suppliers such as:

Brodie and Middleton Ltd
68 Drury Lane
London WC2
Tel: (01) 836 3289

Where limewash is not appropriate, the best alternative is a water-based distemper, which is only manufactured in the UK now by Crown Paints. Some years ago this product (formerly made by Walpamur Ltd) seemed likely to disappear from the market. The SPAB (Society for the Preservation of Ancient Buildings) persuaded the manufacturers to maintain a restricted supply, which can now be obtained only by ordering through the SPAB. 'Walpamur' is obtainable only in five-litre tins and in three colours—white, broken white, and new cream, but it can be tinted with pigment or any commercial coloriser, and can be thinned with water. When ordering from SPAB, please enclose a s.a.e.

The following firms also supply useful products:

Coles of Mortimer Street
This firm has emulsion and oil colours not generally found on other lists.

Coles of Mortimer Street
18 Mortimer Street
London W1
Tel: (01) 580 1066

L Cornelisson & Sons
This firm has pure ground pigments suitable for use in distemper or for mixing with a white lead base.

L Cornelisson & Sons
22 Great Queen Street
London WC2
Tel: (01) 405 3304

Dulux
Dulux undercoat colours such as green, drab, yellow, etc. are useful.

ICI
Imperial Chemical House
Millbank
London SW1
Tel: (01) 834 4444

Manders
Manders manufacture the 'Matsine' range of undercoats and glazes made specifically for graining.

Manders
113 Eastbourne Mews
London W2
Tel: (01) 402) 6625

John Oliver
Specialist wallpaper and paint manufacturer, John Oliver reproduces from original scraps period wallpapers and paints. They can mix any colour to match traditional furnishings.

John Oliver
33 Pembridge Road
London W11
Tel: (01) 221 6466

The following two companies' oil colours may be used for marbling and glazing, etc.

George Rowney & Co Ltd
12 Percy Street
London W1
Tel: (01) 636 8241

Winsor & Newton
24 Rathbone Place
London W1
Tel (01) 636 4231

Furniture Arrangements

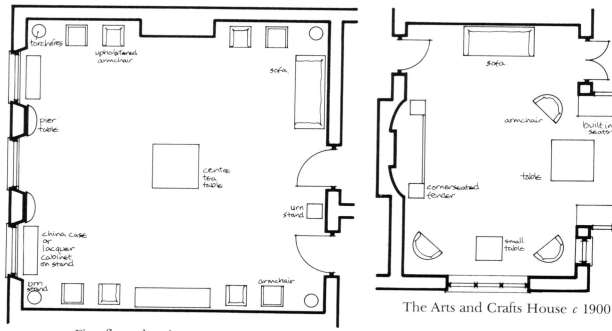

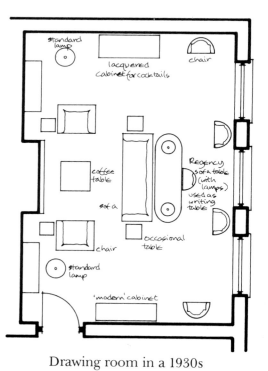

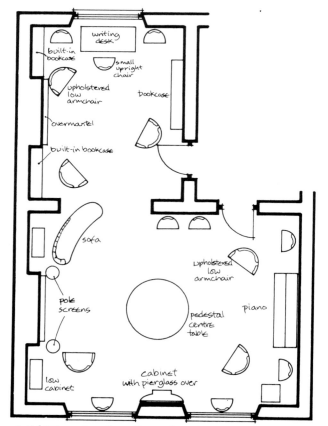

First-floor drawing room *c* 1765

The Arts and Crafts House *c* 1900

Mid-Victorian first-floor drawing room *c* 1865

**Drawing room in a 1930s
mansion flat**

Furniture

The furnishing of any house, whatever its period, must begin with a full assessment of its architectural features. The more obvious of these features, such as doorcases, chimney pieces, the size and height of rooms, the placing of windows and so on, are fairly easily taken in. Equally important but more elusive are details such as cornices, any decorative plasterwork, the intricacy or simplicity of panel mouldings and architraves, the inclusion of carved work, all of which give an idea of the quality of the building, and point to the quality of furniture which it deserves. Of great importance too at this stage is to make a note of all disposable wall space, to be defended at all costs against the intrusion of radiators and other trappings of real life in the twentieth century, which can be placed under windows, or built into the walls behind grilles in less important nooks and crannies.

The problem that now arises is to what extent the choice of furniture for eighteenth and early nineteenth-century houses should be dictated by twentieth-century standards of comfort. Is an attempt at stylistic unity and aesthetic satisfaction worth a degree of moderate discomfort?

Our Georgian forebears took for granted a sense of deportment governed by an easy-going formality. They either stood, sat upright or lay down. The overstuffed comforts of the Victorian drawing room would have shocked the eighteenth-century sensibility; and even more so would the lounging and 'leisure' postures dictated by that very staple of twentieth-century furnishing, the 'three piece suite'. There is probably some compromise required in the solution to this question of comfort.

At least in the Arts and Crafts house it never occurs, since the considerations there must always be aesthetic. A different question might occupy the mind of the owner of a 1930s flat; that of stylistic consistency. Having established the seat furniture with its well-upholstered backs in the form of sunbursts, together with a pair of dwarf cabinets laminated with peach mirror glass, would it then be improper to introduce an alien piece of furniture from a more formal age? My own feeling is that an early piece with sufficiently barbaric qualities would hold its own and be a success. Perhaps a red japanned cabinet-on-stand or a Victorian *papier-mâché* chair flashing with mother-of-pearl would work well, or a gilt-wood feature piece from the Rococo period, such as a mirror or console table.

Stylistic purity is likely to be rather sterile and museum-like, over-aweing one's guests and making them spill their drinks. A house must be a home, must be welcoming and in no sense intimidating, and although the basic furniture of a room should complement its architecture, the accessories, textiles, light fittings, smaller decorative objects, the colour and texture of the walls, will all contribute to create 'atmosphere', in which deliberately placed objects from other periods will give a feeling of continuity and life.

Logically, when starting out to furnish a room, a plan should be made of the wall space available for the larger and dominant pieces which should be chosen and placed first. These will normally not be easily movable and their arrangement should accord with the architecture to achieve balance and a feeling of repose. They will in due course become centrepieces to symmetrical arrangements of chairs, pictures, and light brackets for the more formal setting in an eighteenth or nineteenth-century house, or more dramatically placed in an asymmetrical way in the twentieth-century flat, where the emphasis on horizontal lines and a feeling for spaciousness punctuated with unexpected pieces is desirable. These larger static objects will include chests-of-drawers, clothes-presses, and beds. In the dining room the table itself, together with serving tables or a sideboard, needs to be placed for convenience in relation to the kitchen door as well as for effect. In a drawing room, large cabinets, sofas, centre tables or free-standing desks, and perhaps a piano or harpsichord, will dictate the placing of smaller cabinet furniture and more movable objects.

The rather upright upholstered armchairs of the Georgians, the lower-seated Victorian 'easy' chairs, the lithe and elegant elbow chairs of the Regency period, the many types of small occasional tables for writing, reading or needlework, the folding side tables to be unfolded for tea or cards, the small bookcases for current reading matter; all these help to furnish the 'living room' (a term coined in the early nineteenth century).

In an eighteenth century day room, chairs were placed in a formal way with their backs to the wall, to be brought into use as the need arose. This ordered and rather austere arrangement is also suitable for the Arts and Crafts interior. In the Victorian drawing room, however, the more formal placing of seating furniture gave way to the creation of carefully

organised conversation groups, seemingly little related to either fireplace or windows. In the 1930s interior, to place certain pieces diagonally, though not informally, became smart, with an international feel.

If this all sounds fairly cut and dried let us remember one period when in the living area small movable pieces such as chairs, work tables, footstools, and dispersed nests of tables seem to have been deliberately scattered to create graceful disorder. This period was the Regency, into which a precious insight is given by the painstaking watercolours done by accomplished young ladies and maiden aunts which record so faithfully the domestic arrangements. By comparison the high Victorian interior is more formal but with much more clutter.

The Georgian Terraced House

Under the first two Georges, Baroque styles prevailed in furniture as much as in architecture. The salient feature is the cabriole leg, at first slender and organic with simple pad foot, later a more pronounced curve enriched with carved detail. This revival of carved work is largely due to the introduction of mahogany from the mid-1720s, when supplies of seasoned walnut had run out owing to the severe winter of 1709. The fine grain of mahogany was admirable for richly carved cornices and pediments applied to the 'architectural' cabinet pieces that appeared in response to the Palladian revival. The hairy paw feet, rigid scrolls, acanthus leaves, and fish-scale surfaces of this offshoot of the Baroque style found their place in mahogany furniture, but more specially in the gilt gesso pieces of carved beech or limewood. These mainly decorative 'feature' pieces such as overmantels, pier-glass frames, console tables and *torchères* became yet more spectacular during the last fling of Baroque, the Rococo period of the 1750s. The English version of this style took the rocks, curls, shell borders and broken scrolls of French *rocaille*, interspersing them with Chinese frets, Gothic arches and pinnacles, and rustic branches. Thomas Chippendale's famous *Director* (1754), and Ince and Mayhew's *Household Furniture* (1762), both now available in reprint, give a good idea of the range and complexity of this furniture.

An early eighteenth-century wing chair upholstered in tapestry work, with walnut cabriole legs retaining the square section of the reign of William and Mary.

Left: A satinwood Pembroke table on fluted legs with neo-Classical marquetry details to the freize and serpentine top.

Above: A simple, early nineteenth-century painted chair with cane seat and simulated bamboo front legs.

Contemporary paintings of interiors, for example by Devis, show bare boarded floors, very little furniture, and pictures hung in a formal plan. An attempt to recreate this exclusive sparseness, particularly in panelled rooms, can be wonderful, but should resist the 'after the bailiffs' look. In this context the possibilities of wall furniture, such as mirrors, sconces, china shelves, the would-be or actual ancestral portrait, a barometer or long-case clock, need to be fully explored.

The beginning of George III's reign in 1760 roughly coincided with the neo-Classical style introduced by Robert Adam, which was to be the basis of furniture design until the 1830s. The revival of marquetry at the expense of carved work, together with the introduction of satinwood as a more fashionable alternative to mahogany, plus superlative craftsmanship, gave late eighteenth-century furniture its very special elegance, and an austerity which some of us prefer not to have to live up to. Several new categories of furniture appeared at this time as can be

seen in the illustrations to Hepplewhite's *Guide* (1788) or in the more innovatory *Drawing Book* (1791) by Thomas Sheraton. These new pieces included the dining-room table, usually made up of two D-shaped ends with gate-leg section and spare leaves in between. Until the 1770s, eating rooms had one or more gate-leg tables each seating perhaps eight people. In great houses, these tables were usually removed to the corridor after meals, whilst the chairs were replaced against the wall. The fixed table, with some of the chairs drawn up, superseded this, and called for longer rather than square dining rooms.

Another innovation was the sideboard, which evolved from Adam's designs for side tables with flanking pedestals for plate warming or water cisterns. These three sections merged into one piece of furniture. Pembroke tables, sofa tables and nests called 'quartetto tables' also emerged at this period, as did roll-top desks.

The Regency period (dated for convenience as 1800–1830) replaced satinwood with rosewood as the

*Left: A Regency rosewood sofa
c 1810, with scrolling back rail, lotus-
headed armrests and small details of inlaid
brass on sabre legs.*

*Below left: A double chest of drawers,
with fluted pillar details, a cresting of
urns, and rosette ring handles. From
Hepplewhite's Guide of 1788.*

alternative to mahogany for solid work in joinery, as well as for veneers on cabinets. A number of other woods were also in use for fashionable furniture, notably ebony, amboyna, and the dramatically striped zebra wood. Carved details were used again at this time, as also were cast-metal mounts and panel mouldings of brass or more rarely ormolu. Furniture of this type is very expensive to buy now, but a sophisticated alternative and generally a cheaper one can be found in painted pieces. Cabinets of this type are usually of pine, and chairs are of beech. These woods were sometimes grained to imitate the more expensive ones, or they could be ebonised or japanned in various colours with gilt details added. Very stylish painted country furniture was made in great quantity, and looks very good in a town setting.

From about 1815, panels of marquetry in brass and wood appeared in high-quality pieces. The back rails of chairs and panels of cabinets were decorated in this way using the techniques employed by Louis XIV's great *ebeniste* A. C. Boulle, whose style was to be more consciously imitated in the Victorian period and known then as 'buhlwork'.

The elegance of Regency furniture is unpretentious and easy to live with. The random use of so many surface textures anticipates the eclecticism of the Victorians, but with a lightness of touch and an understanding of throwaway values; the stylish Grecian sofa dressed down with an Indian shawl, the light glazed chintzes for curtains and upholstery, and the cross-stitch bell pulls.

The Victorian Villa

Apart from novelty in furniture-making techniques, the Victorian age stood for a revival of every style that had ever existed. Between 1800 and 1850 the population doubled, increasing the ranks of the shopkeeping and professional classes. The number of books on household management and etiquette published in the 1830s and 1840s suggests a thirst for hard and fast rules and a horror of being thought in

Right: A chair c 1850, with a painted papier mâché *panel in the back combined with spiral-twisted, so-called 'Elizabethan', verticals and Rococo front legs.*

Below: A typical early Victorian button-backed drawing room chair, retaining Regency features in the detail of the front legs and in the line of the back.

any way incorrect. A definition of the prevailing furniture styles appears in Loudon's *Encyclopaedia of Cottage, Farm and Villa Architecture and Furniture* (1835).

Loudon lists the following styles: Grecian, Gothic, Rococo and 'Elizabethan'. Grecian was a late form of neo-Classicism, but heavier in feeling. Gothic, derived from the eighteenth-century 'Gothick', was still at this period a confused and cosmetic mixture based on the three periods of medieval architecture. It would become more correct, but duller, when Gothic was

A satinwood drawing-room cabinet c 1870, with glazed corners for display decorated with fine linear marquetry and a Wedgwood plaque.

Below left: A writing desk in the Japanese taste of the 1870s, with fine gilt incised lines on an ebonised surface framing a painted panel.

adopted as a national style in the 1850s.

Both these styles were considered suitable for gentlemen's quarters—the dining room, library, billiard and smoking rooms. The style considered proper for the ladies' domain of drawing room, boudoir and bedroom was the Rococo, at that time mis-called Louis XIV, based on curving lines, carved decoration and gilding. The shell-shaped backs of *papier-mâché* chairs fitted admirably into this setting. The fourth style, 'Elizabethan', mixed sixteenth-century strapwork and cabochon and table-cut jewel motifs with misapplied Restoration spiral turning. Considered a good style for suburban villas and for updated country houses with a romantic past, the prevailing wood used was light oak seen through a shiny French polish.

The Great Exhibition of 1851 brought further decorative possibilities. 'Naturalism' was not a style, but a copying of natural forms in high-relief carving of a meretricious sort, and applied to any available surface. In appearing to give value for money this detailing tried to distract the eye from inadequacies both in design and craftsmanship, but some pieces still have charm, particularly in the 'cuckoo-clock' or 'Swiss chalet' categories, often in the form of hanging shelves, smoker's companions, what-nots and wall brackets.

The antiseptic approach to furnishing a Victorian villa now would be to select well-made examples of good rosewood or mahogany, using the simpler Classically inspired pieces for dining room or study, and keeping the more florid and gilded mirrors, easy chairs and chiffoniers for the drawing room. With this basis a greater or lesser introduction of delightful pieces of purest tat may be effected, according to taste.

The Arts and Crafts House

Arts and Crafts furniture was founded on two basic influences. The first of these was a vision of thirteenth-century Gothic as expressed in the work of the architect William Burges, and also in the early furniture by Philip Webb for William Morris's firm.

First shown at the 1862 World Exhibition in London, the massive exposed joinery of this furniture combined with an extreme simplicity of form which was often concealed by elaborate painted decoration. The second influence appeared at the same exhibition, and was found in the influx of Japanese wares after trade with the West had been resumed in 1860. The fine proportions, lightness of feeling and decorative surface treatments of Japanese furniture became the basis of the 'Aesthetic movement' of the 1860 and '70s, an important exponent of which was the designer E. W. Godwin who collaborated with the American painter Whistler over the decoration of Oscar Wilde's Tite Street house in 1884. Following in the same influence was 'Art furniture', a good quality department-store line of painted panels on gilt backgrounds

Below: An oak armchair designed by Sir Ambrose Heal, 1928.

A mahogany sideboard c 1900, decorated with Art Nouveau *marquetry details and with beaten copper hinges and mounts on the asymmetrically arranged doors.*

Left: An oak settee by Liberty and Co. c 1905, in Arts and Crafts style. Above: A dramatically composed 1930s cocktail cabinet with satin-birch body suspended between two diminishing pedestals of ebonised reeding.

in an ebonised framework, with many small shelves for the display of blue-and-white Japanese porcelain.

But the Arts and Crafts movement proper grew up from the forming of the various guilds of craftsmen, the first of which was the Century Guild, founded by Mackmurdo in 1882. One of the ideals of William Morris taken up by the guilds was to break down the barriers that existed between artists and artisans, often involving the joint efforts of both within one piece of furniture.

Important guildsmen included Voysey, Lethaby, Ashbee (who founded the Guild of Handicraft in 1888), and Baillie Scott, who worked mostly for Continental patrons. A group of Cotswold craftsmen was led by Gimson, whose successors the Barnsley family still practise in Petersfield, Hampshire. In the early twentieth century the firm of Heal & Son produced Arts and Crafts furniture for a larger market, much as Liberty's had been dealing in *Art Nouveau* pieces since the 1890s.

Other twentieth-century designers who produced some furniture in an Arts and Crafts mould include C. R. Mackintosh, the painter Frank Brangwyn, and Roger Fry who founded the Omega Workshops in 1913.

Cabinet furniture is generally found to be made of indigenous woods such as oak, ash, elm, yew, beech, and the fruit woods, notably pear and cherry. Inlaid decoration sometimes uses ebony or satinwood. Joinery is simple and visible, doors are panelled but sometimes solid with relief carving. A very important feature is metalwork in the form of hinges and mounts of wrought iron or hammered copper, and occasionally as inset plaques. Chairs follow closely in the country tradition of turned joinery with ladder backs and rush seats, but the rather uncomfortably high backed settles often have upholstered seats in the form of loose squab cushions.

The 1930s Flat

A town flat of this period may be furnished very successfully with eighteenth or nineteenth-century objects, but if it is to be 'in keeping', contemporary objects must be sought. The ambience to be established should be one of simplicity and comfort, but with an essential touch of 'luxe'. To achieve this the regular brand of suburban *Art Deco* junk furniture will really not do. Furniture of the 1930s does not age gracefully and needs to be kept in pristine condition. In this connection, the choice of upholstery materials needs careful thought.

If money is not available to buy furniture by named designers or otherwise documented pieces, alternative examples of high quality can be found still. A full exploration should be made of surface textures, from

An Art Deco *corner settee with a small built-in cabinet.*

Below : A painted dining-room chair after a late eighteenth-century model, but with dynamic Art Deco *detail in the back.*

The all-white Syrie Maugham look or the frillier approach of Sybil Colefax, whilst not very practical in real-life terms, are relatively easy to achieve, relying as they do on luxurious upholstery on the simplest and most understated 'Classic' seating, and a variety of textiles in light, toning neutral colours. Introduce into this a flash of chromium, a little distressed gilt, the odd red lacquer screen, and the effect is complete. But cut flowers renewed daily are essential.

The cooler alternative to this would be in the design products of the Bauhaus school, founded by Gropius at Weimar in 1919 and closed down by Hitler in 1933. Copies of seat furniture in leather and hand-finished stainless steel designed by Breuer, and others in laminated wood, are available at a price, but it should be borne in mind that these pieces look their best only in the most austere of settings. The other thing is that they command austerity and make decorative objects look frivolous. In this sense, modern tubular steel with cane seats, leather cushions or plate-glass tops (but only 'in the manner of' Bauhaus originals) is much easier to handle, and strikes an appropriate '30s note.

As important in the '30s setting as in that of any other period discussed here are the small movable and useful objects that add to an interior, from ash-trays to tea-cups. These things, whether decorative objects whose date may be unimportant, or complete services of tableware strictly 'in period' should always be of the right quality, because the overall effect of a room is backed up by its details—and they should never be a disappointment.

cast glass in the manner of Lalique, facetted mirror treatments, fake lacquer, gilding in gold or silver leaf, painted surfaces, leather, parchment, sharkskin, hide, or even leopardskin.

Furniture

Anybody can make mistakes when it comes to buying antique furniture. Even the most experienced dealer will admit he paid too much for something, or that he failed to notice a renewed seat rail on an 18th century chair. For the inexperienced enthusiast, buying antique furniture can be a nerve-racking experience.

One of the most important decisions to make is whether a piece is 'right' of its period or a later reproduction. Throughout the 19th century, innumerable sets of dining-room chairs were made in 18th century styles. By now they have a good patina and are often of fine quality, but they should be appreciably cheaper than the real thing. The carving on such reproductions is usually coarser and more laboured, whereas genuine 18th century work is more lively and has more finesse. Marquetry decoration, too, should be examined closely. Earlier work may be fine or more coarse, but it does not have the perfection of late Victorian or Edwardian reproductions. Polish and surface texture are another hazard, and should have some bearing on the asking price for a piece. A damaged object may have been sensitively repolished wholly or in part, but if it is now covered with a treacly 'refinishing' of French polish it is probably ruined for ever and is best avoided.

The points to watch are legion, but one of the more obvious is the 'marriage': when the *secretaire* below does not tally in proportion or patina with the bookcase above, for example, or when the top of that small pedestal table is of mahogany while the base is certainly of rosewood. Other unfortunate, but not necessarily deliberate, modifications occur, such as later upholstery destroying the lines of a sofa, or the addition of castors to the front legs of dining-room chairs. Both of these modifications can be reversed, but this will involve extra expense. Wooden knobs on chests can be a problem too. They were in use in the very early 19th century, earlier than most people realise, and give a calculatedly underdressed and unpretentious look which was an aspect of Regency taste.

Sometimes they have been wrongly added to update Chippendale period bureaux, and sometimes they are removed from Victorian pieces and replaced by more chic-looking brass ones—in which case the holes probably remain underneath.

When buying at an auction it must be remembered that the catalogue entry is not necessarily a reliable description of the object either in date or condition, and auctioneers print a disclaimer to this effect. Liability will be accepted, though, when the auction house has been asked to certify formally in writing to the seller that the object is genuine, and this has been found by the buyer not to be the case. The larger London auction houses now charge a buyer's premium of 10 per cent, and this in turn incurs VAT. Where to buy can be important: a piece which is the centre of attraction at a country auction might look very modest in a London saleroom, and its selling price there might be less.

It is always wise to form an opinion of potential resale value, but if you have found an object you really like, and it will fit perfectly in the setting you have in mind, price may not be a first consideration. Serious dealers will give their description of the article on their receipt and will normally take it back if you find fault with it. When entering into cash deals without receipt you need to be more wary.

Whilst a fully comprehensive list of antique dealers is to be found in the *British Art and Antiques Yearbook*, the following list has been compiled of those companies who stock fine quality furniture and smaller period items in the middle and upper price ranges. Some of these companies' stock is beyond the means of most private individuals, but they are worth visiting merely to have the opportunity to see some of the finest pieces available. In any case you may be surprised and find that many of these seemingly imposing companies have items that you can afford.

Apter-Fredericks
Established in the Fulham Road since 1946, Apter-Fredericks specialise in fine 18th century English furniture. They have a large stock on two floors.

Apter-Fredericks Ltd
265/267 Fulham Road
London SW3 6HY
Tel: (01) 352 2188

Austins of Peckham
Established *c.* 1865, Austins have an enormous stock of every kind of furniture, ranging from fine and expensive 18th century items to simple secondhand

A pair of Adam satinwood chairs, c 1780 from Apter Fredericks who, operating from their London showroom, specialise in quality pieces of this period.

modern wooden furniture. They also have bric-à-brac and silver.

Austin and Sons Ltd
1–23 Peckham Rye
London SE15
Tel: (01) 639 3163
and
39–41 Brayards Road
London SE15
Tel: (01) 639 0480

Joanna Booth
Established in the King's Road for 17 years, Joanna Booth specialises in fine wood sculpture, 17th and 18th century wood carvings, oak and walnut furniture, needlework and tapestries, period textile cushions, Edwardian fringes, braids, bell pulls and tassles.

Just one example from J. Booth's stock.

Joanna Booth
247 King's Road
London SW3
Tel: (01) 352 8998

Bourne Fine Art
Bourne Fine Art (formerly Steigal Fine Art) opened their gallery in Dundas Street, Edinburgh in August 1981. The gallery specialises in paintings from 1750–1950, Scottish *Art Nouveau* furniture and British art pottery. Bourne Fine Art have sold works to the National Gallery of Scotland, Glasgow City Art Gallery, the British Museum, the Hunterian Museum and the City of Edinburgh Art Centre.

Bourne Fine Art Ltd
4 Dundas Street
Edinburgh EH3 6HZ
Tel: (031) 557 4050

High backed chair by William Birch, c 1910.

W and D Bull
This dealer in Coggeshall has been established since 1961, specialising in 18th century English and continental furniture, constantly maintaining a large and comprehensive stock.

W and D Bull Ltd
85 West Street
Coggeshall
Essex CO6 1TS
Tel: (0376) 61385

Jeremy Cooper
Established for four years, Jeremy Cooper Ltd specialise in fine and decorative arts 1830–1940, with mainly English, but some Continental items. These include Victorian architect-designed furniture by Pugin, Waterhouse, Collcutt, Talbert, Bevan, etc., Arts and Crafts furniture, handmade *Art Deco* furniture, and architectural drawings. The gallery also stocks interesting named architectural details such as fireplace surrounds.

One of a pair of oak carved sidetables designed by A W N Pugin for James Watt of Abney Hall, Cheshire. Made by J G Grace and Sons, 1849.

Jeremy Cooper Ltd
9 Galen Place
London WC1
Tel: (01) 242 5138

Couts
In an authentically restored 16th century building in the Grassmarket, Edinburgh, Paul Couts Ltd have six showrooms displaying probably the largest stock of 17th and 18th century and Regency furniture in Scotland. There is also a good stock of clocks, porcelain and glass.

Paul Couts Ltd
101–107 West Bow (Victoria Street)
Edinburgh
Tel: (031) 225 3238

Dolphin Antiques
Specialists in 19th century decorative and inlaid furniture, Dolphin Antiques have a medium to large stock, reasonably priced.

Dolphin Antiques
13 Holywell Hill
St Albans
Hertfordshire
Tel: (0727) 63080

Edition Graphiques
This gallery has *Art Nouveau* and *Art Deco* glass, ceramics, jewellery, bronzes, lamps, paintings, books and silver, and also original graphics *affiches* from 1880 to contemporaries.

Editions Graphiques Gallery
3 Clifford Street
London W1
Tel: (01) 734 3944

The Fine Art Society

The Fine Art Society was founded in 1876 at 148 New Bond Street with the aim of bringing the arts to as wide a public as possible. This aim was pursued by the publication of engravings after famous paintings such as Holman Hunt's *Light of the World* and an active exhibition programme. Today the Fine Art Society has galleries in London, Edinburgh and Glasgow. All three galleries carry a stock of furniture and decorative arts, though there is a greater concentration in London and Glasgow. The Edinburgh gallery is installed in a fine town house built about 1815 to Sir Robert Reid's design of 1804; the decor, furnishings and exhibition programme all enhance the building and give an insight into the elegance of Regency Edinburgh. In contrast to the domestic setting of Edinburgh, the Fine Art Society in Glasgow is housed in grand 19th century commercial premises at 134 Blythswood Street. The importance of Glasgow's contribution to the decorative arts of the late 19th century is strongly emphasised by the Fine Art Society.

In London in recent years The Fine Art Society has mounted a series of exhibitions exploring different aspects of the decorative arts, such as 'The Arts and Crafts Movement' (1973), 'Morris and Company' (1979), and 'Architect-Designers: Pugin to Mackintosh' (1981).

Roll-top desk designed by J P Seddon for the Gothic Court of the 1862 Exhibition.

The catalogues of these exhibitions remain authoritative reference works on the subject.

Photograph taken at the Fine Art Society's 1972 exhibition The Aesthetic Movement and the Cult of Japan. *The desk in the foreground, designed by Thomas Jeckyll, and the Godwin cabinet, were both in the Handley-Read Collection and are now in London's Victoria and Albert Museum, as is the six fold screen designed by W Eden Hesfield. The screen was made by James Forsyth, who gave it to Richard and Agnes Norman Shaw. The circular table was designed by Philip Webb and was formerly in the possession of Sir Edward Burne-Jones. Drawings by Rossetti and paintings by Tissot and Frederick Sandys adorn the walls.*

The Fine Art Society Ltd
148 New Bond Street
London W1Y 0JT
Tel: (01) 629 5116
and
12 Great King Street
Edinburgh
EH3 6QL
Tel: (031) 556 0305
and
134 Blythswood Street
Glasgow
G2 4EL
Tel: (041) 332 4027

Rupert Gentle

Established 25 years ago, Rupert Gentle Antiques specialise in 18th century furniture, needlework, treen, paintings and objects generally. 18th century brass is also stocked, including candlesticks, boxes, fire tools, skillets, bowls, pipe-tampers, snuffers, locks, alms dishes, coffee pots, ewers, trivets, chafing dishes, etc.

An interesting 18th century serpentine fronted mahogany chest from the stock of Rupert Gentle.

Rupert Gentle Antiques
The Manor House
Milton Lilbourne
nr Pewsey
Wiltshire
Tel: (067 26) 3344

Harvey Ferry and William Clegg

Established for ten years, this firm specialises in 17th and 18th century

English furniture, and also has a small stock of porcelain and treen.

Harvey Ferry and William Clegg
High Street
Nettlebed
Oxfordshire
Tel: (0491) 641533

Hotspur

This is a family firm established in 1924 specialising in very fine 18th century and Regency English furniture. Much of Hotspur's stock is both rare and unusual and consequently their customers tend to be either collectors or museums. Although the prices are prohibitive for most private individuals, it is worth visiting the shop simply to see examples of some of the finest 18th century furniture in London.

Mid 18th century Chippendale Director *armchair carved in the Rococo style, raised on cabriole legs, linked by carved and shaped aprons. Originally part of a set of six.*

Hotspur Ltd
14 Lowndes Street
Belgrave Square
London SW1X 9EX
Tel: (01) 235 1918

Jeremy

Established in 1946 by Geoffrey Hill, Jeremy Ltd specialise in very fine Continental and English 18th century furniture, and are regarded as one of the most important dealers in furniture of this period.

English, George III figured mahogany commode, in the French Louis XV style.

Jeremy Ltd
255 King's Road
Chelsea
London SW3
Tel: (01) 352 0644

John Jesse and Irina Laski

This gallery specialises in the decorative arts from the 1890s to the 1950s with a strong emphasis on *Art Deco* and *Art Nouveau*. They always have in stock furniture, paintings, bronzes, decorative panels, posters, carpets, porcelain, glass and jewellery. They tend to have pieces by well known designers of this period such as Emil Galle, Daum, and Lalique in glass, Joseph Hoffmann in furniture and silver, Lalique and Cartier in

jewellery, chrome furniture designed by Eileen Grey or Louis Sognot, and many other items by lesser known or unknown designers.

John Jesse and Irina Laski Ltd
160 Kensington Church Street
London W8
Tel: (01) 229 0312

Dan Klein

Dan Klein
Dan Klein specialise in objects and pictures 1830–1980. This includes architect-designed furniture from Burges to Lutyens, 1950s paintings, modern designer glass, needlework, tapestries, and carpets, particularly those by Morris and Co, and studio ceramics. The gallery tries to maintain stocks of equivalent items by Continental designers.

Dan Klein Ltd
11 Halkin Arcade
Motcomb Street
London SW1
Tel: (01) 245 9868

Malletts

One of the most famous names in antiques, Mallett and Sons Ltd were founded by Bath silversmith and jeweller John Mallett in 1865. By the 1880s his son Walter had arranged the purchase of the Octagon in Bath, and following their success at the 1908 Franco-British Exhibition Malletts opened a permanent shop in London at 40 New Bond Street. Following Walter Mallett's death in 1930, the business passed to a consortium of six of his employees, who in 1937 decided to close the Octagon and move the whole business to London. In recent years Malletts have specialised in very fine 18th and 19th century English furniture, lamps and coffee tables. Malletts at Bourdon House, established in 1961, specialise works of art in and accessories.

Mallett and Son (Antiques) Ltd
40 New Bond Street
London W1
Tel: (01) 499 7411
and
Mallett at Bourdon House Ltd
2 Davies Street
London W1
Tel: (01) 629 2444

This late 19th century William Burges cabinet from Dan Klein has been bought by the Cecil Higgins Museum, Bedford.

Early 18th century walnut cockfighting chair with its original upholstery and leather.

Phelps

Started by James Phelps around the turn of the century, the company has 20,000 square feet on four floors of showroom, displaying period and reproduction furniture, pictures, *objects d'art* and pianos. Phelps caters for both trade and retail customers. Their contract division undertakes complete furnishing projects.

Victorian chaise longue in mahogany with cabriole legs and velvet upholstery.

Phelps Ltd
129–135 St Margarets Road
East Twickenham
Middlesex
TW1 1RG
Tel: (01) 892 1778/7129

Reindeer Antiques

Reindeer have over 20,000 square feet of showrooms specialising in pre-1830 furniture, and have one of the largest selections of 18th century furniture in the country, as well as paintings, brass, garden statuary and furniture.

Reindeer Antiques
43 Watling Street
Pottersbury
Northamptonshire
Tel: (0908) 542407

Bill Waters

Bill Waters is a dealer in furniture, objects and pictures relating to the Aesthetic, *Art Nouveau* and *Art Deco* periods. He has worked in museums and a private gallery and is the author of two books on Burne-Jones.

Art Nouveau *display cabinet.*

Bill Waters
Cockermouth Antique Market
Main Street
Cockermouth
Cumbria

The companies included in the following list represent those offering quality objects at the sort of prices to encourage and beguile new customers. Their furniture is either in good original condition or sensitively repaired, and many of them show it with other interesting period accessories.

Arthur Brown

Large stock of furniture, mainly from the late 18th and early 19th centuries, and also decorative and smaller objects.

Arthur Brown Ltd
392–400 Fulham Road
London SW6 1HW
Tel: (01) 385 4218

Margery Dean

17th, 18th and 19th century furniture.

Margery Dean
The Galleries
Alma Street
Wivenhoe
Colchester
Essex
Tel: (020 622) 42203

Goodbrey Antiques

18th and 19th century English and Continental furniture and decorative items.

Goodbrey Antiques
29 Double Street
Framlingham
Suffolk
Tel: (0728) 723756

W F Greenwood & Sons

Antique furniture, silver and fine English china.

W F Greenwood & Sons Ltd
37 Stonegate
York
Tel: (0904) 23864
(also in Harrogate)

Betty Meysey-Thompson

Furniture, porcelain and decorative objects

Betty Meysey-Thompson
13 Church Street
Woodbridge
Suffolk
Tel: (039 43) 2144

Stephen Moore

High quality 18th century furniture, mirrors and pictures.

Stephen Moore Ltd
Castle Place
High Street
Lewes
Sussex
Tel: (079 16) 4158

Mrs Monro (Antiques)
Furniture, pictures, prints and china.

Mrs Monro (Antiques) Ltd
11 Montpelier Street
London SW7
Showroom: 7 Relton Mews, London SW7
(by appointment only)
Tel: (01) 589 0686/5052

Merlin Pennink
Large stock of general antiques, prints
and some garden furniture.

Merlin Pennink
23–27 The Pantiles
Tunbridge Wells
Kent
Tel: (0892) 35051

A Roch & Sons
Pre-1830 furniture, including walnut,
satinwood and rosewood.

A Roch & Sons Ltd
99 Crawford Street
London W1H 1AN
(01) 724 0563

W Stockbridge & Sons
Large stock of 18th and 19th century
furniture.

W Stockbridge & Sons Ltd
25–26 Bridge Street
Cambridge
CB2 1UJ
Tel: (0223) 53500

Van Praagh Fine Art
English furniture, porcelain and works of
art.

Van Praagh Fine Art Ltd
30 High Street
Arundel
Sussex
Tel: (0903) 882548

Peter Waldron
Specialist in Arts and Crafts furniture
and oriental decorative arts.

Peter Waldron
105 Kensington Church Street
London W8
Tel: (01) 221 7065

Frank Williams
General antiques and many decorative
small period items.

Frank Williams
The Old Post Office
Burford
Oxfordshire
Tel: (099) 382 2128

Furniture Restorers

(Listed alphabetically
by county)

M Marks
27 Larksleaze Road
Longwell Green
Bristol
Avon
Tel: (027 588) 3483

Thomas Hudson
The Barn
117 High Street
Odell
Bedford
Bedfordshire
Tel: (0234) 721133

Hamilton Havers
58 Conisboro Avenue
Caversham
Reading
Berkshire
Tel: (0734) 473379

Fleetwood Antique Restoration
10 Hewell Road
Barnt Green
Birmingham
B45 8LT
Tel: (021) 445 2212

Browns of West Wycombe
Church Lane
West Wycombe
High Wycombe
HP14 3AH Buckinghamshire
Tel: (0494) 24537

Ron Coleman
Pennyblack Cottage
Church Street
Brill
nr Aylesbury
Buckinghamshire
Tel: (0844) 237752

Peter Wilder (Cabinet maker)
Glaslyn
Wycombe Road
Stokenchurch
High Wycombe
Buckinghamshire HP14 3RS
Tel: (024 026) 3455

W G Undrill Ltd
103/111 Catherine Street
Cambridge
CB1 3AP
Tel: (0223) 47470

John Paynter
River View
Penrhin
St Dogmaels
Cardigan
Tel: (0239) 2815

A Allen Antique Restorers
Arden Street
Newmills
Stockport
Cheshire
Tel: (0663) 45274/42985

Guernsey Woodcarvers
Les Issues
St Saviours
Guernsey
Channel Islands
Tel: (0481) 65373

Roger Leslie Hardy
10 Heol Hyfrydle
Coedpoeth
nr Wrexham
Clwyd LL11 3NL
Tel: (035 280) 611

J Edward-Collins
Trevean
Trevenning
St Tudy
Bodmin
Cornwall
Tel: (0208) 850502

R Udall
Merlin Restorations
Howgill Lane
Sedbergh
Cumbria
Tel: (0587) 20301/20719

Rhodelands Craft
528 Duffield Road
Allestree
Derby
Derbyshire DE3 2DL
Tel: (0332) 558754

Fiona Chichester-Clark
Moyola Park
Castledawson
Derry, Northern Ireland
Tel: (064 885) 606

Cricklepitt Mill
Cricklepitt Mill
Commercial Road
Exeter
Devon EX2 4AE
Tel: (0272) 59692

W T Services
44B Fore Street
Tiverton
Devon EX16 6LD
Tel: (088 42) 3820

George Arthur Matthews
The Cottage Workshop
The Camp Site
Dudsbury
Wimborne
Dorset
Tel: (020 16) 2665

Henry Price
18 Shore Road
Holywood
Co. Down
Northern Ireland
Tel: (023 17) 2643

David Elliott Watts
Penffordd Cottages
Pentre
Boncath
Dyfed
Tel: (023 974) 447

G E Everitt & J Rogers
'Dawsnest Workshop'
Grove Road
Tiptree
Essex
Tel: (0621) 816508

Philip Freedman
54 Osborne Road
Hornchurch
Essex RM11 1HE
Tel: (040 24) 42166

Skillcrafts
5 Park Street
Thaxted
Essex CM6 2ND
Tel: (0371) 8300 162

E J Cook & Son
Severn Road
Gloucester
Gloucestershire GL1 2LE
Tel: (0452) 29716

R H Fyson
Manor Farm
Kencot
Lechlade
Gloucestershire
Tel: (037 786) 223

Aitch Jay
'The Folly'
26 St James Street
Ludgershall
nr Andover
Hampshire SP11 9QF
Tel: (0264) 790477

Bowden Woodcraft
Viables Centre
Harrow Way
Basingstoke
Hampshire
Tel: (0256) 21200

John Small Furnishings
88 Dean Road
Bitterne
Southampton
Hampshire SO2 5AT
Tel: (042 18) 2225

The Tankerdale Workshop
Tankerdale Farm
Steep Marsh
Petersfield
Hampshire GU32 2BH
Tel: (0730) 823839

Paul Weaver Restorations
18 Cavendish Mews
Grosvenor Road
Aldershot
Hampshire
Tel: (0252) 310174

A J Weston
Finches Lane
Twyford
nr Winchester
Hampshire
Tel: (0962) 713162

David Mark Ackroyd
Hellens
Much Marcle
Ledbury
Herefordshire
Tel: (053 184) 618

Ashwood (Cabinet makers) Ltd
143 High Street
Rickmansworth
Hertfordshire
Tel: (092 37) 70194

Adrian J Black
36A Freeman Street
Grimsby
South Humberside
Tel: (0472) 55668

M H P Corkhill
'Mostyn'
Lezayre Road
Ramsey
Isle of Man
Tel: (0624) 813356

Brian Edwin Caudell
55 Stowe Road
Orpington
Kent
Tel: (66) 73631

John D Walters
10 Heather Drive
St Michaels
Tenterden
Kent
Tel: (058 06) 3079

Derek Casement
Slack Lane Works
Slack Lane
Pendlebury
Swinton
Manchester
M27 2QT
Tel: (061) 794 1610

Handsworth Restorations
47A Handsworth Road
North Shore
Blackpool
Lancashire
Tel: (0253) 24994/56847

Don Maddox
47 Church Street
Ribchester
nr Preston
Lancashire PR3 3YE
Tel: (025 484) 512

Brian Green Antiques
26 Evington Road
Leicester
Leicestershire
Tel: (0533) 54344

Treedale Furniture
Garden Cottage
Little Dalby
nr Melton Mowbray
Leicestershire
Tel: (066 477) 535

Edmund Czajkowski & Son
96 Tor-O-Moor Road
Woodhall Spa
Lincolnshire LN10 6SB
Tel: (0526) 52895

**Ashley Stocks
(Cabinet makers) Ltd**
3 Crescent Place
London SW3
Tel: (01) 589 0044

John Chambers
Nugent Terrace
London NW8 9QB
Tel: (01) 289 1393

N M Mkhize
o Lots Road
Chelsea
London SW10
Tel: (01) 352 9876

Fenton House
4 High Street
Harrow-on-the-Hill
London
Tel: (01) 864 2234

Clifford J Tracy
-40 Durnford Street
London N15 5NQ
Tel: (01) 800 4773

E & A Wates Ltd
2-84 Mitcham Lane
Streatham
London SW16 6NR
Tel: (01) 769 2205

Wolff & Son Ltd
Chester Court
Albany Street
Regent's Park
London NW1 4BU
Tel: (01) 935 3636

Church Lane Restorations
Church Lane
Teddington
Middlesex
Tel: (01) 977 2526

**Spadesbourne Antiques and
Reproductions**
Herring House
8 High Street
Henley-in-Arden
Solihull
Warwickshire
Tel: (056 42) 3560

Alma Antique Restorers
The Old Gospel Hall
Dereham Road
Norwich
Norfolk
Tel: (0603) 613184

John Smith
Hill Head Farm
Shilbottle
Alnwick
Northumberland NE66 2HW
Tel: (066 575) 275

Peter Snart
Willowbog Farm
Wark
Hexham
Northumberland
Tel: (043 481) 217

John Berry
48 Longdale Lane
Ravenshead
Nottingham
Nottinghamshire
Tel: (062 34) 2317

Laurence J Grayer
Easter Cottage
Church Street
Bloxham
Banbury
Oxfordshire
Tel: (0295) 720912

Randal J Pakeman
63 Gloucester Street
Faringdon
Oxfordshire
Tel: (0367) 21423

Robin Wardrop
Ardess
Bridgend
Callander
Perthshire FL17 8AG
Tel: (0877) 30446

Francois Greco
40 Vineyard Road
Newport
Shropshire TF10 7DA
Tel: (0952) 813806

John Crane
11 Commercial Road
Shepton Mallet
Somerset
Tel: (0749) 4356

Leslie Stanton
The Joiners Workshop
Ashbourne Road
Rocester
nr Uttoxeter
Staffordshire
Tel: (0889) 590186

Alex Anness
3 Approach Cottages
Withersfield
Haverhill
Suffolk
Tel: (0440) 5895

Jack Whittle
47 Peacocks Close
Cavendish
Sudbury
Suffolk CO10 8DA
Tel: (0787) 280652

Clive T Bristow
32 Waltham Avenue
Stoughton
Guildford
Surrey GU2 6QF
Tel: (0483) 38296

Michael Hedgecoe
Roman House
Burrow Hall Green
Chobham
Woking
Surrey
Tel: (099 05) 8206

A Robins & Sons Ltd
Fairfield
Farnham
Surrey
Tel: (0252) 714233

Victor M Gunn (Antiques) Ltd
14 Clifton Hill
Brighton
Sussex BN1 3HQ
Tel: (0273) 24659

R F Neale
Rowley Farmhouse
Lowfield Heath
West Sussex
Tel: (0293) 21875

A J Swaby
Great Grooms
Antiques
Billingshurst
Sussex
Tel: (040 381) 2263

Mr David M Taylor
No 4 The Arches
Ropetackle
Shoreham-by-Sea
Sussex
Tel: (079 17) 63829

David Burkinshaw
66 High Street
Lindfield
West Sussex
Tel: (044 47) 2826

Munday & Garner
The Moncrieff Barn
off Lower Street
Pulborough
West Sussex
Tel: (079 82) 3610

Noel Pepperall
Dairy Lane Cottage
Walberton
Arundel
West Sussex
Tel: (0243) 551282

D J & Co Antique Furniture Restorers
34 Beach Road
Sutton Coldfield
West Midlands
Warwickshire
Tel: (021) 354 5937

N J W Joyce
Alscot Estate Yard
Atherstone-on-Stour
nr Stratford-on-Avon
Warwickshire
Tel: (082 77) 345

Terence C J Walsh Antique Restoration
Melbourne House
Whichford
Shipston-on-Stour
Warwickshire
Tel: (060 884) 664

Warwick Restorations
7 Emscote Road
Warwick
Warwickshire CV34 4PH
Tel: (0926) 41367

Woodland Furniture Co
3 King Street
Rugby
Warwickshire
Tel: (0788) 61644

Fisher Restorations
The Old Rectory
Aston Somerville
Broadway
Worcestershire
Tel: (0386) 852466

Malvern Studios
56 Cowleigh Road
North Malvern
Worcestershire
Tel: (068 45) 4913

Boulevard Reproductions
369 Skircoat Green Road
Skircoat Green
Halifax
Yorkshire
Tel: (0422) 68628

Derek Hainsworth (Lake Antiques)
Lake House
Welham
Norton
Malton
North Yorkshire
Tel: (0653) 2609

David Lyon
Workshop
57 Hull Road
Withernsea
East Yorkshire
Tel: (3280) 09642

Robert Aagaard Ltd
Frogmire House
Stockwell Road
Knaresborough
North Yorkshire HG5 0JP
Tel: (0423) 864805

Gerald Shaw Restorations
Jansville Quarry Lane
New Park
Harrogate
North Yorkshire HG1 3HR

J K Crooks
842 Ecclesall Road
Sheffield
South Yorkshire S11 8TD
Tel: (0742) 686600

The following companies offer various specialist services for furniture restoration.

French Polishers

V A Manners
47 Chilham Road
Mottingham
London SE 9 4BE
Tel: (01) 857 2592

A R Penfold Ltd
17 Osprey Close
Lordswood
Southampton
Hampshire
Tel: (0703) 737432

T L Turner
131 Manor Road
Caddington
Luton
Bedfordshire
Tel: (0582) 414246

M P Wallis
Norfolk Cottage
1 The Row
Hawridge Common
nr Chesham
Buckinghamshire
Tel: 025 05) 8172

R Warner
11b Salisbury Avenue
Barking
Essex
Tel: (01) 591 6481

Furniture Leather

Antique Leathers
4 Park End
South Hill Park
London NW3 2SE
Tel: (01) 435 8582/7799

Gilders

Thomas Duggan
585 King's Road
London SW6
Tel: (01) 736 7799

David Hagi
91 Troutbeck
Albany Street
London NW1
Tel: (01) 338 1716

Marquetry/Buhl

A Dunn & Son
The White House
8 Wharf Road
Chelmsford
Essex CM2 6LU
Tel: (0245) 354452

Lighting

Artificial light in the home was extremely dim until the advent of the electric light bulb and incandescent oil and gas mantles. The flicker of candles hardly broke the shadows; and they were never used in quantity in daily use because of expense. Candles survived in domestic use, and indeed were preferred by many, through much of the nineteenth century. The candles themselves were either made of tallow, which was a smelly mutton fat that tended to gutter, or beeswax, which burned better with less odour but was up to four times more expensive. Oil lamps had always been more common on the continent, though improvements did not make them a viable alternative to candles until the introduction of kerosene (paraffin) during the 1860s. Gas was used for lighting as far back as the 1780s but could be noisy, snifling, smelly and often dangerous. Paradoxically, electricity was too bright at first; the electric arc was unsuitable for domestic use. Efficient bright light as we know it was not available in the ordinary home until the twentieth century.

Candles

Life in the home was very awkward under candlelight. A candle inadvertently blown out in a draught was quite a problem to relight. A flame was produced either from the main fire, another major source of illumination, or from a tinderbox. These consisted of flints and steel sparked against a dry rag. They required a great deal of patience and were fiddly in the dark. The tallow candle was very uneven in burning and the wick had to be frequently snuffed (trimmed) to obtain a consistent brightness. This was done with a pair of scissors which was fitted with a box on one blade to catch the burnt wick; sometimes this

put the flame out. Beeswax candles were only used by the church, for votive purposes, and by the rich. Their flame was more steady, but in large numbers they were hot and used up a lot of oxygen. Quality improved in the 1840s with the use of steatite (a kind of soapstone) and later with paraffin wax, which is the main component of the modern candle.

Even in the main rooms there would be few candles alight at the same time. Sconces or candlebranches were attached to the mirror frame above the mantelpiece, where candles, often in pairs, would increase their power by reflection. Individual candlesticks would be used for reading or sewing and could include a shade as the flame was relatively bright. Chandeliers were not common in the eighteenth century, except in the homes of the rich. In Parisian society they were often hired for balls and receptions. They devoured candles and were unnecessary in daily use, as the light they give is thrown upwards. A visit by George III to Bulstrode Park in 1779 caused an

Chamberstick of silver-gilt by John Schofield, 1791–2. This portable candlestick is conveniently mounted, with snuffers to trim the wick and an extinguishing cone.

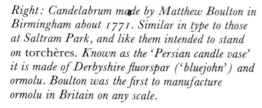

Cut-glass chandelier c 1815 made of highly faceted drops. Such chandeliers should be furnished with candles and not lighted electrically from inside as shown here.

Right: Candelabrum made by Matthew Boulton in Birmingham about 1771. Similar in type to those at Saltram Park, and like them intended to stand on torchères. Known as the 'Persian candle vase' it is made of Derbyshire fluorspar ('bluejohn') and ormolu. Boulton was the first to manufacture ormolu in Britain on any scale.

observer to remark that the hall chandelier had not been lit for twenty years.

The most expensive chandeliers were made of moulded or faceted glass. By the late eighteenth century small drops were strung around an ormolu (gilt brass) frame, reflecting the candles around the perimeter in a glittering cascade of glass. Counterbalances were included in the suspension rope or chain to ease the problem of lighting the candles. Chandeliers were a status symbol for the rich and it was only with cheaper more available light sources that they occurred in the more modest home.

Candelabra were portable free-standing lights with two or more branches. They were again expensive

items, made of silver for the dining table or sideboard. The middle classes could buy Sheffield plate from the late eighteenth century at one-third of the cost of silver. At Saltram Park in Devon, candelabra have always stood on plinths, or *torchères*, in each corner of the drawing room; they are early examples of vases in the neo-Classical taste made by Matthew Boulton. Made of 'blue-john' (Derbyshire fluorspar) and mounted in ormolu, each has six scrolled branches which must have given exceptional brilliance for the time. From the early nineteenth century, candelabra increased in size and proportion and extended designs to sculptural groups in bronze.

Wall-sconces, closely related to the candelabra,

Sheffield plate candlesticks. These were made in large numbers for the rapidly expanding middle class. Similar designs in glass, ceramic, brass, tin, pewter or wood were also common. The three in the centre are in the elegant neo-Classical style of the late eighteenth century, while that on the right is in the broader taste of the 1820s and that on the left is in the Rococo revival style of 1820–40.

were generally carved in wood and gilt, with a large repertory of designs. They were arranged symmetrically in pairs on either side of the overmantel or chimney glass. Only rarely in the eighteenth century was ormolu used. From the late eighteenth century, tall glass shades protected the flame from fluttering. Their design was originally of a swelling baluster form, and they have frequently been mistaken for gas and oil lamp shades.

Lanterns lit the halls and passageways, where draughts could be sudden and strong. The familiar hall lantern had a hanging brass frame filled with glass on its sides. Simple wall lanterns were positioned at strategic points in the corridors, though a chamberstick was usually all there was to light people to their rooms.

Candlesticks were the commonest form of lighting in the house. They could be made in almost any material but from the late eighteenth century the brass candlestick was ubiquitous in baluster form, subtly varying in each period—large numbers were still being made in the inter-war period. Sheffield plate in the gloom gave the effect of silver without the expense. Silver plating and gilding became much cheaper when electrolysis was introduced by the firm of Elkington & Co. in the 1840s. Inspired by French examples, gilt metal fittings became popular. Combinations of candlesticks and ornaments (*garniture*) became standard; a typical example would be a clock or vase flanked by two candlesticks of a very elaborate, vaguely eighteenth-century design, displayed on the mantelpiece. Some of these candlesticks were hung with glass drops known as lustres; versions made

entirely of clear cut glass were followed by coloured and painted glass 'sticks' in the early Victorian era. Also in this era the popularity of *papier mâché* extended to lighting. The material was painted and gilded in glossy black varnish, derived in inspiration from oriental lacquer.

Throughout the nineteenth century the upper classes enjoyed the effect of candles, which when arranged in numbers around the room gave a softer and more even light than the glare of oil and gas lamps. Candles retained their traditional position in rooms even after the introduction of electricity— particularly on the mantelpiece and in the dining room. In the 1920s, John Gloag in his book on decoration recommended a patent candle fitting for the table which 'consists of a hollow cylinder of metal, enamelled white, and in this cylinder is a spring. The candle is inserted and a collar of metal covers the top, allowing the wick to project: as the candle burns away the spring forces it up gradually, and the metal collar at the top prevents any overflow of grease, and removes any chance of the candle shade catching alight.' These were patented under the name of *Green's Arctic lights*, and sold in large numbers.

Oil Lamps

The oil lamp had changed little from the dawn of civilisation until Aimée Argand brought his experimental improvements to England in the 1780s.

Sophie von la Roche visited London in 1786 and related her experience of seeing oil lamps on sale in Oxford Street. 'Most of all we admired a stall with

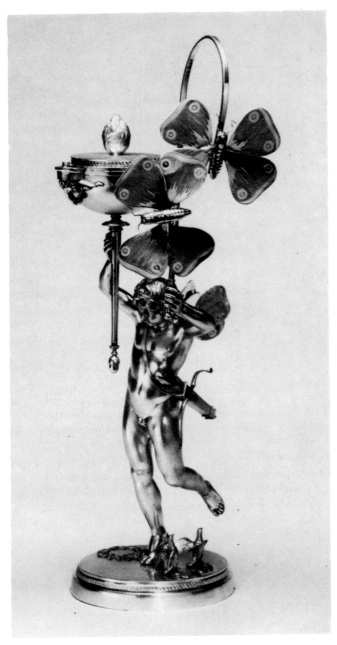

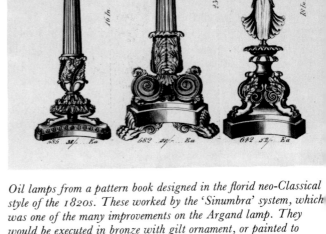

Oil lamps from a pattern book designed in the florid neo-Classical style of the 1820s. These worked by the 'Sinumbra' system, which was one of the many improvements on the Argand lamp. They would be executed in bronze with gilt ornament, or painted to imitate it.

Left: Italian oil lamp made of silver about 1805. Cupid holds the 'torch' containing the oil and the lights; the butterflies act as shades and are adjustable; the snuffers are kept in the quiver. An example of continental neo-Classicism.

Argand and other lamps, . . . forming a really dazzling spectacle; every variety of lamp, crystal, lacquer and metal ones, silver and brass in every possible shade; large and small lamps arranged so artistically and so beautifully lit, that each one was visible as in broad daylight.'

The Argand lamp had a circular wick which improved the combustion of the flame and thus gave it a stronger light. It was fuelled by colza or rape seed oil. Because this oil was heavy the reservoir had to be above the level of the burners. The Argand lamp is distinguished by this reservoir, which is generally in the shape of an urn. It should be mounted as a wall bracket, hung like a chandelier or stand as a table lamp. The designs were elaborately executed in gilt bronze, brass or silver plate. Further improvement

Left: Student lamp. This familiar type of oil lamp was manufactured widely from 1830 onwards. Its principle is based on that of the bird-cage fountain with the oil contained in the brass reservoir. The green shade reduced the glare.

Middle: Victorian paraffin lamp. The highly elaborate base is weighted. Shown lighted.

Right: Table oil lamp made by W. A. S. Benson & Co., about 1895. The Arts and Crafts design is made of copper and brass with the curved vanes of the shade unconsciously anticipating the machine age.

included a clockwork mechanism which forced the oil up the wick.

The student lamp was introduced about 1830, and burned colza oil. It was used for reading with the glare reduced by a green glass shade and was adjustable in height. Prince Albert was known to have used one on his desk and the lamp, with variations, was produced in large numbers during the century.

The arrival of cheap, almost odourless paraffin lamps in the 1860s meant that the most modest household thereafter used several of them for different

purposes. They were cheap and efficiently bright; the table versions had a tall glass chimney and an engraved glass globe to diffuse the light. They stood on japanned, cast-iron and brass bases, or for the rich on a silver plated and brass pillar with heavily weighted bases. Mica 'smoke eaters' were suspended above or attached to the chimney to protect the ceiling. Many variations, such as the standard lamp with an elaborate silk shade, appeared by the end of the nineteenth century, when oil lost its pre-eminence to gas and later, electricity.

Gas Lighting

Experimental gas lighting had been installed in the offices of Lord Lonsdale's coal mines at Whitehaven, Cumberland in the 1760s, and in 1787 Lord Dundonald's hall at his house in Scotland was lit by gas. But it was not until 1807 that gas was brought to public notice by the erection of street lights in London's Pall Mall.

The earliest gas light burned from holes pierced in iron pipes. This resulted in rapid corrosion and the brass burner, developed in about 1810, was found to be a great innovation. At first the flame burned

Caricature on the dangers of gas in the 1820s, when it was extremely uncontrollable.

Right: Gasolier of about 1870. The water-slide system enabled the apparatus to be lowered or raised. It is made of gilt metal in the 'eclectic geometric' style. The shades of cut, etched and coloured glass were interchangeable with oil lamps.

upright in a 'rat's tail'. The wider 'bat's wing' flame was developed in the 1820s and steatite burners, which produced a strong, even light, were invented by Sugg around 1850.

Between 1830 and 1860 gas in the home was an expensive novelty. It gave a flickering flame and an unpleasant smell, together with dangers of asphyxiation or explosion. It was used mainly for street lamps and public buildings. Pugin and Barry's new Houses of Parliament were lit by it (against opposition from the Lords) when they were finished in the 1850s.

Gas fittings followed the general stylistic trends favoured by oil or candle power in the mid-nineteenth century. Wall lights were a distinctive feature, having simple or elaborate brackets with globe shades. These shades were made of opaque, clear, or patterned glass, in a manner similar to oil lamps. Chandeliers or gasoliers did not have the cumbersome reservoirs of oil which meant that their design could be simpler, though they followed the 'eclectic geometric' style of high Victorian design. One of the many inventions at this time was the 'water-slide' chandelier which could be raised or lowered on a counterbalance for easy maintenance. The gas tubes slid inside each other and were sealed with water to prevent the gas escaping. Unfortunately the water tended to evaporate, so some examples had whistles drilled into the pipes to warn of any escape.

At the point when electricity seemed to be taking over in the 1890s, the gas mantle was developed. This meant that the flame burned with a strong incandescent glow. During the period up to the First World War gas was recognised as a bright, efficient and cheap form of lighting, and the invention of the inverted burner furthered its popularity. Between the wars, gas was rapidly superseded by cheaper electricity, despite innovations like the pneumatic switch to improve its convenience. By 1940 it remained only in the homes of the poor, some of whom objected to being converted to electricity because of the extra heat given by gas.

Electricity

The difficulty with electric light in its early days was not its dimness, but its blinding brightness. The electric arc was only suitable for street lamps and railway stations. When the present façade of Buckingham Palace was hurriedly erected in the summer of 1913, work continued at night under arc lamps, though this was not an early instance of its use.

Swan, in Britain, and Edison, in the United States, simultaneously managed to divide the electric arc. Both of them, aided by the invention of the vacuum pump and expert glass blowers, produced electric lamps in 1878–9. After initial disputes over their discovery the two men joined up and formed the Edison-Swan Electric Company in Britain.

The first private house to be lit by electricity was Cragside, a massive Elizabethan-style residence for Sir William Armstrong. He installed his lighting system in 1880 and described it as free from 'all the disagreeable attributes of the arc light. It is perfectly steady and noiseless. It is free from harsh glare and dark shadows . . . [and has] . . . no vitiating effect in the air of a room.'

This last point referred to the fumes given off by candle, oil and gas lighting. Amongst the more snobbish, the 'lack of harsh glare' of electric light was highly disputed, and, like bathrooms and central heating, it was thought 'insufferably vulgar'. Fittings in Cragside were simple electroliers, or clusters of naked light bulbs hanging from the ceiling. In other cases, oil table lamps were converted. Shades were not put onto the hanging fittings until the 1890s.

By this time, all types of lighting had rather similar appliances. The different fuels were in strong competition with each other, so a standard lamp, for example, would be of uniform design whether it was for gas, oil or electricity. The support was usually telescopic in iron, brass or wood, with a very elaborate silk shade that looked like a cross between underwear and millinery. Clusters of wall and ceiling lamps gave the impression of a floral spray, enhanced with etched and coloured glass shades. The temporary advantage of electricity over gas lay in that it threw its light downwards onto the areas where the light was most needed. The brilliance of this arrangement was

A salon in New York lighted by Edison lamps, the earliest electric lighting. The fittings are what might be expected for oil or gas lamps of the 1880s, though electric lamps threw the light downwards.

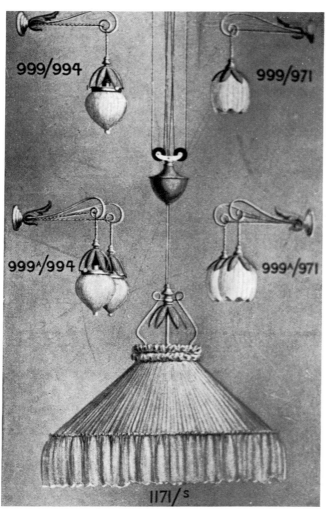

Above: Designs for electrical fittings by W. A. S. Benson & Co., about 1897. These were intended for the dining room, where the silk shaded pendant was to hang over the table and the brass, copper and glass shaded brackets were to hang on the wall.

meet the vastly increased demand. Overhead lighting in a simple cardboard or material shade was still common. More sophisticated table lamps on vase bases and shaded in vellum, parchment or pleated silk gave a soft light for sitting rooms. Indirect 'strip' lighting was concealed in a more formal drawing room by positioning at intervals long tubular light bulbs behind the cornice; although neon lighting was available in the 1930s, it was rarely used in the private home. Modern functional glass and chrome shades gave a clear light for hallways, kitchens and bathrooms. The angle poise lamp for reading and working is still very much of the same design today, its articulated arms derived from the principle of the counterbalanced chandelier.

modified by the First World War, when alabaster or glass hanging bowls, which diffused overhead light, were especially popular. Period-style lighting was common from the earliest domestic use of electricity. Many candle, oil or gas fittings were adapted, and new ones were made in the style of the late seventeenth and early eighteenth century. It was important that electricity did not present too uncompromisingly modern an appearance, since it had to appeal to more traditional tastes.

Cheaper electricity in the 1930s meant an enormous range of appliances had to be produced to

DESIGN. H34.   DIA: 60 %M

Design for a pendant light fitting about 1930. The glass is to diffuse the light. The sharp, angular 'sun ray' form is typical of Jazz Moderne *style, which was popular in the suburban home during the 1930s.*

when furnished with good quality candles, even if they are rarely used. Candlesticks on the dining table have never gone out of use; their position and height is essential so that the flame does not dazzle people's vision. Patent candleholders with conical shades are an ideal solution, though reproductions are not yet being made. Electric 'candles' were produced from the early days of electricity. They have never been entirely convincing. If you must put them onto a glass chandelier of the 'balloon' type avoid supplementing them with extra electric bulbs inside to give more 'sparkle'. In certain areas where direct lighting is needed—as in halls, passages, bathrooms and kitchens—it would be better to avoid the 'period' fitting entirely.

Modern Interpretation

The atmosphere of a room depends greatly on lighting. Period interiors can be greatly enhanced through the clever use of modern electric fittings such as the spotlight, which give a great deal of flexibility in the direction and intensity of light produced.

Candle Fittings

The gloom of candlelight is very congenial for entertaining purposes. Antique chandeliers, candelabra, wall sconces and so on should never be converted to electricity; it is, apart from anything else, detrimental to their value. They look marvellous

Oil Lamps

The Argand burners are laborious and difficult to use. Paraffin lamps for wall and table are made today in 'period' reproductions. They often still use the highly efficient 'duplex' (two flat wicks) system. Antiques are naturally preferable but expensive. The opaque globe used on oil lamps successfully manages to obscure conversion to electricity. Carriage lamps were never intended to light doorways; simpler lanterns hung above the door or behind the fanlight should be adequate.

Gas

The interest in gas lighting in recent years has seen its re-installation in restaurants and pubs, though not very often in houses. The gas wall light is most commonly used nowadays where a weak gas jet is observed behind a *clear* glass shade. Antique gas fittings can, like oil lamps, be converted to electricity; their hollow pipes are ideal for the purpose. This, again, is best hidden behind translucent frosted, coloured or engraved globe shades.

Opposite: Standard lamp designed by Oliver Hill in 1934. The absence of ornament, the functional form and the shining chromium plating exemplify the Modern movement.

Lighting

Lighting is virtually the last subject to be considered when restoring and decorating your house. But placing lights effectively and sensitively can suddenly bring an interior to life, setting a mood and creating an atmosphere of domestic warmth and charm.

Our forbears lived in a level of gloom that we would not find acceptable today. Today, only the Georgian purist would return to lighting his house by candles. The use of electricity makes light fittings an area where the question of using 'reproduction' items has to be carefully thought out, as the market abounds with many gross and vulgar examples. In the following listings every effort has been made to select suppliers of antique or very high quality reproduction fittings.

Acquisitions
Acquisitions stock original *Art Nouveau* and *Art Deco* lighting 1900–30, mainly of French manufacture in cameo glass. They have many signed pieces, and also student lamps, oil lamps, wall mounted lights, and *Art Deco* figure lamps.

Acquisitions (Fireplaces) Ltd
269 Camden High Street
London NW1 7BX
Tel: (01) 485 4955

Clare House
Started by Elizabeth Hanley in 1949, Clare House have the Royal Warrant for lighting, and are regarded as one of the most prestigious companies in the field (a reputation which is reflected in their prices). Lamps are made to order but they also stock antique lamps. Services are available for the conversion of customers' own candlesticks, etc., into lamps, and for the re-wiring and cleaning of lamps. Elizabeth Hanley will travel virtually anywhere to advise on specific lighting enquiries.

Clare House Ltd
35 Elizabeth Street
London SW1
Tel: (01) 730 8480

George and Peter Cohn
This firm has been in existence since 1946 and specialises in the restoration of crystal and ormolu chandeliers, wall lights, candlesticks, candelabra, etc. They also undertake the electrification of such items and will clean large crystal chandeliers *in situ*.

George and Peter Cohn
Unit 21
21 Wren Street
(off Gray's Inn Road)
London WC1

Delamosne
Delamosne are a small firm of specialist dealers in English and Irish glass and European porcelain of the 18th and 19th centuries. They also undertake the restoration of period English chandeliers: perhaps their most arduous undertaking was the complete rebuilding of the celebrated suite of chandeliers in the Assembly Rooms, Bath, in 1938. Established in 1905, the firm has probably restored upwards of 1,000 chandeliers and allied glass fittings for stock and sale all over the world.

Small six-light English chandelier. The single-piece arm, pan and sconce design was soon superseded, and dates this piece at c 1725.

Delamosne and Son Ltd
4 Campden Hill Road
Kensington High Street
London W8 7DU
Tel: (01) 937 1804

Dernier and Hamlyn
Since 1888 Dernier and Hamlyn have been making decorative light fittings which reflect the design, craftsmanship and spirit of the 18th and 19th centuries. Their fine range of chandeliers and lamps includes the 'Dutch' range based on 17th century Flemish designs which was used in the Banqueting House, Whitehall. Dernier and Hamlyn lighting is also found in such buildings as the Palace of Westminster, Liverpool Cathedral, nos. 10 and 11 Downing Street, and Chichester Cathedral. A fine restoration service is offered and spare parts are supplied on request.

A Holbein three-light pendant from Dernier & Hamlyn's range.

Dernier and Hamlyn Ltd
62 Kimber Road
Southfields
London SW18 4PP
Tel: (01) 870 0011

Thomas Goode
In Thomas Goode's Georgian-style interior there are 13 showrooms displaying the finest china and glass tableware, earthenware, silver and cutlery, table lamps, antiques and gift items. They also have probably the largest selection of antique and modern chandeliers in London, which includes handmade reproductions of most periods.

Thomas Goode and Company Ltd
19 South Audley Street
Grosvenor Square
London W1Y 6BN
Tel: (01) 499 2823

Hooper & Purchase

This firm of antique dealers specialises in high quality antique light fittings. All the chandeliers and wall lights have been de-electrified and carefully restored.

Hooper & Purchase
303 Kings Road
London, SW3
Tel: (01) 351 3985

Kelly's of Knaresborough

Kelly's of Knaresborough carry the largest selection of old lighting outside London. This comprises chandeliers, wall lights, lustres, oil lamps, candlesticks, and fittings of all periods up to 1930. They will also undertake to find for customers items that are not in stock at the time.

Kelly's of Knaresborough
96 High Street
Knaresborough
Yorkshire
Tel: (0423) 862041

Joseph Knight Lamp Co

One of Europe's leading producers of high-quality reproduction metalwork lamps and light fittings. Large brochure available. European inquiries should be addressed to the Netherlands branch:
Tel: (02940) 15341

Joseph Knight Lamp Co Ltd
Charles Street
Willenhall
East Midlands
Tel: (0902) 62231/68060

Three fine Victorian oil lamps from Kelly's of Knaresborough, who stock a wide range of period lighting.

Phazia

Phazia have launched a large collection of decorative table lamps and lighting made by Le Dauphin of France. Most of the lighting has an oriental inspiration, but the attractive standard lamps 'Mediez' and 'Desirade' are *Art Deco* inspired. The 'Vermelles' table lamp has an *Art Nouveau* Lalique-style base and is available in white or peach glass.

Lalique-style table lamp from Phazia.

Phazia Ltd
113–117 Highgate Road
London NW5
Tel: (01) 267 6088

D H Sargeant

D H Sargeant have been in business 40 years and are now recognised experts on antique glass, chandeliers, candelabra, and table lights. The stock varies from early Georgian to late Victorian. A restoration and complete re-make service is also offered.

D H Sargeant
21 The Green
Westerham
Kent
Tel: (0959) 62130

W Stitch & Co

Restoration service only. This firm supplies shops such as Harrods and Peter Jones.

W Stitch & Co
48 Berwick Street
London W1
Tel: (01) 437 3776

Sugg Lighting

This firm is probably the only company still manufacturing traditional gas lighting equipment. The firm has a family history of several generations and are often asked for assistance in a wide variety of projects related to a period between 1830–1930. Apart from working gas lamps they manufacture identical electrical models for those who want the convenience of electricity.

Sugg Lighting
Massrealm Ltd
Napier Way
Crawley
Sussex RH10 2RA
Tel: (0293) 21874

Sundial Antiques

Sundial Antiques have a varied and changing stock of decorative items for the home, including a small stock of period oil lamps and brass candlesticks.

Sundial Antiques
Whielden Street
Amersham
Buckinghamshire
Tel: (024 03) 7955

Philip Turner Antiques

The main stock of this shop is Continental furniture 1700–1900 but it also specialises in period lighting with some reproductions. There are generally six or seven chandeliers in stock at any one time.

Philip Turner Antiques Ltd
16 Crawford Street
London W1
Tel: (01) 935 6074

Wendy's World

This firm specialises in all types of lampshades, hard and soft, ranging from manufactured lines to individual shades made to order. The 'Emma' range consists of nine different *Art Nouveau*-style lamps in varying sizes.

Wendy's World
The Old Workhouse
Duck's Hill Road
Ruislip
Middlesex
Tel: (71) 75558

D W Windsor

D W Windsor specialise in Victorian-style exterior lighting. Each lantern, lamp-post or bracket is craftsman-made and individually numbered, using high quality copper with brass fittings.
A limited number of antique cast iron lamp-posts are also available. Unusual commissions have included custom-built lanterns for the GLC restoration of Covent Garden Market, and for Metropolitan Police Stations.

D W Windsor Ltd
Stanstead Abbotts
Ware
Hertfordshire SG12 8HE
Tel: (0902) 870567

Christopher Wray's Lighting Emporium

Probably the most famous name in period lighting, Christopher Wray's shops have a huge selection of antique and reproduction Victorian, Edwardian, and Tiffany lamps. Made of solid brass, hand polished and lacquered, the reproduction lamps are handmade to the original designs, usually with the actual dies that produced them a century earlier. The range is enormous, covering every conceivable form of lighting from oil lamps

The Emma *range of* Art Nouveau-*style lamps from Wendy's World, specialists in both hard and soft lampshades.*

and table lamps to hanging lanterns and brass spotlamps. Over 500 handmade glass shades are also available.

Christopher Wray's Lighting Emporium
600–606 King's Road
London SW6 2DX
Tel: (01) 736 8434
and
62 Park Street
Bristol
BS1 5IN
Tel: (0272) 279537
and
26 Patrick Street
Kilkenny
Eire
Tel: (056) 22776

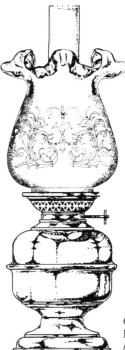

Christopher Wray's Brompton *wall bracket lamp.*

Christopher Wray's Fraser *lamp.*

Fabrics and Wallpapers

Fabrics and wallpapers are two of the elements which contribute most to the overall look and atmosphere of a room. Even an architecturally rather nondescript room furnished with indifferent items can be given a pleasant 'feel' by the skilful use of colour and pattern in upholstery, curtains, carpet and wallpaper. Likewise a 'period feel' can be given to a room, without necessarily investing in expensive antiques, if the right kind of fabrics and wallpapers are chosen.

When choosing fabrics and wallpapers it is a basic rule to pick materials which, as far as possible, are made by the same techniques as they were in the past. In other words, avoid artificial fibres and choose hand-block printed cottons and wallpapers.

In the last ten years or so the range of good reproduction fabrics and wallpapers on the market has increased immensely. The best reproductions are in the more expensive ranges, particularly those where traditional processes are used. Beware of adaptations of old designs, particularly those in the cheaper ranges where modern techniques are used and colours changed by designers to coincide with their ideas of contemporary taste. When buying materials for a period interior, it is worth remembering that better quality not only looks better, but lasts longer.

In the past, as today, economy was a vital consideration to most people. It is certainly not necessary to pay vast sums of money for silk damasks or brocades in order to achieve a period effect. Those kinds of materials, in fact, would be inappropriately grand for most terraced properties, which were essentially middle-class homes.

In the days when houses were entirely heated by coal fires, 'spring cleaning' really did mean something. It was then that the heavy wool or velvet curtains were taken down to be replaced by printed chintz, usually with matching slip covers for the upholstered furniture. This ritual was instigated in Victorian times when the machine production of fabrics made them cheaper and more accessible to middle-class households. In the eighteenth century complete changes of furnishing fabrics from winter to summer was less usual, but the use of slip covers to protect expensive silk, velvet or embroidered upholstery from everyday wear and tear was certainly common. These covers were sometimes made of printed cotton or chintz, but more usually of checked cotton or linen gingham. By using the right kind of printed cottons or linens for slip covers and curtains an authentic-looking period interior can be created quite inexpensively.

The Georgian Period

The Industrial Revolution in the second half of the eighteenth century particularly affected the production of textiles. Innovations like 'Crompton's Mule' and the 'Spinning Jenny' made for enlarged production of cheaper fabrics. New techniques had less effect on wallpapers because, although a machine for producing lengths of paper had been invented in France in 1739, it took the best part of a hundred years for its use to be allowed in this country. Until the 1830s, therefore, papers continued to be produced in strips instead of rolls.

Taste in the mid-eighteenth century tended to elaborate patterns based on those of fashionable imported French textiles. However, in the latter part of the century fabrics and wallpapers generally played a less dominant role in interiors; this does not mean that less were used, but that there was a growing taste for plain unpatterned surfaces, or patterns of a single colour, or with small multicoloured motifs. A Classical effect was wanted, cool or even austere. This was the period when the Adam brothers dominated fashionable taste. The gloss of satin and watered silk was much admired, presumably for its cool but expensive effect. Colours were on the whole pale: white, cream, pale blue, grey and green. Only in the 1810s did clear

Left: English block-printed cotton chintz '1774–80. This kind of pattern was based on cottons imported by the East India Company for the European market.

Opposite right: Block-printed English cotton, early nineteenth century. This kind of naturalistic tour de force *was very popular in the mid-Victorian period.*

Opposite left: One of a portfolio of English, mid-nineteenth century patterns for printed cottons.

bright colours come back into fashion, possibly through the influence of the Prince Regent's Brighton Pavilion.

Woven Fabrics

In grand rooms, even at the height of the Classical vogue, 'where a high degree of elegance and grandeur are required' as Hepplewhite suggests in his *Guide* of 1788, 'silk or satin, figured or plain, also velvet with gold fringe' should be used. Plain velvet or single-coloured damasks were generally of muted shades such as drab green or dull red. The velvet or silk was stretched on batons to cover the walls (not something to be attempted by the amateur!) with matching upholstery and curtains or, more usually, 'Roman'

blinds. These are pelmets with material suspended beneath them, which forms a ruched effect when drawn up during the day (examples may be seen in the drawing room at Osterley Park House in Middlesex).

Printed Fabrics

The name 'chintz' comes from the Indian painted and dyed cotton material which had been imported into this country by the East India company and achieved great popularity. The patterns of printed fabrics are usually floral, and of Indian or Oriental inspiration. They are block-printed in bright, clear vegetable dyes in a range of blues, reds, violets, yellows and greens, usually on a white ground. Frequently based on the 'Tree of Life' pattern, chintzes usually have branches

eandering over the fabric with bright flowers on the
d of rather thin stems.

In the last twenty years or so of the eighteenth
ntury the growing fashion for all things Classical
perseded these floral prints with severely Classical
atterns, imports from France known as '*Toiles de
uy*' (referring to the Oberkampf factory at Jouy near
ersailles). These chintzes were printed from en-
raved copper plates, making a more accurate
npression than the wood blocks used for the floral
intzes; they were usually produced in a single
lour—red, blue, violet or sepia—on a white ground,
ut occasionally additional colours were added by
lock printing.

arpets

grand rooms carpets were boldly patterned,
eflecting the Classical plasterwork of the ceiling. But
more ordinary rooms patterns were usually rigidly
eometrical, in diapers, squares or roundels. In the
te eighteenth century the Wilton factory developed
technique imported from Brussels, where the pile of
he carpet is cut in such a way as to give a dense,
elvet-like effect. This was produced plain, or with
old geometric patterns in narrow widths intended to
e joined together rather like a modern 'fitted carpet'.
Iany carpets were imported from Turkey, Persia and

India for use in this country. Their patterns undoubtedly had a considerable influence on British
manufacturers. It is clear, however, from paintings
and engravings, that most interiors—apart from the
very affluent—were generally uncarpeted until well
into the nineteenth century, and that bare boards with
rugs was the norm. The boards were scrubbed with
dry sand rather than polished; the silvery effect which
this achieved appealed to the cool neo-Classical taste.

Wallpapers

Wallpaper patterns have always tended to be based on
the imitation of more expensive materials. Flock
wallpapers, imitating the expensive imported 'Genoa
velvets', were favoured in grand rooms in the first half
of the eighteenth century. In the middle years of the
century wallpaper imitated the costly and fashionable
silk brocades which were imported from France as
well as chintzes. The Chinese silk papers, made
especially for the European market and imported into
this country by the East India Company in the mid-
eighteenth century, usually came in sets of five

Left: A panel of Chinoiserie wallpaper, c 1760. This example was made in England, copying imported Chinese examples made for the European market.

Opposite right: Length of French wallpaper from the series Les Monuments de Paris, *produced by Dufour and Leroy, 1814.*

Opposite top: Wallpaper with a Trellis and Rosette pattern from Uppark, Sussex. Late eighteenth or early nineteenth century.

Opposite middle: Wallpaper frieze, wood block printed c 1800. Friezes are still printed in sheets in this manner and have to be cut up for use.

Opposite below: Wallpaper borders. English, c 1840, printed in colour from wood blocks, some with flock.

lengths, hand painted with a tree pattern (like the chintz, based on the 'Tree of Life' pattern) decorated in bright colours with flowers and birds. These were extremely expensive and therefore copied in block-printed versions by English wallpaper manufacturers. In the late eighteenth century a more stripey effect was common to wallpapers and fabrics—not like the 'Regency Stripe' of the 1950s, but designs where stripes alternated with meandering floral motifs. Papers imitating watered silk were also produced.

The French have tended to lead the field in wallpapers, as in textile design, from the eighteenth century. High taxes both on British and imported wallpapers meant that papers were generally used sparingly in this country until the Victorian period. From the 1770s until the French Revolution in 1789 the firm of Reveillon produced complex neo-Classical designs, and in the 1800s Parisian firms produced expensive panoramic wallpapers with subjects like 'Les Monuments de Paris'.

'Print Rooms' were fashionable in the second half of the century, which are amusing and easy to reconstruct. The prints or engravings are glued in groups to the wall which has been papered with an unobtrusive pattern. They are then 'framed' with paper architectural borders printed in black and white, and grey. Other areas are then filled in with paper swags and roundels to give a Classical effect

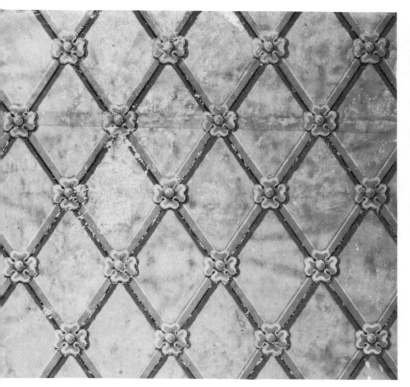

Window Curtains and Trimmings

From the 1790s onwards the arrangement of draperies around windows became more and more complex. The arrangements were both symmetrical and asymmetrical, but basically they consisted of draperies looped over and under a pole or pelmet, behind which hung floor length curtains of the same or contrasting colour with sub-curtains (mainly for use during the day) or some other transparent material behind those. When open, the curtains were looped to the side by means of a curtain loop attached to the wall on a curtain pin. The fabrics used were usually plain but decorated with heavy fringe braids and looped cords, as well as Classical motifs such as Greek anthemions or laurel leaves.

Some of the more complicated arrangements took many yards of material. Using silks these arrangements would be astronomically expensive to reproduce, but a very pleasing effect can be achieved by using glazed calicoes, which come in a variety of good colours. The most important element, the fringes and braids, are also available and much fun can be had trying out different arrangements.

The Victorian Period

The heaviness of effect which we associate with the Victorian period begins to be noticeable in fashionable

Both pages: Illustrations from The Cabinet Maker and Upholsterer's Guide *by George Smith (1808). These styles also served as a basis for Victorian window draperies.*

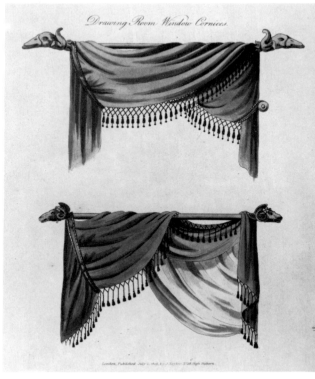

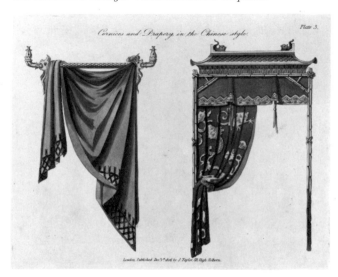

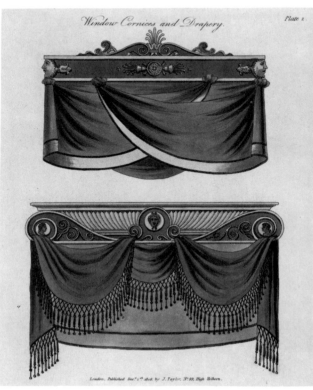

interiors as early as the mid 1820s. Elaborately patterned fabrics were coming back into fashion by the early 1830s, but throughout the 1840s bright clear colours continued to be fashionable. After about 1850, heavy fabrics dyed in such ponderous shades as crimson or bottle green were favoured, and remained generally in vogue well into the 1870s.

Woven Fabrics

From about 1830 onwards the widespread use of a technical innovation—the 'Jacquard loom' (a method of programming patterns on to the loom)—facilitated the production of increasingly complex woven designs. Manufacturers vied with each other in the production

of more and more elaborate patterns to show off their technical ingenuity. The patterns range from abstract designs of Elizabethan strapwork to naturalistic ones of fruit and flowers. Patterns frequently had dark coloured backgrounds in order to make the fruit and flowers look more realistic. In the 1850s, the taste was for more and more exotic types of plant.

Heavy patterned velvets were also favoured for draperies in drawing rooms, after the introduction in the 1820s of Manchester or cotton velvet led to its widespread use in middle-class houses. It was often used in conjunction with elaborately patterned, machine-woven, cotton-lace inter-curtains. Fabrics woven out of horse hair (which comes in a variety of colours as well as black and is extremely hard-

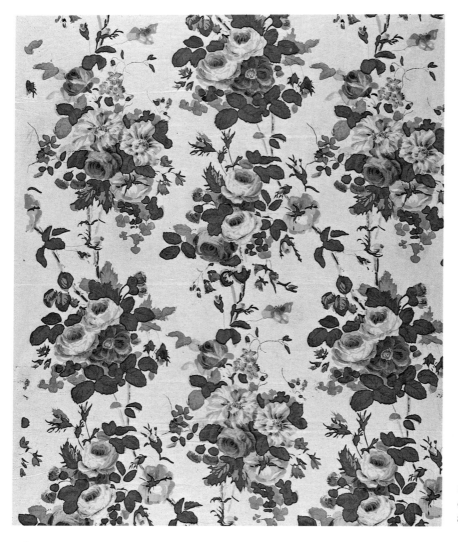

Left: Block-printed chintz Victoria and Albert, c *1850 (a twentieth-century reproduction from the original blocks).*

Opposite: English roller-printed cotton, c *1836. The introduction of roller printing made for more and more elaborate designs.*

wearing) and leather (or imitation leather) were considered suitable for upholstery in dining rooms and libraries.

Printed Fabrics

The naturalism seen in the design of woven fabrics is even more aggressive in the patterns of printed ones. In the 1830s two technical innovations, chemical dyes and roller printing, made for elaborate and highly coloured patterns.

The naturalistic fruit and flowers which form the most characteristic motif throughout the period tend to be superimposed on Classical architectural backgrounds during the 1830s, but by the 1840s elaborate scrolls and cartouches with flowers weaving around them are more usual, the patterns covering the whole surface of the fabric to disguise the repeats. In the mid to late 1840s there was a vogue for overlapping rosebud patterns on a dotted or trellis background; like many mid-nineteenth century cottons, these often had their surfaces glazed to give a luxurious satin-like

effect. By the 1850s the realistic depiction of flowers had more or less taken over printed cotton patterns.

Carpets

The early Victorian period saw great technical strides in the development of machine woven carpets. Fitted carpets were occasionally seen in affluent homes from the 1820s, and by the 1850s some form of carpet was within the reach of all but the poorest. There were two main kinds of machine-made carpets available: 'Brussels' carpet, which had a looped uncut pile, and 'Geneva', which was made on the same principle but with the pile cut to give a velvety effect. In the 1840s and '50s, the patterns followed the current vogue for naturalism so that carpets with dark backgrounds had the appearance of having had flowers strewn over them at regular intervals. In the 1840s, too, Queen Victoria's acquisition of Balmoral in the Highlands of Scotland started a vogue for tartan.

Wallpapers

Wallpaper patterns as usual tended to follow fabrics. However, in the early nineteenth century the distinction between what was considered appropriate to

Left: English roller-printed chintz, c. 1831.

Below: Wallpaper designed by Owen Jones, 1852. This kind of flat pattern was cultivated taste in the 1850s and 1860s.

drawing room, dining room or bedroom became more pronounced. An elaborate pattern consisting of bunches of cabbage roses tied with blue silk ribbons and weaving in and out of Rococo scrolls was considered 'right' for the drawing room. Gothic tracery would be correct for the dining room or library and a simple sprig pattern for the bedroom. Surprisingly wallpaper only came into common usage in this country after 1836, when the taxation on home produced papers was lifted. It was only in the 1830s, too, that papers began to be produced in rolls, in the form that we know them today. Until then the paper used was much thicker, more like card and was usually hung by professionals employed by the manufacturer. It was usually nailed into position in sections. For these reasons wallpaper was only mass-produced from the 1840s onwards.

In cultivated circles in the mid 1850s there was a reaction against naturalism, and flat patterns by designers such as Pugin and Owen Jones came into favour.

Window Draperies

There were no great innovations in the arrangement of window draperies in the early Victorian period except that pelmets became more elaborate and the general effect more solid and heavy; they could be in any style and made of oak, mahogany or deal, with painted or gilded applied decorations. Below the pelmet was hung a pleated valance, trimmed with a wide and often elaborate band of braid, a wide fringe, and tassels. Behind this, curtains of the same material as the valance were hung on ordinary rods, with sub-curtains of machine lace or muslin hanging on subsidiary rods.

From about 1850, muslin or 'net' curtains started to be used to cover only the bottom part of sash windows, stretched in taut folds from rings on small brass rods. In the 1840s elaborately patterned net curtains, known as 'Madras Muslins', were introduced giving what we have come to see as a typically 'Victorian' effect. Curtains were usually made of a plain heavy fabric (often velvet), relying on trimmings for effect.

The Arts and Crafts

William Morris started the firm of Morris, Marshall, Faulkner and Co. in 1861 because he was unable to obtain the kind of furnishings he wanted for his new house on the commercial market of the time. He liked simple, country-type designs. In the early 1860s he produced three designs for wallpapers, the first in the long list of famous works which were mainly produced in the '70s and '80s. In the 1870s he turned his attentions to chintz patterns, and designed some of the best-known patterns ever to be produced.

Although Morris is famous for his wallpaper designs, he did not wholeheartedly approve of their use. He looked on them as substitutes for tapestries or wallhangings of embroidery or chintz. Chintz was to be hung in folds around the walls from just below the picture rail down to the skirting board, like curtains. His 'Daffodil' design can be seen hung in this way at Standen in Surrey. If these abundant lengths of fabric were not available, he favoured simple whitewash.

By the 1880s Morris had become a 'grand old man', and his ideas and designs became the starting point for many young designers.

Trellis block-printed wallpaper designed by William Morris and Philip Webb, 1864. This pattern was intended to have the simple feel of a country garden.

Printed Fabrics

The design innovators of the 1850s had been un-
animous in insisting that good design should be flat,
and that fabric and wallpaper designs should not
'jump off the wall at you' as did many early Victorian
designs. Nature was to be the source of inspiration for
drawings, which should be formalised into patterns.
This can be seen in Morris's earliest wallpaper
designs. In the 1870s, however, he became more and
more interested in historical patterns, which tended to
make his designs become more complex. His hand-
block and natural dye methods were time consuming
and necessarily expensive, but with his designs and
colour ranges Morris established printed textiles once
and for all as fashionable items.

In the 1880s, Liberty's in Regent Street, London,
established their new 'Art Fabrics' department,
aiming at the same cultivated middle-class clientele as
Morris and Co. They used the same subtle colour
combinations as Morris, known as 'greenery yallery'
in the slang of the time. They produced designs
printed in coarse silks and cottons, in simple formalised patterns based on Indian designs, and became
famous for their ranges of 'Fade Silks' in 'Sage greens',
'Russet browns', 'Peacock blues', 'Venetian reds' and
'Ivories' (white would have been vulgar!).

Woven Fabrics

The rather austere feel inspired by Morris's taste for
country-made goods ruled out shop-bought woven
textiles for Arts and Crafts houses. It was only after the
crafts experiments in the Cotswolds in the early 1900s

that any number of people took to the non-professional hand-loom weaving which we now associate so strongly with 'arty-craftiness'.

Morris designed brocades and damasks for his more prestigious commissions, notably St. James's Palace in the 1880s. He also produced 'doublecloths', a complex process in which a thick cloth is produced by means of weaving on two levels at once. The most famous of these patterns is 'Bird'. These heavy cloths were intended for wallhangings, and so are sometimes referred to in Morris and Co. catalogues as 'Tapestries'. Voysey designed 'doublecloths' in silk and wool so that the two textures contrasted. 'Velveteen', a fine cotton velvet described by Sullivan as having 'a tender bloom like cold gravy', was often printed with designs by people like Voysey. 'Utrecht', or stamped velvets, were also popular.

Window draperies were on the whole simple—perhaps a 'Morris' fabric hung on large wooden rings from a thick dark wooden rod.

Wallpapers

As early as the 1860s, writers on interior decoration had been suggesting that walls in hallways and reception rooms should be divided into three distinct areas. Above the skirting board, the dado up to the line of the chair rail was usually papered in embossed 'Lincrusta' paper and then painted. The area of the wall above this and below the picture rail was papered with a patterned paper, and the area above the picture rail and below the cornice was left plain, or sometimes stencilled with a frieze. The ceiling was often papered with a lightly embossed 'Lincrusta', or a lightly patterned paper. From the 1870s onwards many manufacturers produced papers with designs divided up into sections as described above. They were usually in 'Morris colours' with designs often using Japanese motifs.

Carpets

Morris designed a range of expensive hand-knotted rugs which he called 'Hammersmiths' (because he happened to be living in Hammersmith at the time of designing them!). He also designed a machine-woven carpet called 'Lily', which was produced by Axminster. Liberty's sold a range of hand-made 'Donegal' rugs, but the most usual floor covering for the Arts and Crafts home were oriental rugs—these too could be bought from Liberty's.

Opposite: Wandle *block-printed chintz by William Morris, 1884. This example is printed using Madden (red) and Indigo (blue), both traditional natural dyes revived by Morris.*

Right: Two block-printed wallpaper borders. English, c 1870.

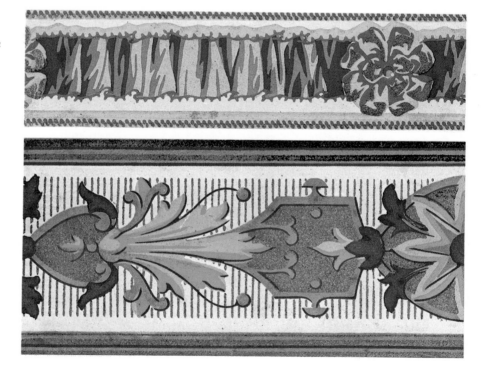

Bullerswood, *hand-knotted woollen carpet. Designed by William Morris, 1880, for Bullerswood House, Chislehurst, Kent.*

Opposite: Jacquard woven cotton and rayon rug designed by Barbara Hepworth in 1937.

The 1930s

The overall 'look' of the 1930s interiors is in direct reaction to the brightly coloured 'Jazz' patterns of the '20s. The so-called 'all white' interior, thought to have been invented by the interior decorator Syrie Maugham (estranged wife of the novelist Somerset Maugham), had great influence on the taste of the period. In the early '30s there was almost no colour to be seen in fashionable interiors; they relied almost entirely on textures to achieve a decorative effect. But if colour was restricted, there was an amazing variety of subtle variations within that restriction. Marion Dorn, perhaps the most famous textile designer of the period, had a colour range especially dyed for her of five hundred different shades (including six shades of white and three of black) to be used in combination with dozens of browns, beiges and greys. Blue, dull orange and red were the only positive colours used to give a decorative accent.

The importance of textiles in the '30s interiors was less in terms of colour than as the one element which tended to soften the effect of otherwise very austere rooms.

Woven Fabrics

Texture was much appreciated in woven fabrics of the 1930s. The combination of different threads—wool, linen, and even the new 'Rayon'—gave an interesting variety. In the years of the 'slump' many fine artists looked towards designing for the applied arts as a source of income. Painters and sculptors like Ben Nicholson and Barbara Hepworth both designed textiles during the period, bringing their own feeling for abstract design to the medium. They were excited by the vast assortment of differently spun and treated fibres which became available in the mid '30s, many of them the results of experiments done in the weaving workshops of the Bauhaus in Germany in the late '20s, and brought to this country by refugee designers when the Bauhaus was closed in 1933.

An authentic-looking 1930s effect can easily be achieved by the use of any off-white or fawn 'slub' fabric, which has an irregular surface. 'Crash', a coarse, plain linen, was a great favourite with the not so well off, as it was cheap, had an appealing texture and came in a variety of off-whites and beiges. The typically square three-piece suites of the period were

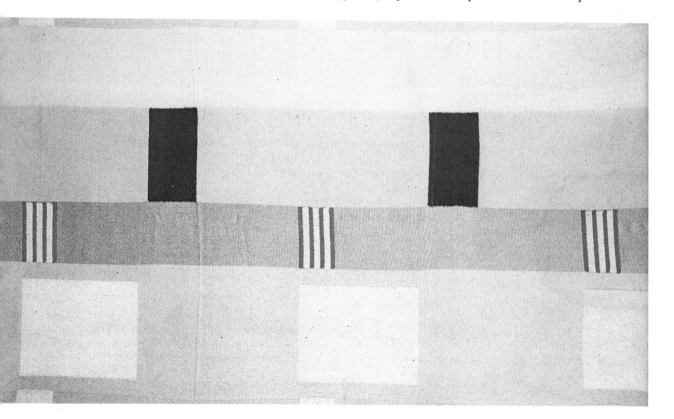

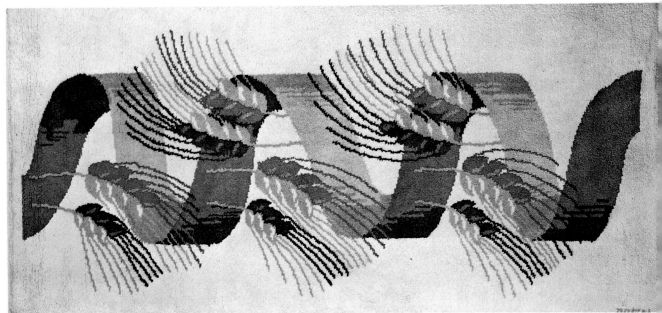

Opposite top : Hand-knotted carpet designed by Ashley Havinden and manufactured by Royal Wilton, 1936.

Opposite below : Hand-knotted rug designed by Marion Dorn and made by Royal Wilton, c 1935.

often given loose covers of crash or off-white linen, the square shape of the furniture further emphasised by the use of dark-brown piping.

Printed Fabrics

Screen printing (the normal technique for printed textile production today) was introduced in the early 1930s and rapidly taken up because of its flexibility and cheapness. Rayon with a mixture of cotton or linen was used effectively for printed fabrics, its satin-like floppy texture being particularly suitable for the sweeping designs of the later '30s. The fabric was also particularly suitable for glamorous Hollywood-style bedrooms !

In the first half of the decade the design was almost entirely restricted to small neat patterns in fawns and greens, or fawns with an occasional touch of red or orange. But by 1938 Marion Dorn had produced a design called 'Langton' in two shades of green with salmon pink and beige on pink; and another called 'Aircraft' in navy, green, yellow and turquoise on natural. These were part of a general move in the late '30s back to pattern and colour.

Curtains were usually hung behind simple plain pelmets, sometimes with a strip light behind the pelmet to highlight the fabric at night.

Carpets

The *sine qua non* of the 1930s drawing room was the hand-knotted rug. Some of the most prestigious were designed by Marion Dorn in the Wessex range for Royal Wilton. They were also produced by other designers for other firms, but if you could not afford to buy one, you could always buy a kit and make one yourself. The patterns were usually abstract and ranged from simple geometric shapes superimposed on one another in a limited range of browns and beiges to huge shaded swirls based on Ionic capitols. The floors beneath these rugs were either highly polished parquet, or fine-pile fitted carpets formed of narrow strips, usually in fawn or occasionally pale grey-blue, or in small geometric patterns.

Wallpapers

In the 1930s it was felt that wallcoverings should form a suitable 'background'. Hence, as with woven fabrics, texture was what was looked for rather than pattern. Ranges of textured papers known unkindly at the time as 'porridges' were produced in tones of beige, cream and oatmeal. Sometimes papers were produced in ranges of different shades intended to be hung horizontally with the lightest tone at the top of the wall, working down to the darkest. Papers were usually produced with borders intended to be placed at the top of the wall or beneath the picture rail. They were usually in darker colours than the paper and came in abstract geometric shapes or conventionalised autumn leaves or flowers. Scenic wallpapers of seascapes with sailing boats, or underwater scenes with fish weaving in and out of coral, were produced for bathrooms.

Bibliography

Aslin, Elizabeth *The Aesthetic Movement* (1968)

Battersby, Martin *The Decorative Thirties* (1970)

Clark, Fiona *William Morris Wallpapers and Chintzes* (1974)

Montgomery, F. M. *Printed Textiles 1700–1850* (1970)

Naylor, Gillian *The Arts and Crafts Movement* (1971)

Oman & Hamilton *Wallpapers* (1982)

Thornton, Peter *Baroque and Rococo Silks* (1965)

Fabrics and Wallpapers

Selecting wallpaper and fabrics is one of the most enjoyable aspects of refurbishing a house. The demand for patterns and colours of the past has greatly stimulated the wallpaper and furnishing textile industries in recent years. As a result, there has never before been a greater profusion of colours, patterns and price ranges to choose from.

The following listings should help you steer a path through the bewildering variety of fabrics and papers now available, whether you are decorating a late 18th century house or jazzing up a 1930s *Moderne* property. See also the listings following the chapter on colour.

Laura Ashley

Bernard Ashley began printing textiles in a small workshop in Pimlico in 1953, using the hand silk-screened method. His wife, Laura, designed small items. By 1975 the firm had shops throughout Great Britain, the Continent, the USA, Canada, and Japan. Designs are small in scale and in mute colours. In addition to printed cottons for curtains and draperies, the company produces table linen, cushion covers, quilted fabrics and wallpapers. There are 33 branches throughout Great Britain.

Laura Ashley
40 Sloane Street
London SW1
Tel: (01) 235 9728

One of the many attractive reproduction chintzes available from Colefax and Fowler.

G P & J Baker

This long established company has an enormous range of glazed chintz, printed cotton, cotton twill, and cotton and linen union. Many of Bakers' designs have combinations of Chinese bird and plant motifs, though not all of the designs have an Eastern inspiration: the 'Provençal' design, for example, is taken from a French 18th century child's bodice.

G P & J Baker
18 Berners Street
London W1
Tel: (01) 636 8412

The Colefax & Fowler Chintz Shop

This elegant shop is an offshoot of the well known Colefax & Fowler interior design partnership founded by John Fowler and Sybil Colefax in 1936. The Colefax & Fowler chintzes are based on original designs of the 18th and early 19th centuries. Specialist services include *trompe-l'œil*, hand-painted furniture and floors, and an exclusive range of painted wood wall lanterns based on mid 18th century originals.

The Colefax & Fowler Chintz Shop
149 Ebury Street
London SW1 9QN
Tel: (01) 730 2173/4
and
Colefax & Fowler (Interior) Design
39 Brook Street
London W1 1AU
Tel: (01) 493 2231

Coles of Mortimer Street

Coles have the Royal Warrant for wallpapers and paints. They have a fine range of traditional hand-blocked wallpapers, and some fabrics. Some of their wallpapers are to the original designs of Owen Jones.

Coles of Mortimer Street
18 Mortimer Street
London W1
Tel: (01) 580 1066

Colour Counsellors

Started in 1970 by Virginia Stourton, Colour Counsellors offer a service which allows customers to choose a co-ordinated colour scheme for fabrics, carpets and wallpapers in their own homes. Following an inquiry by a customer, a Colour Counsellor will visit him or her with the eight 'Black Boxes', each of which contains examples of wallpapers, carpets and fabrics whose tones and patterns will be grouped round a central colour.

Colour Counsellors Ltd
187 King's Road
London SW6
Tel: (01) 736 8326/7

Liberty & Co

Founded in 1875 by the Japanist, Arthur Lazenby Liberty, the shop was originally called East India House and played a significant role in the English Aesthetic Movement. The store is famous for its huge range of printed fabrics, jewellery and rugs. Liberty printed chintzes are 100 per cent cotton with a high satiny glaze and are usually floral in design. Liberty also sell an enormous range of printed floral dress fabrics which, when lined, can have the necessary body for curtains or bed hangings.

Liberty & Co Ltd
Regent Street
London W1R 6AH
Tel: (01) 734 1234

Mrs Monro

Founded 60 years ago, this shop keeps a small but exclusive set of authentic chintzes. These are primarily revivals of 19th century designs using the original patterns such as the 'Bird Dog' collection, a reprint of a Currier & Ives design of 1857. The lower floor of the shop is devoted to small items of antique furniture, porcelain, and prints.

Mrs Monro
11 Montpelier Street
London SW7
Tel: (01) 589 5052

sborne & Little

others-in-law Peter Osborne and
thony Little started this firm in 1968
th the aim of filling a gap that had
veloped in the fine quality wallpaper
rket. They launched an exotic range
hand-prints, many of them based on
signs to be found in the Victoria and
pert Museum and the Cooper-Hewitt
useum of Design in New York. Today
borne & Little offer a huge range of
nd-printed and machine-printed wall-
pers, fabrics, and co-ordinates,
luding the 'Plains' collection of wall-
pers and fabrics which has been
signed to reproduce the brush effects
ated by craftsman painters. It is
ailable in three ranges: stipple, drag,
d marble.

borne & Little Ltd
₄ King's Road
ndon SW3 5UH
l: (01) 352 1456/7/8

display showing the Parrot Tulips *design
om Osborne Little's* Pergola *collection, one of
e company's large range of hand and machine
inted wallpapers, fabrics and co-ordinates.*

uenby Prints

uenby Prints was started in 1980 by
lith de Lisle. It has three ranges of
brics: the 'Edith de Lisle Designs'
llection, composed of modern designs
th a traditional flavour; the 'Gold of
ru' collection, printed using gold
wders which give it a look reminiscent
18th century brocades; and a range of
xpensive co-ordinates.

*A fine bedroom setting incorporating the cotton
fabric from Quenby Prints' recently introduced*
Gold of Peru *range.*

Quenby Prints
86 Baggrave Street
Leicester
LE5 3QT
Tel: (0533) 23056/7

A Sanderson & Sons

Founded by Arthur Sanderson in 1878,
this firm has an enormous selection of
fabrics and wallpapers. Their Perivale
factory currently produces and stocks
four exclusive collections: the 'Heritage'
collection, comprising 113 colourways,
two Sanderson Handprint Collections,
and 'Elite', a collection of 40 screen-
printed metallic foils. Sanderson hold the
entire collection of original William
Morris wallpaper blocks and Morris
papers are still produced using both hand
and machine printing methods. A total of
54 patterns are produced in both original

Sanderson's Pink and Rose *wallpaper. An
1890 design hand printed from the original
wood blocks made by Morris & Co.*

Aldworth by C F A Voysey, from the Sanderson Handprint Collection. It is available in three colourways.

and contemporary colours to cater for all tastes.

Arthur Sanderson & Sons Ltd
53 Berners Street
London W1A 2JE
Tel: (01) 636 7800

Sekers English Country House Collection

Designed by Bernard Neville, former design consultant to Liberty prints, 'The English Country House Collection' reflects the different moods of the English country house during the Victorian, Edwardian and pre-war periods. Using original wooden hand-blocks he has skilfully recreated designs in the traditional style, taking care to achieve the characteristic mis-fitting found in original hand-block printing. There are 14 designs in the collection, each named after a different country house, and each reflecting a different mood and period.

Sekers Ltd
15/19 Cavendish Place
London W1
Tel: (01) 636 2612

Watts & Co

Watts & Co offer a unique collection of Victorian fabrics and wallpapers for domestic use. The wallpapers are printed in the traditional way, using the original pear wood blocks, some of which are over 100 years old. Each colour is blocked on to the paper by hand and allowed to dry naturally before the next blocking can start, thus giving each paper its own individual character which varies slightly from craftsman to craftsman. Many of the fabrics in Watts' collection were designed by the founders of the company, Bodley, Garner and Scott. Colours conform as closely as possible to the original, but fabrics can be specially woven in any chosen colour. The design

Bernard Nevill's Earlywood *design from* Sekers *English Country House* range, *available in cotton Ottoman and chintz.*

Pugin Pineapple *wallpaper from Watts & Co.*

Bodley, *also from Watts & Co., used in the restoration of the Old Union Bank, Tasmania.*

and production of fine silverware and needlework, and a comprehensive restoration service, are also undertaken by Watts & Co.

Watts & Co Ltd
7 Tufton Street
Westminster
London SW1 3QB
Tel: (01) 222 7169

Architectural Salvage

House owners are increasingly rejecting the boring designs of post war 'box-style' estate houses in favour of the detail in older homes. The good proportions and interesting decoration and craftsmanship that went into the construction of older properties are a welcome relief from the modern mass-produced monotonies.

Somehow there is a lasting attraction in the exquisitely detailed Georgian, Victorian and Edwardian buildings and in the lively visual interest of the 1920s and '30s properties. Their individuality has become important and respected in an age of so much poor planning and impersonal design. And with this renewed interest many owners of older houses are now eager to restore them to their original architectural glory.

Unfortunately many otherwise fine houses have been deprived of their original interest by the removal or alteration of architectural details and decorative features. Sometimes the effects of these losses can be devastating, not only to the house, but to the rest of the terrace or surrounding environment too.

Much of the mutilation is the result of misguided, haphazard modernisation and improvement over the years. Additionally, areas affected by general wear and tear have been repaired with no regard to original styles.

But happily, most badly 'modernised' houses can be refreshingly brought back to life. An 1820s terraced house I know of had its modern casement windows replaced by sash windows of original design. The owner then put in an original delicate fanlight, panelled front door and cast-iron railings. The effects were pleasing to the eye and uplifting to the general character of the area. In this chapter we will look at the various methods of undertaking a sympathetic restoration which will improve, and indeed enhance, the value of the property.

One of the finest ways to put back the character of a house is in the correct use of salvaged features such as Georgian fanlights and doors—'correct' being the operative word. A Regency doorway put into a 1920s house is as damaging as a poor alteration or modernisation.

In the last ten years there has been a growing market in rescued period details. These come mainly from demolition sites and include Victorian stained glass, decorative doors, windows and fireplaces. Many firms now specialise in this field. At the end of the chapter there is a comprehensive list of these and other firms involved in restoration, and of advisory services.

The restoration of a house can be an interesting, enjoyable, and, in the end, profitable exercise for the owner. Many aspects of 'getting it right' may be expensive but are thoroughly worthwhile.

Discovering the Lost Style

Finding out the original designs of the missing details, especially external ironwork doors, windows, bargeboards and roof finials is a most important stage of a sympathetic restoration. These components are vital to the overall design of a house and greatly affect its appearance. Proper research should be undertaken before any work begins.

Depending on your situation there are several ways of tackling this problem. If your house is in a terrace or road where all of the houses were built about the same time (and this is almost certainly the case with terrace houses), you should examine a well preserved neighbouring house. Make sure that what you are looking at is contemporary to the build of the house, not a later addition. The glazing pattern of windows, door panelling arrangements and ironwork types usually provide the necessary clues. If any doubts remain, however, you should consult your local museum or library. They might have early prints, watercolours or photographs showing you how it looked before it was altered. Old estate agents' details, where they exist, can be helpful too. Failing this, you can always consult the advice of a specialist (see list at end of chapter). Only when a clear idea of these facts has been established can and should you set about finding original details, or having replacement features made.

How to Find Architectural Features

There are three basic ways of finding the panelled front door, window balcony, fireplace and other features you may require for your period restoration.

One of the cheapest and most interesting methods is to approach some of your local demolition contractors (they will be listed in the Yellow Pages) and enquire about work they might have in hand. The success of this method depends on the contractor. Some will only be too pleased to help, and will sell you the odd door or fireplace from a house they are demolishing, while others will have strict time limits to finish their work. Try and arrange a visit to the site with the foreman and have a good look around. It is surprising what you might find. You may even pick up small fittings like porcelain finger plates and decorative shelf brackets.

When you agree a price for items of interest you may be asked if you are removing the material yourself from the building. Providing the site is safe this is always worth attempting, especially in the case

of delicate items like fanlights, marble chimney pieces etc. If you can do it yourself it will possibly make the price more reasonable. Do not forget, though, that extracting something like a marble chimney piece requires a certain amount of knowledge and muscle, and it might be worth calling on a friend or someone who has some experience in this field. There will be situations where for safety reasons there will be no question of you removing the material yourself.

In that case a realistic price should be negotiated for the careful removal of objects from the structure in the contractor's time.

Some contractors have yards in which they store salvaged material, including decorative elements from demolished buildings. These sorts of places are always worth visiting, even if the contractor seems vague about his stock. You might well find a Georgian front door buried behind piles of modern joinery.

But if you cannot find the items you require from this source then it is worth approaching some of the firms engaged in architectural salvage. Prices vary considerably, depending on the age and design of the object. Movement of stock makes inventories hard to keep up to date, so a visit is the best answer.

Many items, like decorative ironwork and lead fanlights, are now almost impossible to acquire and

A selection of architectural ironwork salvaged from demolished buildings or salvage yards and now stocked by House of Steel Antiques (see page 169).

the only option open to restorers is often to have original designs copied by specialist firms using traditional methods.

Ironwork

The house that has lost its front railings and balconies, probably in the scrap drive of the last war, is quite a common case but fortunately there are various companies specialising in modern copies.

Sometimes you will find it hard to locate ironwork of the correct period or dimensions, and here it would be best to approach a specialist foundry. Iron fittings are often covered in many layers of paint, obscuring the original design details. Traditional paint stripping methods are time consuming in the extreme and are not always very effective so it is advisable to have the ironwork shot-blasted and primed for painting. The fixing of railing and other external features requires specialist expertise to be called in.

Doors

Doors of all periods and designs can be found on demolition sites. Firms engaged in reconditioning older property are often worth approaching as they are responsible for removing fittings in many of these schemes.

The front door fanlight or surrounding decorative sidelights are a very important feature and great care should be taken when choosing a replacement. Once again, it may prove impossible to find early nineteenth-century lead fanlights and the only answer is to have them made up by experts. Victorian and Edwardian etched stained and coloured glass doors are more numerous, and several salvage firms in Britain have a wide selection. Damaged leaded panels in front doors can be repaired by firms listed at the end of the chapter. Door furniture, architraves, dado rails, picture rails and skirting boards can all be obtained from sources I have already mentioned. If a design is hard to find then a profile can be taken with a profile comb and some joinery firms will make sections in the required pattern.

Cast-iron door knockers and letter plates, coated in paint, are best cleaned by soaking in caustic soda. This method does not damage the metal in any way.

Woodwork was not generally left in its natural state in the past, although there are notable exceptions including varnished pine and polished oak. When

Top: Bow latch from the bedroom door of a semi-detached villa c 1815 in Reigate, Surrey.

Above: Draw-back lock with sliding latch rescued from the front door of West Strand Improvements in London and designed by John Nash 1831–2. Draw-back locks were the main type of front-door locks used in the late eighteenth century and for most of the nineteenth century. There were several variations and some were quite large.

Below: Two bell pulls of the 1870s–1880s.

Left: Carved pine brackets from a doorway in Great Titchfield Street, London, built c 1793, showing the amount of detail that can be lost under successive coats of paint. These brackets were not carved from one piece of wood, and the small scrolls at the side are also separate pieces glued on. Great care must be taken when stripping paint, as water-based strippers can dissolve old glues.

Opposite: Two carved limewood rams' heads, shown before and after removal of paint. Salvaged from 51 Portland Place, London, which was built by Adam Helam in 1785.

Brass letter plate from basement servant entrance of a large c 1860s–1870s house in Queensbury Place, London. This letter plate has been half-stripped of its many coats of paint and restored to its original burnished relief lettering and decorative borders, illustrating again the detail so often lost under layers of accumulated paint.

stripping paintwork it is a good idea to examine the original finish. Traces of varnish can nearly always be detected, as can the odd lead primer, which indicates that it was painted by earlier owners. Whatever you do, resist the temptation to strip woodwork in caustic soda tanks as this takes out the natural oils too, and opens up the joints.

People with houses of the 1920s and '30s who are having problems with Crittall steel-framed doors due to corrosion can now largely overcome the problem. Crittall are manufacturing some parts and units to the original designs. Other firms also re-make steel casements to original glazing patterns.

Windows

It is very often hard to locate windows of the correct period and dimensions when you are renovating a building where several windows are required for the façade. A friend of mine was fortunate enough to acquire a set of three typical 1860s four panel sash windows, exactly the right size, from an identical neighbouring house which was being demolished. But he was lucky—you would probably be better off having your windows made up by a joiner rather than waiting until the size you need becomes available locally.

For window shutters, and window ironmongery, it is again worth approaching a demolition company or salvage firm. Perhaps surprisingly, early glass often survives in windows of all types of buildings and it is worth salvaging, especially if it is Crown glass. Old glass can be cut from frames and used to fine effect. Crown glass should only be used in buildings up to the 1850s. Many Victorian and Edwardian buildings have larger panes of glass which retain that pleasant, reflecting and slightly undulating surface, so different from that of modern glass which is completely flat.

The same should be said for the typical acid-etched patterned glass and those amber, deep blue and ruby red panes so often used in landing and hall windows. If you want to find leaded-light stained glass and other types of decorative window, the sources mentioned earlier should be able to help you.

Whenever possible, retain the original joinery. You would be surprised how much a skilled joiner can repair. Once again, it is worth contacting Crittalls when you have problems with metal windows.

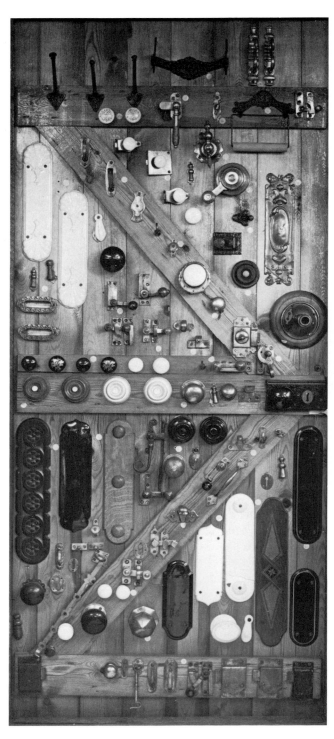

Door furniture of the 1850–1914 period salvaged from demolished buildings in London and Guildford. Preserved for the Brooking Collection (see page 168).

Other External Decorative Details

The decorative features on the roofs of houses are often missing. Terracotta ridge tiles, chimney pots, finials, cast-iron crestings, ornamental hopper heads and shaped roof tiles and slates, all become victims of time. But if you are prepared to wait a little you should be able to find replacements through a salvage company.

Edwardian porch on a house up for demolition in Guildford.

Ornamental bargeboards and decorative porches, such as the typical Victorian and Edwardian type, with their turned supports and balusters, may be possible to find but it is unlikely they will be of the design you need to match. Whether you use designs that are different from the original depends entirely on the situation. If you have a terraced house or semi-detached villa, with porches and bargeboards of the same pattern, this departure would matter. On the other hand, where designs vary from house to house, there is less harm in departing from the original design.

Patterned bricks and tiles and geometrically tiled hall and porch floors were popular in the second half of the nineteenth century. But it is not easy to find replacements now and the specialist manufacturing of broken and missing parts is frequently the only answer.

Interior Features

Staircase handrails and balusters are normally fairly easy to find, including the cast-iron type that became more common after 1840. In the case of one or two turned wood balusters that are broken or missing, these can be remade by a good wood turner.

The decorative plaster brackets of various designs that grace many nineteenth-century hall arches can be found quite easily in houses of the period scheduled for

demolition. The layers of white distemper covering them can be washed away using a soft brush and warm water, taking great care for often they are very brittle. Plaster ceiling roses and cornices can sometimes be salvaged too, if originally made up in sections. Some later examples were however made of *papier mâché*, and screwed through the plaster to the joists.

Fireplaces

There is a wider choice of period fireplaces. Designs often varied slightly from room to room. The best way to discover what your fireplace originally looked like is to examine the interior of a well preserved house of the same age and design (if one exists) near your own. A friendly neighbour is a real bonus here.

The sad demolition and gutting of houses is providing a glut of all types of fireplaces. Most end up in a salvage firm's yard, or in a shop specialising in these items. Whenever you are in doubt over an original design, take advice from a specialist.

The fixing of marble chimney pieces is more difficult than it would at first appear. It is best to contact a builder who is well versed in the subject, or a specialist fireplace firm.

If your late Victorian or Edwardian tiled fireplace interior is damaged beyond repair there are some very fine examples lying around in yards.

Above left: Two carved-mahogany handrails with cast-iron newel posts from large terraced houses in Cromwell Road, London, c 1878. Cast-iron newel posts, although appearing in the late eighteenth century, did not become widely used until the 1830s–40s, when many designs were produced. They remained very popular until the 1880s. Some designs are very common and were made in different sizes for all types of property.

Left: Copper light-switch plate with Art Nouveau *decoration from West Mount in Guildford, c 1900–8.*

Architectural Salvage

Salvage yards are the graveyards of architecture, but the fact that there is now a ready market for such items is an encouraging sign that traditional building craftsmanship is once again valued by the young. Compiled by one of Britain's leading experts on the subject, the following pages list the major suppliers of architectural salvage in Britain. Look through these for everything, from runs of antique tiles to stained glass front doors.

The Brooking Collection

This museum and information centre of architectural features covers the period 1700–1935 and has large selections of architraves, mouldings, windows, doors, fireplaces, ironmongery and other features of known date. These details can be examined, and advice and technical information will be given to those seeking to carry out accurate restorations of buildings. The dating of buildings and alterations to the same are undertaken.

The Brooking Collection
Woodhay
White Lane
Guildford
Surrey
Tel: (0483) 504555/68686

Architectural Heritage of Cheltenham

Architectural Heritage supply period English and Continental architectural pieces to private and professional people converting and restoring houses, hotels, restaurants and shops. The range of items that Heritage can supply includes: period oak, polished mahogany and stripped pine internal doors; solid studded oak, panelled, lead glazed and stained glass external doors; fine period and fielded panelling in oak, mahogany, and pine; fire surrounds; balustrading; carved wood cornices; decorated columns; Victorian shop and pub interiors;

Victorian pub interior from Architectural Heritage of Cheltenham, who are also pleased to help with less ambitious projects.

stained, etched and cut glass; lead and cast iron hoppers; and much more.

Architectural Heritage of Cheltenham
Boddington Manor
Boddington
nr Cheltenham
Gloucestershire
Tel: (024 268) 741
    (0242) 22191

Architectural Salvage

This is a register service. People wishing to sell materials are put on a register which is published in the *Architects' Journal* for a fee which depends upon the price wanted for the item. The same applies for a 'wanted' advertisement. Interesting items are always on offer, ranging from balconies to bell pulls.

Architectural Salvage
Hutton and Rostron
Netley House
Gomshall
nr Guildford
Surrey GU5 9QA
Tel: (048 641) 3221

Crittall Windows

Crittalls were the leading manufacturer of steel doors and windows in the 1920s and '30s. They now manufacture some replacement parts to the original designs and offer advice on all aspects of repair and replacement of steel doors and windows.

Crittall Windows Ltd
Manor Works
Braintree
Essex CM7 6DF
Tel: (0376) 24106

T Crowther & Son

This long established family business, founded *c.* 1882, operates from a large late Georgian building with extensive showrooms of fine Georgian furniture, carved wood and marble chimney pieces with metalwork accessories. They also stock oak and pine room panelling and

The main courtyard of T. Crowther showing their range of statuary and ornaments.

have a large joinery works on hand to adapt it to suit clients' requirements, and to install it if necessary. Alternatively they can produce a complete room made from old timber in any style and with either carved or plain mouldings.

T Crowther & Son Ltd
282 North End Road
Fulham
London SW6 1NH
Tel: (01) 385 1375/7

Crowther of Syon Lodge

Founded by Bert Crowther in 1929, Crowther of Syon Lodge occupy elegant Georgian premises, originally built by the Adam brothers in the 1770s, at Busch Corner in Isleworth. Today Derek Crowther directs a skilled team of restorers and knowledgeable sales staff in the constant pursuit of items of interest. The restoration team, consisting of carpenters and stonemasons, works on the acquisitions which comprise the five divisions of the company's present interests—panelled rooms, chimney pieces, marble and bronze statuary, wrought iron gates, and garden ornaments. Prices range from about £100 to £60,000.

One of a fine pair of 19th century carved stone chimney pieces from Millcorne House, once the family seat of the Drummonds of Blair Drummond. A superb item from Crowthers of Syon Lodge.

Crowther of Syon Lodge
Busch Corner
London Road
Isleworth
Middlesex TW7 5BH
Tel: (01) 560 7978/7985

N J A Gifford-Mead

Gifford-Mead hold a rapidly changing stock of coloured and stained glass windows, Victorian fireplaces, etc. The firm specialises in stained glass front doors.

N J A Gifford-Mead
The Furniture Cave
533 King's Road London SW10
Tel: (01) 352 9904

Glover and Stacey

Dealing mainly with the public, Glover and Stacey specialise in period doors, both exterior and interior, such as Georgian front doors, French doors, carved door surrounds, fanlights, etc. Also in stock are large amounts of scrap oak, turned balusters and handrails. The emphasis of the stock is on the more simple, functional period items.

Glover and Stacey
Malt House Bungalow
Kingsley
nr Bordon
Hampshire
Tel: (0402 03) 5754

Goddard and Gibbs Studios

Founded in 1868, the Goddard and Gibbs Studios at Shoreditch are the biggest firm of their kind in Britain, if not Europe. Engaged in the design, making and restoration of stained glass and decorative windows for religious and secular

A typical example of heraldic stained glass, produced by Goddard and Gibbs' ancient processes of staining, painting and firing handmade 'Antique' glass.

buildings at home and overseas, the studios also specialise in modern glass techniques such as Dalle-de-Verre and glass applique. Examples of Goddard and Gibbs' best work can be seen at Westminster Abbey, Westminster and St Paul's Cathedrals, the Houses of Parliament, and Windsor Castle. Potential customers are encouraged to visit the Studios to see the craftsmen at work on the many processes involved in current projects.

Goddard and Gibbs Studios
41–49 Kingsland Road
Shoreditch
London E2 8AD
Tel: (01) 739 6563

Hale Farm Building Materials

All types of windows, doors, fireplaces, ironwork, architraves, handrails, balusters, and stained and coloured glass are stocked. There is also a good selection of door furniture. Prices are reasonable.

Hale Farm Building Materials
32 Guildford Road
Farnham
Surrey
Tel: (0252) 726484

House of Steel Antiques

House of Steel have 5,000 square feet of warehousing, showrooms and workshops where a complete restoration service for their own and customers' items is

An unusual cabinet constructed of cast iron and marble. The fine decorative work has been carefully restored by House of Steel's workshop.

provided. Their stock covers every aspect of architectural salvage with some special items such as original ship's gear, pub fittings, hand carved and painted signs, working London traffic lights and Victorian post boxes.

House of Steel Antiques
400 Caledonian Road
Islington
London N1 1DN
Tel: (01) 607 5889

The London Architectural Salvage and Supply Co

This company stocks a very large selection of all kinds of architectural items. The stock changes rapidly and covers every conceivable aspect of architectural salvage, including shop fittings, balustrading, masonry and timber. The firm also undertakes conversion, extension, modification, repair and installation to stock items, through their own workshops and through recommended associate tradesmen.

The London Architectural Salvage and Supply Co Ltd
Mark Street (off Paul Street)
London EC2A 4ER
Tel: (01) 739 0448/9

Mimram Stained Glass Studio

This firm will replace any kind of stained glass detailing, from large scale windows to missing panels from Edwardian doors. The colours are lovely and the standards of craftsmanship high.

Mimram Stained Glass Studio
Digswell House

Monks Rise
Welwyn Garden City
Hertfordshire
Tel: (0707) 26169

The Old Maw Tileworks

The Old Maw Tileworks can reproduce many old Maw tile designs for fireplace, wall, and floor tiles.

The Old Maw Tileworks
Jackfield
Shropshire
Tel: (0952) 882030

Solopark

Solopark specialise in supplying reclaimed building materials. Their comprehensive range of stock, covering three acres, includes bricks, roofing tiles and slates, timber, joinery items, and steel.

Solopark Ltd
The Old Railway Station
Station Road
nr Pampisford
Cambridgeshire
Tel: (0223) 834663

Townsends

Started on a market stall by Matt Townsend ten years ago, Townsends now have two shops in St John's Wood. At No 1 Church Street they have a constantly changing stock of 2,000–3,000 original Victorian tiles, which are priced individually and sell from £2–£6 on average. These include older 18th century and Delft examples. They also carry a stock of 200–300 Victorian stained glass windows. Their other shop

specialises in stripped pine fireplaces, cast iron stoves and fireplaces, stained glass doors and other architectural items. Period fireplace accessories are also stocked, and there is a stained glass repair service.

Townsends
1 Church Street
London NW8
Tel: (01) 724 3746
and
81 Abbey Road
London NW8
Tel: (01) 624 4756

Walcot Reclamation

Walcot Reclamation stock a wide range of traditional building materials divided into three basic categories. Firstly, there are 'volume' materials: pennant paving, Bath stone ashlar, Welsh slates, ridging and chimney pots, pine and wood block flooring, etc. Secondly, there is a large stock of period bathroom fittings, Victorian baths, taps, sinks, etc. Thirdly, Walcot Reclamation have a range of upwards of 600 doors arranged by type and size, Georgian six-panel doors being a speciality, and also an enormous collection of period fireplaces. Woodwork and ironwork restoration is also a speciality.

Walcot Reclamation
108 Walcot Street
Bath, Avon
BA1 5BG
Tel: (0225) 310182

Whiteway and Waldron

Decorative ironwork, doors, architraves, skirting, fireplaces, staircases, balusters, flooring, door furniture, and stained glass are available. The firm specialises in the restoration of stained glass and can also restore leaded lights; painted panels typical in late Victorian work can be made up. There is also a section entirely devoted to pine doors, cupboard doors, architraves and old pine timber for constructors of old pine kitchens.

Whiteway and Waldron Ltd
305 Munster Road
London SW6 6BJ
Tel: (01) 381 3195

A photograph of Townsend's Church Street premises which gives a good idea of their wide and rapidly changing stock of Victorian tiles, cast iron stoves, fireplaces, stained glass and other architectural items.

Garden Furniture

The small town garden is something which the natives of many European cities envy the British: invariably used as a kind of extra, outdoor room it offers possibilities far beyond the tiny terrace or window box that a Parisian, for example, has to be content with.

These back gardens, reminders of the fact that medieval town houses had generous strips of ground attached, became smaller as the pressure on land became greater in the eighteenth and nineteenth centuries but lack of dimensions does not seem to have proved discouraging. Most back gardens doubled as serviceable yards and as a spot in which to grow a few plants—often in most inhospitable conditions, short of light and with a heavily polluted atmosphere. Detached and semi-detached villas made much of their gardens, emphasising formality in the front garden, with a more haphazard approach to the private garden behind. At all the periods dealt with in this chapter some kind of furnishing was thought suitable—both practical objects such as cisterns or planters, seats and benches, and the more purely decorative statues and other ornamental touches.

As the great gardens developed styles of the period in question, as much through their furnishings as their plants, so the small urban garden followed suit—remarkably, considering the obstacles which stood, and still stand, between making a dingy, undernourished patch into a tempting place in which to sit, eat and pass a few minutes in discreet self-congratulation.

Eighteenth-Century Terraced House

While subsequent periods offer a wide range of literature full of hints to the town gardener, the uses and

A lead cistern of a type which provided a handy source of rainwater in a small garden as well as being extremely decorative in its own right. As in this case, such cisterns are usually dated.

*Variants upon the urn and vase, shown
above, were mass-produced in Coade stone
(a kind of composition stone) in the late
eighteenth and early nineteenth century,
often derived from Classical prototypes.
The elaborate stone bench (top left), again
Classical in inspiration, is at the furthest
extreme from the delicate Regency ironwork
bench (left), made of ribbon-like strands
of metal and elaborated by a foot rest for
the weary gardener.*

Above: Eighteenth-century lead vase.

Left: A rather grand early eighteenth-century garden at Mapperton, Beaminster in Dorset. Gardens such as these provide superb examples of authentic features, which can be modified to suit a more modest garden.

arrangement of the individual back garden within the Georgian speculative development must have been various, according to plot size and the social status of the occupant. Certainly the gardens of such housing did not emulate the parks of the landed gentry, dotted with statues depicting Flora, Diana or other suitable deities or mythological beings. For the small garden a small faun was quite sufficient, and with the production of Coade stone figures, there was a wide demand for such ornament. Within a limited space a careful line had to be trodden between the practical and decorative. On the Grosvenor Estate (*Survey of London* Volume 39, part I (1977)) a garden on Grosvenor Street contained a Doric-style alcove, complete with panelled, wainscotted and seated interior, and paved in Portland stone.

Cisterns, often in lead, were the one item which perfectly fulfilled both practical and ornamental requirements, and few gardens with any pretensions toward horticulture could have been without one. Certainly Mrs. Delany's garden, also on the Grosvenor Estate, which was, she reckoned, the size of her sister's parlour in Gloucestershire, held a fine range of blooms, though her philaria were 'some dead, some alive'. Vases were another combination of the attractive and the expedient. It was much easier to tend plants, and keep them weed-free, and they could be moved around and taken under cover if the climate threatened them. Urns of classical form (including Coade stone replicas of the Borghese, Albani, Warwick and other great antique vases) were suitable for even the smallest gardens, together with terracotta or lead planters. Urns were lidded and so took a purely ornamental function, surmounting walls or balustrades. Formality, echoing the symmetry of the house itself, was the key-note to such gardens.

Trellising along the walls or, a reminder of earlier practices, espaliered fruit trees, helped to emphasise this trim and neat approach to horticulture. The walls were often substantial and sometimes offered an alcove in which a bench could be placed. Here again Classical prototypes, made in artificial stone, were popular in the later years of the eighteenth century while a few years on, the slim ironwork Regency seat, sometimes with a foot-rest, took its place. Sundials were popular, usually free-standing and placed symmetrically at the focal point of the garden. Simplicity and clarity were the aims, and hence the style of the garden which echoes it today has to be governed by the same criteria.

The Victorian Terraced House

It was the Victorian garden which exploited the possibilities of garden furniture and ornament to the furthest extreme. In reaction to the sparse and orderly arrangement favoured in the eighteenth century,

Shirley Hibberd, writing in *Rustic Adornments for Homes of Taste* (1856), considered that embellishment, however small, 'will offer more and more to interest the eye and occasion pleasurable emotions in the mind'. For the Victorian garden writers it was not the practical or the functional that mattered, but pleasing vistas and uplifting sensations. To that end garden furniture was rustic, either of unbarked branches or elaborate wrought iron (itself often emulating the branches), and generally rather uncomfortable. Presumably the Victorian lady carried cushions which could deal with the skirmishes of sharpened twigs or knobs of iron long before they reached the flesh. Charles McIntosh's *Book of the Garden* (1853) listed variations of types of seating, including folding types which may be carried from 'place to place, even by ladies who may wish to avoid the sun or enjoy a fresh object or views'. The gardens of houses that Hibberd called 'hump-backed town houses' must have offered less scope for such wanderings, but then 'the smallest plot may be so ornamented as to convey an impression of luxurious completeness'. With the seating, which took the motifs of such favourite Victorian plants as ferns, brambles and vines, came tables and stools, trellising, arbours and a vast range of statues and plant-holders, in particular the elaborate cascades of metalwork *jardinières*. J. C. Loudon's lists of garden furniture in his

The Victorian mass-manufacturer touched the garden as he did every other corner of the house. This fern-leaf bench was one of a number of favourite patterns for cast-iron garden furniture, designed more for ornament than for comfort. It was recommended that cushions be carried on a walk into the garden. The fern was perhaps the most appropriate of all the plant patterns, for the plant proliferated in the Victorian house. Where there was a conservatory, it achieved especially favoured status.

The sundial, as seen here at the Court, Holt, in Norfolk, is a useful object around which to plan the axes of a garden. Although shown here in a large, rather informal garden, the sundial was prescribed as an important element in town gardens for all periods—regardless of whether the sun ever fell upon it and thus whether it had any useful function as a time-keeper. Sundials on a wide variety of pedestals were available. Here, a Classical baluster-form serves as an elegant support.

Encyclopaedia (1834) includes 'stone or cast iron mushrooms, painted or covered with moss, or mat, or heath'. The considerable discomfort must have been masked by the Victorian ladies' outdoor dress. Loudon suggested an 'elegant structure of iron rods, wire and painted canvas' in mushroom or Turkish tent form, and he even included mention of swings and see-saws. Sundials were popular according to McIntosh (but are better when placed in the sun, he adds—rather unnecessarily, one might think). There are some 'pretended connoisseurs', he says, 'who object to statuary altogether, unless clothed with more than a fig-leaf . . . we may answer "honi soit qui mal y pense."'

There was a vast range of ornament for the Victorian town garden: statues, vases (of cast iron, ceramics, imitation marble or bronze, or artificial stone), and furniture of every conceivable form and shape. It must have been difficult at times to move around the garden at all, and much of the advice offered indicates that it was in any case thought of largely as an outdoor room. Indeed McIntosh suggests it should be either entirely portable or entirely glazed over.

The density of furnishings within the house is echoed in the garden. Anyone seeking to reproduce such an atmosphere today would probably opt for a modified version, relying on the wide range of reproductions of the iron furniture of the time and perhaps omitting the Minton, Doulton or Copeland vases, statues and tazzas, in order to include a modicum of vegetation.

Right: A simple wooden garden bench at Polesden Lacey, Surrey, facing out over a splendid landscape. In a smaller Edwardian garden, the view would more likely be inward—perhaps down a vista or along the length of an herbaceous border. Garden furniture at this period emphasised the simplicity of objects customarily used by country people, the first stirrings of a conscious attempt to record the vanishing artefacts of the countryside. This led to a reaction against the manufactured items of the Victorian period, and against the mechanistic processes and unsympathetic materials of that era. Iron was displaced by wood: ceramics by terracotta.

The Arts and Crafts House

For the Arts and Crafts gardener the attitude towards garden furniture and knick-knacks was quite simple: as Charles Thonger, in his *A Book of Garden Furniture* (1903) put it, 'the less of it the better'. What was chosen should be 'good of its kind, simple and artistic in construction', for the watchwords were utility and

That most Victorian appendage to the house, the conservatory—here at Wallington in Northumberland. Here are terracotta urns, a portrait bust upon a pedestal, and a pair of iron folding chairs, as well as an ingenious mobile garden seat.

congruity. The garden writers were in retreat from the preceding half century of contorted ironwork and self-consciously rustic furniture. William Robinson, high priest of all that was least contrived in gardening, had said 'it is rare to see a garden seat that is not an eye-sore', and thus the simple wooden furniture of the 1890s and early 1900s substituted the 'supreme discomfort' of the rustic garden seat for plain oak or elm seats, with panelled backs. Sometimes they were semi-circular, sometimes they encircled the great trunks of mature trees. A summer house, similarly constructed in the plainest style, was a recommended feature, if for nothing else, as one author suggested, as a place to which to banish the children.

Arches, trelliswork and, of course, the ubiquitous

The carefully measured mix of the informal and the formal is the mark of Sissinghurst garden in Kent, which has its roots in the Edwardian garden revolution begun by Gertrude Jekyll. The paving, with planting between and the low planter as centrepiece, typify that perfect balance between the planned and unplanned aspect of the garden.

pergola were part of the Arts and Crafts garden in its later manifestations, under the influence of Gertrude Jekyll, but these were confined to the extremities or excluded altogether in the smaller scale garden. The sundial produced no such problem of space. It was important to place it correctly, certainly not in 'the exact centre of a microscopic grass plot' as Thonger had seen it once 'in a villa garden of my acquaintance'. It was not comfortable in the villa strip or methodically arranged suburban plot, he felt, but was ideal for a small enclosure or as an eye-catcher at the end of a walk. Manufacturers produced a wide range, including a classical type based on a simple column or baluster, or in more elaborate shapes, twisted or ornamented. As at other periods, the use of 'portable receptacles for containing shrubs and flowering plants had much to recommend it, and comparatively uninteresting gardens may be much improved by

their judicious employment'. Terracotta was the favoured material for such planters.

The visual sources for the furnishings of the Arts and Crafts garden were those suggested by the cottage garden: the wooden butt to catch rainwater, the stone sink filled with a few rock plants, the trelliswork porch (perhaps echoed in the form of the summer house), and the wooden bench which country people usually placed inside the porch. The grand effects offered by changes of level, terracing, the play of water and gardens within gardens, were not available to the owner of a quarter acre. But the use of dense planting, parting to reveal a simple curved oak seat or a walk between herbaceous beds to the sundial beyond, echoed the ideas of Jekyll and Lutyens, and were available tricks to the owner of all but the very smallest garden. The furniture played its part, but a subsidiary one.

Revolving timber garden hut of a type that is well suited to the garden of both Edwardian and later periods. French windows allow the hut to be weather-proof, yet light and open to the sun.

The 1930s House or Flat

For a 1930s villa, detached or semi-detached, the *Daily Express* publication *The Home of Today* (n.d.) offered guidance of a firm and authoritative sort. They counselled that 'even the cultivated backyard or miniature grass plot will look better for the presence of a suitable seat or a bird bath and—in some instances—a statuette'. Regarding position, the authors suggested that 'garden furniture should be placed with care, in such a manner as to make it harmonious to its environment'. Wooden seats could be moved around, allowing respite to different patches of lawn in turn. Stone or cement seats, if used, should be built when the garden was being planned. More seasonal were 'gaily painted deck and other kinds of canvas chairs', which would 'lend a colourful note to the garden in warm weather and provide restful accommodation. Canvas hammocks slung on wooden stands are also a feature of the modern garden'. Even a small garden could contain a summer house; ideally it would be thatched and weather-boarded. The inside could be enlivened by the addition of decorative canvas. A revolving summer house would allow for best use of sunshine or shade, as desired.

Bird baths were suggested as both a necessity and an ornament. A salutary note warns owners to add a piece of stone if the bath is on the deep side to give the birds a perch, 'otherwise they are liable to drown'. For 'garden figures', the watchword was to be sparing: great care should be taken not to have too many, as it is the individuality of one or two that adds to the charm of the garden'. It is not hard to imagine the kind of over-crowded arrangement the writers had in mind.

There was really only one item on which this *Daily Express* publication agreed with the contemporary books by more artistic specialists, and that was the sundial. It generally appeared placed formally in the exact centre, surrounded by, and at a respectful distance from, a few carefully sited tubs or vases. As the *Studio* special number, *Modern Gardens* (1926–7) made clear, a small garden offered 'perfection of detail

. . . that the scale of a larger one might make impossible'.

Whether the house was crisply neo-Georgian, or something more continental with flat roof and modernist leanings, a sculptural rather than horticultural emphasis was evident. Only the survivals from the turn of the century could treat the hard landscaping and furnishings as secondary. Paving was much used, sometimes geometrically patterned, and water played an important part in the form of small pools or even as wall fountains. One publication featured an immaculate tiny town garden, floored in white marble and with a *trompe-l'œil* perspective trellis on the end wall. For the modern white-washed house, whitened concrete tubs containing dwarf cypresses were *de rigueur*. For a flat, when the space was limited to patio, balcony or, unusually, a roof garden, advice pointed to metal furniture (tubular steel designs which doubled for indoor use) or canvas deck chairs in clear bright colours, which could be stacked neatly away when not in use. For a brief period, the delights of living on the roof were much in vogue, at least in the sales literature, but for the English, beleaguered by an utterly unpredictable climate, roof gardening never developed very far. The 1930s garden, furniture and all, was—despite all the options—much more at home on the ground.

Garden Furniture

Even in a town house with a tiny yard, it is possible to have an attractive and refreshing garden space in which you can relax during the summer and which you can enjoy throughout the year. The following list gives suppliers of Classic garden furniture for period houses. Although it is unlikely that anyone would have used an inner-urban yard as a garden during the 18th and 19th centuries, there is no reason today why this tiny and often scruffy space should not have the fresh charm of its suburban and country cousins.

Barlow Tyrie
Barlow Tyrie manufacture the 'Braintree' range of traditional and functional teak seats and benches. Matching benches and tables are available.

Barlow Tyrie Ltd
Springwood Industrial Estate
Rayne Road
Braintree
Essex CM7 7RN
Tel: (0376) 22505

Chilstone Garden Ornaments
This firm is well known for its range of handmade reproduction garden ornaments such as obelisks, benches, statues, urns and vases. They even produce a wooden and stone dovecot. Items are made in reconstituted stone, in a colour between Portland and Bath stone, although various shades can be produced to blend with existing architecture. Chilstone will undertake restoration work and will copy, from photographs or drawings, cornices, coping, lintels, balustrading and many other architectural details.

Chilstone Garden Ornaments
Sprivers Estate
Horsmonden
Kent TN12 8DR
Tel: (089 272) 3553

Classic Garden Furniture
Classic Garden Furniture have a small factory in the heart of the Midlands, where they produce a range of cast iron furniture using methods unchanged since they were first applied over 100 years ago. Their reproduction Victorian garden furniture is all handmade and available in either black or white, though special colours can be supplied. Most items are bolted together and can be easily dismantled

Classic Garden Furniture Ltd
Audley Avenue
Newport
Shropshire
Tel: (0952) 813311

T Crowther & Son
Crowther's specialise in furniture and architectural salvage but their joinery works have recently produced a very fine chinoiserie garden temple and a large bridge in similar style. They also have a large courtyard and garden laid out with statuary and ornaments of every description, including temples and wrought iron gates.

Garden temple with stone columns supporting a copper covered panelled timber dome.

T Crowther & Son Ltd
282 North End Road
Fulham
London SW6 1NH
Tel: (01) 385 1375/7

Crowther of Syon Lodge
Apart from specialising in period panelled rooms and fireplaces, Crowther of Syon Lodge have a large selection of antique garden ornaments ranging from temples to vases.

Crowther of Syon Lodge
Busch Corner
London Road
Isleworth
Middlesex TW7 5BH
Tel: (01) 560 7978/7985

Garden Crafts
Garden Crafts have been established for over 56 years. They have a very large selection of statues, vases, troughs, fountains, seats, animals, balustrading, birdbaths, sundials, wall plaques, gazebos, tables and chairs, etc., made in a variety of materials ranging from terracotta to cast iron. They import from Italy some of the best classical figures and fountains available.

Garden Crafts
158 New King's Road
Fulham
London SW6 4LZ
Tel: (01) 736 1615

Grahamston Iron Company
Grahamston manufacture two models of ornamental garden table in cast iron and aluminium, and also two models of cast iron bench ends to be fitted with wooden planks.

Grahamston Iron Company
PO Box 5
Falkirk
FK2 7HH
Tel: (0324) 22661

Haddonstone
Haddonstone is a special form of reconstructed limestone with a surface texture resembling that of natural Portland stone. It develops character rapidly and, with care, it has a lifespan of many generations, resisting the effects of weathering, which cause so much damage to the laminated structure of natural stone. Using this material, this firm produces almost every type of decorative or non-structural stonework. Their standard range, with a choice of three finishes, is one of the most extensive available. They also have a special services department where private clients, architects, and designers can have original work produced or existing items copied or restored.

19th century wrought and cast iron folly of large proportions adapted to form an aviary. From Crowther of Syon Lodge.

Haddonstone Ltd
The Forge House
East Haddon
Northampton NN6 8DB
Tel: (060 125) 365
Also small show garden at:
The Building Centre
26 Store Street
London WC1

House of Steel Antiques

This firm specialises in its own cast garden furniture: benches, seats and tables. It is soon to open a garden centre incorporating stone and cast ornaments, urns, pots and planters. Apart from reproductions, a varied range of original and antique items are kept in stock.

House of Steel Antiques
400 Caledonian Road
Islington
London N1 1DN
Tel: (01) 607 5889

Jardine Leisure Furniture

Jardine produce aluminium furniture in traditional designs which is suitable for both indoor and outdoor use. It is light, completely weatherproof and available in convenient cartons ready to assemble. The attractive 'Gardencast' range includes chairs and tables adapted from the neo-classical designs of Robert Adam.

Jardine Leisure Furniture Ltd
Rosemount Tower
Wallington Square
Wallington
Surrey SM6 8RR
Tel: (01) 669 8265

L F Knight

Established at the turn of the century, L F Knight's specialise in the manufacture of timber buildings for the garden. Six models of summer house are produced in varying sizes and can be personalised as the customer wishes. Some of the summer houses can even be fitted with revolving gear so that they can be turned to follow the sun. L F Knight also produces an extensive range of garden ornaments, greenhouses and sheds which can be viewed at the Reigate factory.

L F Knight Ltd
Reigate Heath, Reigate
Surrey RH2 9RF
Tel: (07372) 44811

The London Architectural Salvage and Supply Co

This City of London firm specialises in every aspect of architectural salvage, including statuary and garden furniture. Also available is Staffordshire Cable Twist path edging. Items are reasonably priced and range in period from 1680 to 1920.

The London Architectural Salvage and Supply Co Ltd
Mark Street (off Paul Street)
London EC2A 4ER
Tel: (01) 739 0448/9

J Newall

J Newall Ltd design and make a very large selection of cast aluminium patio, garden and terrace furniture based on both traditional and modern designs. Original Georgian, Regency and Victorian designs can be reproduced accurately. As well as supplying the public and domestic trade they also supply hotels, restaurants and wine bars throughout the world.

J Newall (Interior) Ltd
171 Lavender Hill
London SW11
Tel: (01) 228 2595

The Olive Tree Trading Company

The Olive Tree Trading Company is an importing company started in 1973 by Robert and Marzia Montagu as 'Imports from Tuscany'. It originally dealt with Italian wines but over the years Marzia introduced a selection of terracotta, ceramics and kitchenware, often tracing sources in remote villages where pottery is worked as it was centuries ago. The company has now built up the most comprehensive range of plain and ornate Italian terracotta in the country, including flower pots, window boxes, statues, and ornate vases and urns.

The Olive Tree Trading Company Ltd
Church Wharf
Pumping Station Road
Chiswick
London W4 2SN
Tel: (01) 995 5281/2/3

Charles Verey

Charles Verey specialises in making and selling wooden garden furniture. There are four bench designs, as well as the Chelsea Folding Seat, an Iroko octagonal bench to surround a tree and some 'dismantables', which are fixed with slotted brackets. Charles Verey is always keen to develop ideas to the particular requirements of individual customers and designers.

Charles Verey
Unit 10
New Mills Estate
Slad Road
Stroud
Gloucestershire GL5 1RN
Tel: (045 36) 79000

The Architect and the Period House

The neglect that many older houses have suffered through lack of regular maintenance often poses the dilemma of what to restore and what to replace. In most cases a limited budget must be distributed in some order of priority, in which modernising the plumbing and electrical systems will be higher on the list than, for example, repairing plaster cornices or panelled doors. There is an understandable desire to get all things dealt with as rapidly as possible, and perhaps to take short cuts by, for example, removing the whole of a damaged cornice rather than waiting to have it repaired, or replacing rotten skirtings with cheaper minimal modern skirtings.

There is also perhaps some reluctance to accept that any item should remain in an unfinished state. It is better to wait for the right fireplace to come along to replace one that is missing or damaged, rather than to fill in the opening to obtain a 'finished' appearance. It is difficult without experience to organise this work so that mistakes are avoided and so that the best value is obtained both in terms of money and the quality of the end result.

Most people employ an architect to survey a house before purchase. The object of the survey is basically to identify any more serious defects which could affect the decision to buy or the level of offer made. An architect's time is relatively expensive and there is therefore some reluctance to go beyond this first level of consultation, particularly with all the other expenses involved in house purchase.

To employ an architect to carry out all the work from preparation of specification to looking after the work on site takes up as much time on a small contract as it does on a contract of three times the size, therefore the fee can become disproportionate to the value of the work. To use the full services of an architect in this way is worthwhile only if the client cannot provide any of the necessary organising and supervising of the work himself and if by employing an architect he can

free himself to do other things, such as earning more to pay for the work. Many architects would in any case advise that his services be retained on a limited basis to help prepare a budget and programme for carrying out the work, to identify which repair items must be dealt with immediately and which can wait until money is available, and to advise on the most appropriate methods of repair and restoration of the architectural detail. On the basis of say two or three days of his time, sufficient guidance can be given to avoid serious mistakes and to help ensure that the money available is spent wisely.

There are two main approaches adopted by architects to restoration and modernisation. The true restorer advocates the retention and restoration of all the period detail with the minimum of alteration other than the careful integration of modern plumbing and electrical systems. Rooms are retained largely as they are, and if any changes are made they are entirely in character with the period of the house. If it is necessary to build an extension it is carried out as inconspicuously as possible, and in a matching architectural style.

The other approach goes further in adapting the building to meet today's requirements while still respecting the style and retaining all the important period features. The main departure is in the treatment of any new building work, which is carried out in a modern style on the basis that it is better that new work should reflect the time in which we live rather than imitate the past. There are many examples in which different styles are brought together with entirely satisfactory results. The success of this approach depends on the skill of the architect in achieving harmony between old and new.

Like other professions, architects specialise in specific areas, and therefore not all are experienced in this type of work. A record is kept by the RIBA Professional Services Department of the type of work firms of architects carry out, and they will provide on

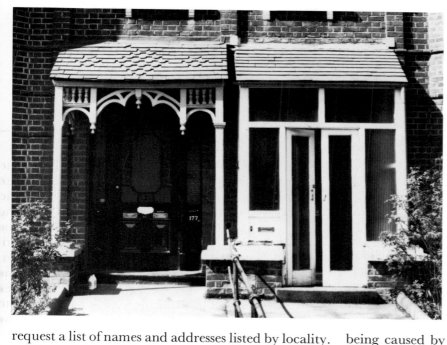

If you have a lovely Edwardian porch and door, do not do this!

request a list of names and addresses listed by locality.

The quality and style of our domestic architecture has been very much undervalued except at the level of the country mansion, pretty village or the grander urban squares and terraces. Anything less spectacular or appealing has been regarded as expendable in a process of redevelopment and road improvement sometimes carried out on a massive scale and with appalling insensitivity and destructiveness. The uncertainties arising from such projects have been the main cause of the neglect of large areas of Victorian, Edwardian and later housing in our cities and towns.

A combination of public concern and a change of Government policy has provided the basis on which to reverse the neglect. At national level, resources have been switched from new housing to the better use and modernisation of the existing housing stock. Substantial grants are now available through local authorities for the repair and improvement of older houses. Local authorities are much more sensitive to local opinion on the question of redevelopment and have been given powers to designate conservation areas when preservation could not easily be justified for outstanding architectural merit. Lastly building societies, banks and local authorities are now providing mortgages for older properties on a level not previously available.

Unfortunately there is increasing evidence that serious damage to the period detail of many houses is being caused by the process of repair and modernisation made possible by this release of resources. Some of this destruction arises from what might be called the Hollywood approach. In the quest for a film image or dream, the quality of what is there is ignored, the stylistic features are destroyed and the result is bad Modern style wrapped up in an old shell. Usually such transformations are expensive and therefore, fortunately, not perpetrated too often. Most of the damage is caused by a combination of ignorance, bad building practice and plain commercial opportunism.

The type and shape of the windows make an important contribution to the style of the house. Regrettably it is only too common to see them replaced with something entirely different in style, usually modern windows which are readily available through builder's merchants. These windows are produced primarily for the new housing market and are often of a quality, design and performance which has done considerable harm to the appearance and reputation of modern housing, let alone to older houses. The total replacement of windows to match the existing can be expensive, hence the importance of regular maintenance to prolong life. It is often possible to renew the more vulnerable parts of windows such as the sills, and carry out other repairs which will bring the window virtually up to new standard at a fraction of the cost of total replacement.

There is a temptation when faced with a mainten-

Above: Late Victorian house with all its original features intact.

Above right: The same type of house with all the brick detailing knocked off and covered with pebble-dash render. Note also the cheap replacement windows, the type that the 'cowboy' builder may offer when in all probability the careful repair of the original window would not only fit in better with the style of the house but may also be considerably cheaper.

Right: Resist the temptation to coat your house with artificial stone facing. Brick is a very durable material in its own right and requires a minimum of maintenance.

ance problem to find the 'once and for all' solution. One or two rotten window sills prompt a search for the magic 'no-maintenance' answer. This is an understandable reaction when faced with a problem the implications of which are not understood. Hard-selling replacement-window companies often rely on this ignorance to achieve a sale when they are offering a product entirely inappropriate to the style of the house at a cost which often far exceeds much more straightforward maintenance measures.

An important peg on which replacement-window companies hang their sales pitch is to combine low maintenance appeal with double glazing. It is important to understand that double glazing makes a

Do not be persuaded that it is necessary to ruin period windows by this type of replacement, when very often repair is not a major undertaking.

far smaller contribution to heat loss per £ spent than, for example, loft insulation, for which grants are available, or simple measures such as making the existing windows more draught-proof.

If these possibilities are exhausted, windows can be insulated more cheaply, without the need for total replacement, by means of a secondary window inside the first. The secondary windows can be made up to match the shape and size of the existing windows, thereby minimising their visual impact.

Security is becoming an increasing problem in the face of the rising number of burglaries and higher insurance premiums. An extreme reaction is to turn the house into a fortress with metal screens on all the windows which look appalling and transform the house into a cage. It is worth considering how a house can be protected without making it less pleasant to live in. Reputable lock manufacturers and insurance companies provide advice on locks and security devices for doors and windows, which is the first line of defence. A burglar will make for the windows most protected from view, for example in basement areas or perhaps rear lavatory windows. The use of bars here, particularly the folding type, are useless unless massively strong, because they can be levered open comparatively easily with a crowbar. Good locks combined with toughened glass (which is difficult to break without a lot of noise) is a better answer. Wooden shutters, which are a period feature in many older houses, are well worth restoring, not only in the interest of security but also for their value in conserving heat. Another more expensive discourage-

ment to the burglar is to install discrete lighting which is switched on by an alarm system.

The shape and detailing of older roofs are very dependent on the use of slates or clay tiles to maintain their characteristic period style. Slates and tiles can easily be replaced as they become damaged or missing, and the life of the roof therefore greatly prolonged at little cost. Ultimately the slating and tiling nails will rust through in increasing numbers, and recovering becomes necessary. The existing slates and tiles, if of good quality, will have decades of useful life in them—certainly equal to, if not more than, the life expectancy of modern alternatives. They should therefore be re-used if possible. If the quality is such that re-use is not feasible, good second-hand slates and tiles can be obtained as a cheaper alternative to new ones, and should certainly be considered before the nearest modern alternative is adopted.

Anyone who has a leaking roof without having some understanding of the causes and remedies is vulnerable to 'cheap repair' offers. These usually take the form of a bituminous coating reinforced with fabric, which is applied over the slates or tiles. The advantages of this system are said to be that it is a low-cost alternative to recovering the roof; the slates and tiles are held in place, and cracked or damaged slates or tiles are made waterproof. However attractive the price may appear, there are overwhelming reasons why these treatments must not be used. The life of the coating is short—about two to three years; tiles and slates that have been treated in this way cannot be re-used or sold for re-use; the coating prevents the roof

Value your period front doors and porches, and avoid this type of soulless conversion.

from 'breathing', and therefore increases condensation problems in the roof space beneath; the covering is seldom fully waterproof and results in water being trapped under the lap of the tiles or slates, causing deterioration of the surface and rot in the battens; and lastly, these coverings turn a previously attractive roof into a black mess.

Chimney stacks are often a period feature in many older houses and as such should be preserved. With the growth in the use of central heating and the corresponding decline in the need for open fires, there has been a tendency to remove chimney pots and seal off the flues, and sometimes also to reduce the height of the stack or even remove it altogether. Usually repair work to chimneys is a matter of repointing the brickwork, possibly replacing one or two chimney pots, and re-cementing the top of the stack.

If the flues are not in use, simple flue ventilators are available which fit into the top of the pots without spoiling their appearance to prevent rain from entering. A further argument in favour of preservation is that the traditional chimney gives scope for other forms of heating in the face of the escalating costs of gas and electricity, as well as providing indirect ventilation to keep rooms aired.

Water penetration through walls caused by defective guttering, rainwater pipes or poor pointing is sometimes wrongly diagnosed as resulting from 'porous' brickwork. The brickwork is then unnecessarily coated with some form of cement rendering to make it 'waterproof' with disastrous results to the appearance and period quality of the house. In practical terms, to treat brick in this way is, to say the least, counter-productive. Good quality brick is one of the most durable and maintenance-free materials available; it only requires repointing and possibly a good cleaning every 60 or 70 years to maintain it in good condition. No other man-made material offers

Far left: The cornices and other details on this property have been chopped off and the parapet reduced in height, disastrously altering its appearance (compare with picture on right). It is rare that these features are so badly damaged that they cannot easily be restored and given protection against the weather by, for example, covering the top surface with lead flashings.

Left: Cornices and decorative features around windows and doors are retained here, giving this nineteenth-century terraced house great charm. But the traditional sash windows have been replaced by aluminium windows, which are totally out of character with the rest of the property.

the same durability combined with good appearance. The quality of brick can be uneven to the extent that a few may be more susceptible than others to deterioration under severe weather conditions, or when subjected to continuous damp. Under these circumstances the surface of the brick may deteriorate and soften. Here again the answer is not to resort to a rendering treatment but to simply cut out the defective bricks and insert new bricks in their place.

The attitude of many jobbing builders to maintenance work is 'quick in—quick out'. In many cases they look for the easiest and most profitable way to deal with a problem. For example they will propose a replacement window in the interest of speed but, 'to save money', offer a standard window or something made up to fit which in no way matches with what is replaced. Rather than repair a decorative cornice or other feature they will knock it off. The damage caused in this way is probably more common than any of the other reasons. Regrettably, matters are further complicated by the traditional separation of the trades in the building industry. A plumber and electrician will often run their pipes and cables through cornices and across walls to make life easier for them, but with a sublime disregard for the problems they are causing the decorator or plasterer.

When repairing and converting an historic house, the amount of expert advice needed will depend both on the age of the property and on the amount of detail,

such as carved woodwork, painted plaster, moulded ceilings, and so on. Generally speaking, those houses which are at least partly pre-Georgian and have developed over several periods and styles require the greatest care. But the character of later houses can also be lost in improvements, unless expert help is sought.

The Society for the Preservation of Ancient Buildings gives advice on these later houses as well as on pre-Georgian buildings, and has records of architects, suppliers, builders, and specialist contractors in various parts of the country.

Other national amenity societies such as the Georgian Group, the Victorian Society and the Ancient Monuments Society may also be able to help with nominations. Such advice can also be obtained from local authorities in some areas, though the capacity to help varies greatly from one authority to another. The historic buildings departments of county councils are often the best bet. The Craft Council tries to maintain a full list of all builders and craftsmen recommended by county councils, while the National Federation of Building Trades Employers has area lists of qualified builders who specialise in restoration. Nominations for architects, structural engineers, and surveyors can of course be obtained from the Royal Institute of British Architects, the Institute of Structural Engineers, or the Royal Institute of Chartered Surveyors.

Useful Societies and Organisations

Ancient Monuments Society
St Andrews By the Wardrobe
Queen Victoria Street
London EC4
Tel:(01) 236 3934
Founded in 1924 for the study and conservation of ancient monuments, historic buildings and fine old craftsmanship. Publishes an annual volume on the conservation and restoration of period properties.

Art Workers Guild
6 Queen Square
London WC1N 3Ar
Tel: (01) 837 3474
Guild of artists, craftsmen and others engaged in the design and practice of the arts. The Guild is involved through its work with such organisations as the SPAB, the National Trust and the Crafts Council.

Association of Studies in the Conservation of History
c/o James Elliott
6 Woodland Place
Bathwick Hill
Bath Avon BAZ 6EH
Tel: (0225) 4576
Information and technical advice by letter to the general public on all aspects of the conservation of historic buildings.

BRE Scottish Laboratory
Kelvin Road
East Kilbride
Glasgow G75 ORZ
Tel: (035 52) 33001
Information available on research topics such as the durability of walls and roofs etc.

Brick Development Association
Woodside House
Winkfield
Windsor
Berkshire SL4 2DP
Tel: (034 47) 5651
Inquiries on bricks and bricklaying from the general public can be answered by the Association. Their publication *The Conservation of Brick Buildings* is also available.

British Antique Dealers Association (BADA)
20 Rutland Gate
London SW7 1BD
Tel: (01) 589 4128
Produces useful booklets listing members in London and the rest of the country. The BADA will authenticate and value items for a small fee.

British Ceramic Tile Council
Federation House
Station Road
Stoke-on-Trent ST4 2RU
Tel: (0782) 45147
Free technical advisory service on the installation of tiles.

British Decorators Association
6 Haywra Street
Harrogate
North Yorkshire HG1 5BL
Tel: (0423) 67292/3
The Association has 1,000 members who specialise in the decoration of period homes.

British Wood Preservation Association
Premier House
150 Southampton Row
London WC1B 5AL
Tel: (01) 837 8217
Leaflets and a technical advice service for the general public on wood preservation.

Building Conservation Trust
Apartment 39
Hampton Court Palace
East Molesey
Surrey KT8 9BS
Tel: (01) 943 2277
Promotes proper conservation, maintenance and alteration of buildings of all types and ages.

Chartered Institute of Building Services
Delta House
22 Balham High Road
London SW12 9BS
Tel: (01) 675 5211
The Heritage Group of the CIBS gives advice concerning plumbing, heating, ventilation etc. in old houses. Written inquiries are preferred.

Civic Trust
17 Carlton House Terrace
London SW1Y 5AW
Tel: (01) 930 0914
General advice on environmental problems.

Crafts Council
12 Waterloo Place
London SW1Y 4AU
Tel (01) 839 1917
Organisation promoting Britain's artists and craftsmen. The Crafts Council operates an information service which answers queries from the general public, and a non-selective national register of conservation craftsmen is available.

Georgian Group
2 Chester Street
London SW1X 7BB
Tel: (01) 235 3081
Advice to owners of Georgian buildings on repair and preservation.

Historic Buildings Bureau
22 Savile Row
London W1X 2BT
Assists owners of listed buildings to find new uses for their buildings.

Historic Buildings Council for England
25 Savile Row
London W1X 2BT
Tel: (01) 734 6010
Advises the Department of the Environment on the awarding of grants for the repair of historic buildings.

Historic Buildings Council for Wales
St David's House
Wood Street
Cardiff CF1 1PQ
Tel: (0222) 397083
Advises the Secretary of State for Wales on matters concerning historic buildings.

Historic Houses Association
10 Charles II Street
London SW1Y 4AA
Tel: (01) 839 5345
Advice and support for owners of historic houses.

Institute of Architectural Ironmongers
15 Soho Square
London W1V 5FB
Tel: (01) 439 1753
General information and advice on architectural ironmongery.

Interior Decorators and Designers Association
24 Ormond Road
Richmond
Surrey TW10 6TH
Tel: (01) 948 4151
The Association will recommend to members of the general public interior decorators and designers in their own area.

London and Provincial Antique Dealers Association (LAPADA)
112 Brompton Road
London SW3 1JJ
Tel: (01) 584 7911
LAPADA issues two useful booklets listing their members in London and the provinces. Its Consumer Liaison Department will answer inquiries from the public on the buying, selling, valuation and authentication of antiques.

National Federation of Building Trades Employers
82 New Cavendish Street
London W1M 8AD
Tel: (01) 580 5588
The Federation can recommend stone masons, painters and decorators, plasterers etc. in an inquirer's area. Technical information is also available.

Paint Research Association
Waldegrave Road
Teddington
Middlesex TW11 8LD
Tel: (01) 977 4427
A private organisation offering advice on paint and painting problems.

Royal Commission on Ancient and Historic Monuments in Wales
Edleston House
Queen's Road
Aberystwyth
Dyfed
Tel: (0970) 4381
Answers queries from the general public concerning the age, type and function of buildings.

Royal Commission on Historical Monuments (England) / National Monuments Record
Fortress House
23 Savile Row
London W1X 1AB
Tel: (01) 734 6010
The National Monuments Record Library, open Mon-Fri 10.00 – 5.30, has approximately 1 million photographs, arranged topographically.

Royal Incorporation of Architects in Scotland
15 Rutland Square
Edinburgh EH1 2EE
Tel: (031) 229 7205
Advice available to the public on the selection of an architect, or any other general matter concerning architecture in Scotland.

Royal Institute of British Architects (RIBA)
66 Portland Place
London W1N 4AD
Tel: (01) 580 5533
The RIBA Client's Advisory Service will recommend local architects, and the library and bookshop are open to the public.

Royal Institute of Chartered Surveyors (RICS)
12 Great George Street
London SW1P 3AD
Tel: (01) 222 7000
Has 42,000 Corporate Members, many of whom are concerned with conservation and rehabilitation. The Information Service will recommend local surveyors.

Scottish Civic Trust
24 George Square
Glasgow G2 1EF
Tel: (041) 221 1466
General advice on environmental problems in Scotland.

Scottish Georgian Society
39 Castle Street
Edinburgh 2
Tel: (031) 225 8391
Advice to owners of Georgian buildings on repair and preservation.

Society for the Protection of Ancient Buildings
55 Great Ormond Street
London WC1N 3JA
Tel: (01) 405 2646/4541
The oldest conservation society, founded by William Morris in 1877. The SPAB can recommend architects, structural engineers, builders and craftsmen.

Victorian Society
1 Priory Gardens
London W4 1TT
Tel: (01) 994 1019/5143
Specialist information available on restoration, interior design and decoration of Victorian homes.

Glossary

acanthus Plant used as decoration on Corinthian capitals and other ornaments.

alabaster Translucent form of gypsum.

anthemion Pattern based on stylised honeysuckle.

architrave Moulded frame surrounding a door or window.

Art Deco Angular decorative art style of 1920–30s.

Art Nouveau French decorative art style of late 19th century, with exaggerated sinuous lines.

Arts & Crafts Decorative movement of the late 19th century based on traditional country craftsmanship.

astragal Small convex moulding; frequently used for glazing bars.

baluster One of a series of posts supporting a handrail and forming a balustrade.

balustrade (see baluster)

bargeboard Ornamental board as decoration of gable.

Baroque Style of the 17th and 18th centuries, characterised by expansive and exuberant forms.

Bauhaus German school of architecture and design, 1919–33.

block print To print on paper or fabric using an engraved piece of metal or wood.

bolection Convex moulding used in late 17th and early 18th century.

box cornice Moulded timber cornice, often used with panelling.

breeze-blocks Lightweight building blocks.

brocade Fabric with raised pattern.

cabochon Polished gem with no facets.

cabriole Curved leg popular in Queen Anne and Chippendale furniture.

cames Metal strip used in leaded lights.

cartouche Tablet, imitating scroll, used ornamentally or bearing inscription.

capital The head or top of a Classical column.

Carron Name of a Scottish ironworks.

casement windows Metal or timber window hung vertically and opening inwards or outwards.

chair rail Moulding round a room which protects walls from damage when chairs are pushed back.

chevron A V-shaped design, popular in Art Deco.

chiffoniers Low, movable cupboard with sideboard top.

chimney piece Frame surrounding a fireplace, sometimes including a mantel or mirror above.

chinoiserie Patterns in furniture, etc. resembling Chinese motifs.

Classical Harmonious, well-proportioned style constructed in accordance with Roman and Greek forms of art and architecture.

Coade stone Artificial stone invented in late 18th century England and manufactured by Mrs Coade at Lambeth, London.

colonnade Series of columns.

console table Table supported against a wall by a bracket.

corbel Stone or timber projection from wall intended to support weight.

Corinthian One of the five Classical Orders. This one has its capital formed of acanthus leaves.

corner quoins (see quoins)

cornice Ornamental moulding around the walls of a room, just below the ceiling.

corona Vertical face of a cornice, usually projecting.

crestings Decorative finish along the top of a wall or roof.

Crown glass Small pane of glass, used before the invention of plate glass.

dado Pedestal of an Order, and hence the part of an interior wall beneath the chair rail.

damask Woven material with pattern visible on both sides.

dentil One of a series of small squares or rectangular blocks resembling teeth, used under a cornice in Classical architecture.

dog grate Small semi-circular iron grate for burning coal.

dog-leg stair Two flights of stairs at right angles, joined by a half landing.

door case Structural part of the door frame.

Doric Oldest and sturdiest of the five Orders.

drip stone Projection, usually over a window, which throws off rainwater and prevents it from running down the wall below.

eaves Overhanging edge of roof.

eaves cornice A cornice attached to the eaves.

ebonise Paint finish which resembles ebony.

Edwardian Period based on King Edward III's reign, 1901–10, but usually taken loosely to be 1900–14.

entablature The upper part of the Classical Order, encompassing the architrave, the frieze and the cornice.

enrichments Ornaments, decorations, additions.

escutcheons Pivoting key-hole cover.

fanlight Semi-circular window over a door in Regency or Georgian buildings.

fascia Long, flat surface of wood or stone under eaves or cornice.

fielded panel Panel with raised central area.

fillet Narrow flat band separating two mouldings.

finials Ornament finishing off a pinnacle, e.g. of roof.

flax Plant cultivated for its fibre (used in textiles) and its seed (linseed).

Flemish bond Type of building construction in which stretchers and headers are laid alternately in the same layer of bricks.

floral swags Carved or moulded chain of flowers.

fluorspar A mineral (calcium fluoride) often used for decorative vases.

fluting Semi-circular vertical grooves.

fresco Method of painting in which paint is applied to wet plaster.

gable Triangular part of wall at end of roof.

garniture Adornments, trimmings.

Georgian Chronological period covering the reigns of the first four Kings George (1714–1830).

gesso Plaster of Paris.

geyser Apparatus for heating water, introduced in Victorian times.

gilding Thin covering layer of gold or golden colour.

glazing bar One of two or more bars, wood or metal, which supports the glass in windows.

Gothic Of the pointed-arch style in Western Europe, 12th–16th century.

Gothic revival Reversion to Gothic style in 19th century.

Gothick Decorative 18th century Gothic revival style.

graining Painting technique which imitates the appearance of wood.

greenery-yallery Late 19th century 'aesthetic' taste.

half-timbered A building made of a timber frame filled with bricks or plaster.

harled Treatment in which surface is coated with lime and gravel.

hip (on roof) A roof with sloping ends and sides.

hip bath Bath in which the bather is immersed up to the hips, popular in the early Victorian era.

hob grate Small iron grate for burning coal, with flat side pieces on which to rest kettles, etc.

hopper head Type of rainwater pipe forming junction with gutter.

impost Top of pillar, which carries an arch.

ingle nook Large open fireplace, often with corner seats.

Ionic One of the five Classical Orders. This one has its capital decorated with volutes.

Italianate Of Italian style or appearance.

jamb Side post of a window, doorway or fireplace.

japanning Varnishing with a hard, black varnish resembling lacquer.

keystone One of two wedge-shaped stones forming the summit of an arch.

lath Thin strip of timber, used in trellises, Venetian blinds and as backing for plaster.

leaded lights Window glass made up from small panes held in place by strips of lead forming a diamond or other pattern.

lincrusta Wallpaper covered with embossed patterns.

lustre Prismatic glass pendant on a chandelier.

louvres Series of overlapping strips of glass, metal, plastic, etc, (as in Venetian blinds), which admit air but exclude rain or light.

marbling Decorative finish simulating the appearance of marble.

margin light Side light.

marquetry Inlaid decorative patterns in ivory, wood, etc.

metallic painting Paint finish resembling metal.

modillion Decorative bracket supporting the upper section of a cornice.

mortice and tenon joint Joint made by fitting a projecting piece of wood (tenon) into a correspondingly sized socket (mortice).

mottling Irregular spotting or blotching of coloured paint.

mullion Vertical bar separating a window into two or more parts.

mutule Projecting block under a Doric cornice.

newel post Upright post supporting a stair banister at top or bottom.

ogee An 'S'-shaped moulding.

ormolu Gilt bronze.

overdoor Decorative painting above a door frame.

overmantel Decorative unit often comprising display shelves and a mirror fitted above a fireplace.

Order Essential component of Classical architecture comprising a column, base shaft and capital, and an entablature with frieze and cornice.

palisade Fence of iron railings or wooden stakes.

Palladian Classical style associated with the late 16th century architect Andrea Palladio.

pantile Interlocking 'S'-shaped roof tile.

parchment Skin of sheep or goat prepared for writing, painting, etc.

parquet floor Floor made up from hard-wood blocks, often arranged in a pattern.

patina Deep gloss developed on old wood or metal from constant polishing.

pediment Triangular form resembling a gable above an entablature, often used as a decorative element over doors and windows.

pergola Covered garden walkway formed with upright posts and horizontal beams.

pier-glass Looking glass between windows.

pilaster Projecting rectangular column forming part of a wall.

plinth The base of a column or pedestal.

pongee silk Soft, unbleached Chinese silk.

Queen Anne Architectural period corresponding to the reign of Queen Anne in the early 18th century. Revived by Norman Shaw in the late 19th century as the 'Queen Anne style'.
quirk V-shaped slot in, or between, mouldings.
quoins Stones or bricks forming corner piece, laid alternately to look large and small.

reeding Decorative mould in reed pattern, often used with fluting.
Regency Architectural and decorative style characteristic of the Regency, 1810–20. Often used loosely to mean early 19th century.
risers Vertical surface between treads of staircase.
Rocaille Ornamental style of 18th century, employing shapes of rocks or shells.
Rococo Style of decoration popular in 18th century, featuring scroll work and shell motifs.
roundel Small decorative medallion.

rough cast Plaster made from lime and gravel, used on walls.

sash horns Small projections on the ends of window sashes. Invented by the Victorians and not found in 18th century windows.
sconces Flat candlestick, either with handle or with bracket for fixing to wall.
segmental arch Shallow arch.
shellac Type of varnish.
sitz bath Form of hip bath.
size Glue-like solution used to stiffen textiles, etc.
soffit Underside of architrave, window recess, balcony, etc.
spandrel Space between shoulder of arch and surrounding rectangular moulding.
squab cushion Small square cushion forming the seat of a chair.
steatite A form of soapstone.
stippling Painting or engraving by plaited straps.
stock brick Yellow brick used in London.
strapwork Decoration imitating

string Sloping piece of wood which supports ends of staircase steps.
string course Horizontal band or course of bricks on a building.
stucco Cement or plaster used for coating surfaces or for mouldings.

table-cut (of jewels) Cut so as to give a large flat top.
tallow Substance made from animal fat, used for candles, soap, etc.
template Piece of thin board or metal used as pattern or guide when cutting wood, stone, metal, etc.
terracotta Hard, artificial material of baked clay, usually brownish-red in colour.
torchères Tall stand with a small table-top for candlesticks etc.
transom Wooden or stone bar dividing window horizontally.
trompe l'oeil Painting which deceives viewer that painted objects are real.
truss Supporting framework of building, roof, etc.
Turkey carpet Woollen rug or carpet

with thick pile and bold design.
Tuscan Order One of the five Classical Orders. A simplified version of Doric.

valance Short curtain above window, around bed-frame, etc.
vellum Skin of calf prepared for writing and painting etc.
verdigris Green substance (copper oxide) used as pigment in paint, varnish etc.
vernacular Indigenous, native to country or area.
Victorian Style of architecture etc. characteristic of the reign of Queen Victoria (1837–1901).
vitruvian Scroll pattern used in frieze decorations, etc.
volutes Spiral scroll pattern, based on rams' horns.

watered silk Silk treated with water in manufacturing process to resemble damask.
what-not Stand with shelves for small objects, popular in 19th century.

Picture Acknowledgements

Swallow Publishing Limited would like to thank all the authors who provided illustrations for their chapters, and the following: Architectural Press, Country Life, T. Crowther & Son, Crowther of Syon Lodge, Dan Klein, Design Council, L. F. Knight, House of Steel Antiques, Nairn Floors, National Trust, John Prizeman, Science Museum, Victoria & Albert Museum, Victorian Society. Should we have omitted to acknowledge anyone who supplied us with photographs, we apologise.

Index